T0174642

SECURITY
SOFTWARE
DEVELOPMENT

Assessing and Managing Security Risks

SECURITY SOFTWARE DEVELOPMENT

Assessing and Managing Security Risks

DOUGLAS A. ASHBAUGH, CISSP, CISA

CRC Press
Taylor & Francis Group
Boca Raton London New York

CRC Press is an imprint of the
Taylor & Francis Group, an **informa** business

AN AUERBACH BOOK

CRC Press
Taylor & Francis Group
6000 Broken Sound Parkway NW, Suite 300
Boca Raton, FL 33487-2742

First issued in paperback 2019

© 2009 by Taylor & Francis Group, LLC
Auerbach is an imprint of Taylor & Francis Group, an Informa business

No claim to original U.S. Government works

ISBN-13: 978-1-4200-6380-6 (hbk)
ISBN-13: 978-0-367-38660-3 (pbk)

This book contains information obtained from authentic and highly regarded sources. Reasonable efforts have been made to publish reliable data and information, but the author and publisher cannot assume responsibility for the validity of all materials or the consequences of their use. The authors and publishers have attempted to trace the copyright holders of all material reproduced in this publication and apologize to copyright holders if permission to publish in this form has not been obtained. If any copyright material has not been acknowledged please write and let us know so we may rectify in any future reprint.

Except as permitted under U.S. Copyright Law, no part of this book may be reprinted, reproduced, transmitted, or utilized in any form by any electronic, mechanical, or other means, now known or hereafter invented, including photocopying, microfilming, and recording, or in any information storage or retrieval system, without written permission from the publishers.

For permission to photocopy or use material electronically from this work, please access www.copyright.com (http://www.copyright.com/) or contact the Copyright Clearance Center, Inc. (CCC), 222 Rosewood Drive, Danvers, MA 01923, 978-750-8400. CCC is a not-for-profit organization that provides licenses and registration for a variety of users. For organizations that have been granted a photocopy license by the CCC, a separate system of payment has been arranged.

Trademark Notice: Product or corporate names may be trademarks or registered trademarks, and are used only for identification and explanation without intent to infringe.

Library of Congress Cataloging-in-Publication Data

Ashbaugh, Douglas A.
  Security software development : assessing and managing security risks /
Douglas A. Ashbaugh. -- 1st ed.
    p. cm.
  Includes bibliographical references and index.
  ISBN 978-1-4200-6380-6 (alk. paper)
  1. Computer security. 2. Application software--Development. 3. Computer networks--Security measures. I. Title.

QA76.9.A25A8246 2008
005.8--dc22   2008015213

Visit the Taylor & Francis Web site at
http://www.taylorandfrancis.com

and the Auerbach Web site at
http://www.auerbach-publications.com

Contents

Preface xiii

Acknowledgments xv

Author Biography xvii

1   Current Trends in Application Security 1
    1.1   Recent Data Security Breaches 1
    1.2   Definition 3
    1.3   Legislative and Regulatory Requirements Affecting Application
         Security 4
    1.4   Industry Standards Requiring or Affecting Application Security 6
    1.5   Risks Associated with Current Trends 10
    1.6   Introduction to Test Case That Relates to Current Trends 14
    1.7   Conclusion 18
    References 18

2   Security Risk Assessment Methodologies 19
    2.1   Definitions 20
    2.2   Quantitative Risk Assessment Methodologies 21
         2.2.1   Exposure Factor 21
         2.2.2   Single Loss Expectancy 21
         2.2.3   Annualized Rate of Occurrence 22
         2.2.4   Annualized Loss Expectancy 23
         2.2.5   Cost-Benefit Analysis 23
    2.3   Qualitative Risk Assessment Methodologies 25
         2.3.1   Likelihood of Occurrence 26
         2.3.2   Magnitude of Impact 27
         2.3.3   Risk Level 28
    2.4   Published Methodologies 31
         2.4.1   Software Engineering Institute's OCTAVE 31
         2.4.2   STRIDE 31
         2.4.3   DREAD 32
         2.4.4   TRIKE 33

		2.4.5	Australian/New Zealand Standard 4360:2004	34
		2.4.6	Common Vulnerability Scoring System (CVSS)	34
	2.5	Automated Risk Assessment Tools		34
	2.6	Tips in Selecting a Methodology		35
	2.7	Selecting a Methodology for the Test Case		37
		2.7.1	Arguments for Using a Quantitative Risk Analysis Method in the Test Case	38
		2.7.2	Arguments against Using a Quantitative Risk Analysis Method in the Test Case	38
		2.7.3	Arguments for Using a Qualitative Risk Analysis Method in the Test Case	39
		2.7.4	Arguments against Using a Qualitative Risk Analysis Method in the Test Case	39
	2.8	Checklist for Deciding on a Security Risk Assessment Methodology		39
	2.9	Conclusions		40
3	**Identifying Assets**			**41**
	3.1	Definition		42
	3.2	Types of Assets Typically Found in Software Development		43
		3.2.1	Information Assets	44
		3.2.2	External Databases	44
		3.2.3	Business Rules	46
		3.2.4	Services and Functions	46
		3.2.5	Software	46
		3.2.6	Proprietary Formulas	47
		3.2.7	Encryption Software and Encryption Keys	48
		3.2.8	People	48
		3.2.9	Accounts, Transactions, and Calculations	49
	3.3	How to Identify Assets in Application Development		49
		3.3.1	Business and User Management Involvement	49
		3.3.2	Review of Organizational Documentation	50
		3.3.3	Other Methods of Identifying Assets	50
	3.4	Determining Assets for the Test Case		52
	3.5	Asset Checklist		55
	3.6	Summary		56
4	**Identifying Security Threats**			**59**
	4.1	Definition		60
	4.2	Information Security Threats to Software Development		61
		4.2.1	Business Threats	61
		4.2.2	System Threats	62
		4.2.3	Human Threats	63
		4.2.4	Technical Threats	66

                4.2.5   Environmental Threats 70
                4.2.6   Natural Threats 72
        4.3   How to Identify Security Threats...73
                4.3.1   Attack Histories...73
                4.3.2   Current Headlines..73
                4.3.3   Internet Sites 74
                4.3.4   Threat Modeling...75
        4.4   Test Case Threats... 77
                4.4.1   Test Case Business Objectives 78
                4.4.2   Test Case User Roles 78
                4.4.3   Test Case Use Cases 79
                4.4.4   Test Case Components..96
                4.4.5   Test Case Architecture...97
                4.4.6   Test Case Threats... 101
        4.5   Conclusion 104
        4.6   Threat Identification Checklists..104
                4.6.1   Typical Threats (the "Usual Suspects") 104
                4.6.2   Sources of Threat Identification.....................................106
                4.6.3   Threat Modeling...106

5   **Identifying Vulnerabilities 109**
        5.1   Definition 109
        5.2   The Importance of Identifying Vulnerabilities 110
        5.3   Identifying Vulnerabilities 111
        5.4   Common Vulnerabilities.. 113
                5.4.1   Buffer Overflows 113
                5.4.2   Injection Flaws 113
                5.4.3   Information Leakage and Improper Error Handling 115
                5.4.4   Cross-Site Scripting.. 116
                5.4.5   Nontechnical Vulnerabilities 117
        5.5   Methods of Detecting Vulnerabilities during Software
              Development 118
                5.5.1   Review of Current Controls.. 119
                5.5.2   Code Reviews... 119
                5.5.3   Testing 120
                5.5.4   Static Code Scanning 120
                5.5.5   Dynamic Code Scanning 121
                5.5.6   Web Application Scanning..121
                5.5.7   Network Vulnerability Scanning.....................................121
                5.5.8   Review of Best Practice Standards 122
        5.6   Secure Coding Techniques to Avoid Vulnerabilities.....................135
                5.6.1   Validate Input..135
                5.6.2   Validate Output to Be Displayed on Browsers 135

	5.6.3	Keep It Simple	136
	5.6.4	Follow the Principle of Least Privilege	136
	5.6.5	Practice Defense in Depth	136
	5.6.6	Practice Quality Assurance	137
	5.6.7	Adopt Coding Standards	137
	5.6.8	Define Security Requirements	137
	5.6.9	Practice Threat Modeling	137
5.7		Vulnerabilities Associated with the Test Case	138
5.8		Conclusion	140
5.9		Checklists	140
	5.9.1	Sources of Education about Software Vulnerabilities	140
	5.9.2	OWASP Top 10 (2007)	141
	5.9.3	SANS Top 20 for 2007	141
	5.9.4	Methods for Finding Vulnerabilities	142
	5.9.5	Secure Coding Practices to Avoid Vulnerabilities	143

6 Analyzing Security Risks ... 145

6.1		Threat–Vulnerability Pairs	146
6.2		Risk Likelihood or Probability	147
6.3		Control Analysis	152
6.4		Impact or Severity of Threat Actions	154
	6.4.1	Impact on Confidentiality	155
	6.4.2	Impact on Integrity	155
	6.4.3	Impact on Availability	156
6.5		Determining Risk Levels	158
6.6		Sources of Scales and Tables	160
6.7		Determining Security Risks for the Test Case	160
	6.7.1	Human Threats	161
	6.7.2	Technical Threats	161
	6.7.3	Vulnerabilities	162
	6.7.4	Threat-Action Statements	162
	6.7.5	Likelihood of Occurrence	164
	6.7.8	Control Analysis	164
	6.7.9	Magnitude of Impact	166
	6.7.10	Risk Levels	168
6.8		Conclusion	169
6.9		Common Risk Scales and Tables	169
	6.9.1	Likelihood of Occurrence Scales	169
	6.9.2	Magnitude of Impact Scales	170
	6.9.3	Risk Matrixes	170
	6.9.4	Risk Assessment Reporting Template	172
	6.9.5	Alternate Risk Assessment Reporting Template	175
6.10		Risk Assessment Summary	176

	6.10.1	Overview	176
	6.10.2	OCTAVE Risk Assessment Methodology	177
	6.10.3	Identified Assets	177
	6.10.4	Critical Assets	177
	6.10.5	Vulnerability Assessment	178
	6.10.6	Security Requirements	178
	6.10.7	Sources and Potential Impacts of Threats	180
	6.10.8	Impact Descriptions	182
	6.10.9	Current Protection Strategies	184
	6.10.10	Risk Analysis	186
	6.10.11	Risk Mitigation Plans	186
	6.10.12	Summary	187

7 Managing Security Risks 201

7.1	Definitions	202
7.2	Risk Mitigation Strategies	202
	7.2.1 Risk Assumption	203
	7.2.2 Risk Transference	203
	7.2.3 Risk Avoidance	205
	7.2.4 Risk Limitation	206
7.3	Protection Strategies	207
7.4	Mitigating Risks in the Test Case	209
7.5	Conclusion	211
7.6	Risk Mitigation Checklists	212
7.7	Risk Mitigation Reporting Template	213
	7.7.1 Risk Mitigation Documentation	213
	7.7.2 Risk Mitigation Options	213
	7.7.3 Risk Mitigation Strategy	214
	7.7.4 Control Implementation Approach	215

8 Risk Assessment and Risk Mitigation Activities in the SDLC 217

8.1	Requirements Gathering and Analysis	218
8.2	Design	220
8.3	Development	221
8.4	Test	222
8.5	Production and Maintenance	223
8.6	Risk Management Activities within the Test Case	223
	8.6.1 Test Case Assets	224
	8.6.2 Test Case Threats	225
	8.6.3 Test Case Vulnerabilities	227
	8.6.4 Test Case Risks and Mitigation Efforts	228
8.7	Conclusion	230
8.8	Risk Assessment and Risk Mitigation Activity Checklist	230

9 Maintaining a Security Risk Assessment and Risk Management Process..233
9.1 Definitions.. 234
9.2 Risk Management Plans 235
9.3 Supporting Risk Management Practices 238
    9.3.1 Top-Down Support 238
    9.3.2 Support from Policies and Procedures 240
    9.3.3 Legislative, Regulatory, or Compliance Support..........241
    9.3.4 Certification and Accreditation Support......................242
    9.3.5 Support from Change Management 254
9.4 Continuous Evaluation and Improvement 254
    9.4.1 System Security Plan Scope 255
    9.4.2 Identifying Key Infrastructure 257
    9.4.3 Identification of Key Personnel....................................257
    9.4.4 Determining System Boundaries.................................258
    9.4.5 Physical Inspections and Walkthroughs 259
    9.4.6 Interview Key Personnel..259
    9.4.7 Incidental Documentation 259
    9.4.8 Prepare Documentation 260
    9.4.9 Discuss SSP with Management 260
    9.4.10 Finalize Documentation..261
9.5 Risk Management Policy 261
9.6 Conclusions 261
9.7 Risk Management Plan Template 262
    9.7.1 Purpose 262
    9.7.2 Objective 262
    9.7.3 References 263
    9.7.4 Legal Basis...263
    9.7.5 Definitions...263
    9.7.6 Risk Management Overview 264
    9.7.7 Importance of Risk Management 264
    9.7.8 Integration of Risk Management into the System Development Life Cycle (SDLC) 264
    9.7.9 Key Roles 264
    9.7.10 Risk Assessment 266
    9.7.11 Preparing to Assess Risks.. 266
    9.7.12 Phase 1: Build Asset-Based Threat Profiles.................267
    9.7.13 Phase 2: Identify Infrastructure Vulnerabilities 267
    9.7.14 Phase 3: Develop Security Strategy and Plans 268
    9.7.15 Risk Mitigation 268
    9.7.16 Risk Mitigation Options 269
    9.7.17 Risk Mitigation Strategy 269
    9.7.18 Control Implementation Approach...............................270

	9.7.19	Evaluation and Assessment	271
9.8	Risk Management Policy Template		272
	9.8.1	Purpose	272
	9.8.2	Overview	272
	9.8.3	Scope	273
	9.8.4	Statutory Authority	273
	9.8.5	Compliance	273
	9.8.6	Updates	273
	9.8.7	Definitions	273
	9.8.8	Policy Details: Risk Management	274
	9.8.9	Integration of Risk Management into the System Development Life Cycle (SDLC)	274
	9.8.10	Key Roles	275
	9.8.11	Risk Assessment	276
	9.8.12	Risk Mitigation	277
	9.8.13	Risk Mitigation Options	278
	9.8.14	Risk Mitigation Strategy	278
	9.8.15	Control Implementation Approach	279
	9.8.16	Evaluation and Assessment	280
9.9	System Security Plan Template		281
	9.9.1	Section 1: System Identification	281
	9.9.2	Section 2: Management Controls	284
	9.9.3	Section 3: Operational Controls	285
	9.9.4	Section 4: Technical Controls	288
	9.9.5	Section 5: Appendices and Attachments	289
	9.9.6	Secure Product Development Policy Template	290

Index 299

Preface

Application security is a relatively new, yet very exciting field. It is being driven by a number of open source, government, regulatory, and industry organizations, but the need for application security is, sadly enough, the fact that software continues to be developed that isn't secure. For example, buffer overflows continue to plague software development despite the fact that buffer overflows and the methods for preventing them have been known for more than 20 years. The author believes that the primary reasons that secure software hasn't been developed lies with two factors:

- First, software development teams have not been sufficiently trained in how to identify vulnerabilities associated with their software development projects.
- Second, software development teams falsely believe that if perimeter security controls are in place, then the software they develop will also be secure, or at least will not affect the perimeter security.

The author was one of those developers who believed that as long as perimeter security (i.e., firewalls, intrusion detection and prevention, anti-virus, etc.) was in place, flaws in his code could not possibly affect the security of that perimeter. That may have been the case when applications were primarily mainframe- or client/server-based. However, the paradigm shifted with the introduction of Web-based applications, as the author painfully discovered.

Traditional firewalls must let Web-based traffic through the perimeter in order for Web-based applications to function. Therefore any attacker who can exploit flaws in the code of a Web application is already within the perimeter! There are additional controls that may be added to secure this perimeter including application and database firewalls, but many organizations have not yet recognized the need for such controls, as headlines sadly continue to point out. When you couple this with the fact that organizations are often slow to adopt new security controls because security is often seen as another expense, it becomes even more imperative for software development teams to understand the vulnerabilities associated with their software development efforts.

The author believes that education is truly the key. Software development teams, including project managers, technical analysts, business analysts, business managers, developers, quality assurance analysts, and testers must all be aware of the vulnerabilities that could plague any software development effort. However, with more than 3400 new vulnerabilities discovered in the first half of 2007 alone, this becomes an almost impossible task.

That is why the author believes in the process of assessing risks within the software development process. Through techniques such as threat modeling, software development teams can quickly begin to learn how to measure the risk associated with their software development projects. Once potential risks are understood management can at least make informed decisions on how to deal with those risks.

It is the sincere hope of the author that you can improve the security of the applications that you develop by following the techniques outlined in this book.

Acknowledgments

The author would like to thank R. J. Droll and Sue Horsman for their assistance in pulling all of the desperate ramblings of the author together to meet the submission deadlines for this manuscript. There is no way I could have done it without your assistance. You're the best!

The author also wishes to thank Jim Bridges, president of Software Engineering Services for taking a chance on a fellow Air Force veteran. You provided me with the chance to prove myself and my abilities at a time in my life when few others would. I truly appreciate all of the faith that you have placed in me and my abilities to get the job done right for you and SES. Thanks Jim!

The author would also like to thank his step-children, Stephanie Bennett and Brody Bennett, for putting up with his surly attitude and closed doors when attempting to put some serious thought into this volume!

Finally, the author would like to thank his wonderful wife Debi for all of the love, support, chiding, and comfort provided during the writing of this book. My love, I could not have done this without your love, patience, understanding—and most of all prodding—to finish writing the book.

And the author also wishes to thank almighty God for providing him with the wisdom and knowledge required to produce this work.

Author Biography

Douglas A. Ashbaugh is a Certified Information Systems Security Professional (CISSP) and member of the International Information Systems Security Certification Consortium (ISC²), as well as a Certified Information Systems Auditor (CISA) and member of the Information Systems Audit and Control Association (ISACA). Mr. Ashbaugh is also the manager of information assurance for Software Engineering Services (SES) where he leads a team of dedicated information security analysts in providing security strategy and solutions, evaluation and assessment services, application security services, and security remediation services to corporate as well as various federal, state, and municipal government clients.

A dedicated information security professional, Mr. Ashbaugh has extensive experience in project management, application development, and information security. His 18+ years of information systems experience in both government and commercial environments provides a solid foundation to achieve outstanding results. He has a Bachelor of Science in engineering operations from Iowa State University. He served eight years in the U.S. Air Force as an acquisition project officer performing project management duties on a number of different development projects ranging in size from $50,000 to $3 billion. He has also worked as a software developer/analyst for the financial services industry for a period of more than six years. For the past five years, Mr. Ashbaugh has been providing information security services to a number of clients for SES. SES provides leading-edge IT solutions to DoD, government, state agencies, and the private sector. Mr. Ashbaugh may be reached through the Iowa branch office of Software Engineering Services.

Mr. Ashbaugh is married to a wonderful woman named Debi and lives in the great Midwest with her and a menagerie consisting of two yellow Labrador retrievers, Sam and Barbara Jean, a lop-eared rabbit named Fast-Girl, a red-eared slider (turtle) named Moses, and the head of the household, a black and white tabby named Sassy Marie.

Chapter 1

Current Trends in Application Security

Information is among the most important assets in any organization. Organizations are constantly building more complex applications to help them accomplish their mission; they are entrusting their sensitive information assets to those applications. But are those information assets secure as they are transmitted, modified, stored, and displayed by those applications? One only has to look at today's headlines to realize that information stored by organizations is not as secure as it could, or should, be.

1.1   Recent Data Security Breaches

Let's look at some of the recent data security breaches in the news today:

- July 27th, 2007: City Harvest, New York. Improper access to systems that contained donor credit card information resulted in the improper exposure of approximately 12,000 records.
- July 26th, 2007: Names and Social Security numbers of 10,554 U.S. Marines were found through the Google Internet search engine.
- July 25th, 2007: The private medical information, including Social Security numbers and treatment details of 25 people who sought medical assistance from the county was posted on the Hidalgo County, Texas Web site.

- July 24th, 2007: A security lapse compromised names, addresses, and Social Security numbers of more than 51,000 employees and patients of St. Vincent's Hospital in Indianapolis, Indiana.
- July 23rd, 2007: A security hole on a Fox News Web server exposed sensitive content to the public, including log-in information that allowed hackers to access names, phone numbers, and e-mail addresses of at least 1.5 million people.
- July 21st, 2007: University of Michigan databases were hacked. More than 5500 names, addresses, Social Security numbers, birth dates, and in some cases, the school districts where former students were teaching were exposed.
- July 20th, 2007: A Pentagon contractor may have compromised personal information, such as names, addresses, birth dates, Social Security numbers, and health information about 580,000 military personnel and their relatives because it did not encrypt data transmitted online.

These incidents represent just one week's worth of recent incidents reported by the Privacy Rights Clearinghouse (PRC) (http://www.privacyrights.org/) with a grand total of 2,159,079 records that were potentially compromised. The PRC has reported a total of 218,621,856 compromised records since the beginning of 2005. In reality, the number is probably much larger, because for many of the breaches listed by the PRC, the number of records actually compromised is unknown, and there are many data breaches that go unreported.

By conservative estimates at least 230 million records held by private companies, private and public organizations, universities, state and local governments, and the federal government have been compromised over the past three years. How were these records compromised? What security controls have failed to protect this valuable resource called information? The answer is that many different controls have failed. Some breaches are caused by the simple loss or theft of media containing confidential information. Theft (or misplacement) of laptops, hard drives, flash drives, backup tapes, and CD/DVD ROM account for many of the data breaches. Still others are caused by operator error, improperly configured or protected systems, improperly or poorly trained people, and transmission of information in the clear or just plain ignorance. Finally, many of these record losses can be attributed at least indirectly to poor, inconsistent, or nonexistent application security.

What is application security? Inasmuch as this book is about secure software development—which means that it is really all about application security—a definition is in order.

1.2 Definition

Application Security: The use of software, hardware, and procedural methods to protect applications and their data from threats to confidentiality, integrity, and availability.

The goal is to build security measures into applications, in order to minimize the likelihood that individuals with malicious intent will be able to manipulate applications and access, steal, modify, or delete sensitive and important data. For many years, security was an afterthought in software design. Even today, many organizations do not include Information Security (IS) personnel in the decisions made during the Software Development Life Cycle (SDLC) until they are ready to implement a fully developed application. Many software developers, system analysts, software architects, business analysts, and project managers believe that information security is the responsibility of the network administration staff, and as long as servers, firewalls, routers, and other hardware are configured properly, and that operating system software is configured properly and patched regularly, then any applications they deploy on those servers, behind the firewalls, will be secure.

At best, that is a naïve approach. Especially when you consider that all software, including operating systems, as well as the firmware that resides within hardware such as routers and firewalls is an application. Everyone reading this book is probably well aware of Microsoft's "Patch Tuesday" when Microsoft releases "patches" for vulnerabilities (or weaknesses) found within its software. If a software giant such as Microsoft, who does practice application security, can continue to develop software with vulnerabilities, then what are the odds that smaller organizations who don't understand the concept of application security have vulnerabilities within the software they develop?

Applications developed by organizations are becoming more accessible to larger audiences over networks, intranets, and the Internet. This also means that they are becoming more vulnerable to a wider variety of threats. We have already seen the results of making applications (and the data processed, transmitted, or stored by those applications) more available to larger audiences: 160 million compromised records since January 1st, 2005. And each compromised record has a cost associated with it. Consider the following facts from a study conducted by Vontu, Inc. and PGP Corporation during 2006:

■ $182 total cost per record lost/compromised (an increase of 30 percent over 2005 costs).
■ Average total cost per reporting company: $4.8 million.
■ Twenty percent of customers terminated their relationship with the company once informed that their private and confidential information had been mishandled with a further 40 percent considering either terminating their relationship or taking some sort of financial action.

- Only 14 percent of customers receiving notices that their private and confidential information had been mishandled were not concerned.
- Cost of new preventive measures put in place after the fact: only four percent of breach cost.

If you extrapolate these figures, then the cost of the 2,159,079 records compromised during our one week in July of 2007 is $510,838,091.40. If a half-billion dollar loss during one week isn't enough to convince you of the need for application security let's look closely at some other driving factors behind the push for good application security.

1.3 Legislative and Regulatory Requirements Affecting Application Security

In addition to the financial impact of data breaches, there is also a legislative and regulatory aspect to consider. Legislators in federal, state, local, and international jurisdictions have become increasingly concerned over the privacy and security of information held by various organizations. This has resulted in an increasing number of laws designed to protect the confidentiality, integrity, and availability of different types of data held by different types of organizations. In addition, regulatory agencies such as the Internal Revenue Service (IRS), Social Security Administration (SSA), Office of Management and Budget (OMB), Centers for Medicare and Medicaid Services (CMS), and the National Institute of Standards and Technology (NIST) all publish their own set of regulations for those organizations doing business with them.

A brief listing of some of the laws and regulations covering the privacy and security of information includes the following:.

- Public Law 74-271, *Social Security Act*, as amended, §1816, Use of public agencies or private organizations to facilitate payment to providers of services
- Public Law 74-271, *Social Security Act*, as amended, §1842, Use of carriers for administration of benefits
- Public Law 93-579, *The Privacy Act of 1974*, as amended
- Public Law 99-474, *Computer Fraud & Abuse Act of 1986*
- Public Law 100-235, *Computer Security Act of 1987*
- Public Law 104-13, *Paperwork Reduction Act of 1978*, as amended in 1995, U.S. Code 44 Chapter 35
- Public Law 104-106, *Clinger–Cohen Act of 1996* (formerly known as the Information Technology Management Reform Act)
- Public Law 104-191, *Health Insurance Portability and Accountability Act (HIPAA), 1996* (formerly known as the Kennedy–Kassenbaum Act) http://www.cms.gov/hipaa

- Public Law 104-231, *Freedom of Information Act (FOIA) of 1974*, as amended by Electronic Freedom of Information Act of 1996
- Public Law 106-398, *Government Information Security Reform Act (GISRA) of 2000*
- Federal Information Security Management Act of 2002 (FISMA)
- Presidential Decision Directive/NSC-63 (PDD 63), Critical Infrastructure Protection, May 22, 1998 http://www.info-sec.com/ciao/paper598.pdf
- Office of Management and Budget (OMB) Circular No. A-123, Management Accountability and Control, June 21, 1995 http://www.whitehouse.gov/omb/circulars/index.html
- OMB Circular No. A-127, Financial Management Systems, Transmittal 2, June 10, 1999 http://www.whitehouse.gov/omb/circulars/index.html
- IRS Publication 1075, Tax Information Security Guidelines for Federal, State, and Local Agencies, June 2000 http://www.irs.gov/pub/irs-pdf/p1075.pdf
- Public Law 107-204, *Public Company Accounting Reform and Investor Protection Act of 2002*, http://frwebgate.access.gpo.gov/cgi-bin/getdoc.cgi?dbname=107_cong_bills&docid=f:h3763enr.tst.pdf
- Public Law 106-102, 113 Statute 1338, *Gramm–Leach–Bliley Financial Services Modernization Act*, November 12, 1999, http://banking.senate.gov/conf/confrpt.htm
- *California SB 1386, *California Security Breach Information Act*, February 12, 2002, http://info.sen.ca.gov/pub/01-02/bill/sen/sb_1351-1400/sb_1386_bill_20020926_chaptered.html

All of these laws and regulations place both financial and legal burdens on those who do not comply with the legislation. The penalties will vary according to the legislation or regulation, but include both civil penalties, as well as criminal penalties that can lead to fines or imprisonment. Some of these penalties can be cumulative and can be significant figures, especially to small- and medium-sized organizations. Failure to comply with yet other regulations can mean the loss of government contracts and the inability to compete for similar contracts for various periods of time.

Legislatures and regulatory agencies aren't the only organizations publishing their own information privacy and security standards and regulations. Industry organizations are also publishing their own security standards enforcing application security.

---

* Although California was the first to pass security breach notification laws, as of January 9, 2007, 35 states have enacted breach notification laws. In addition, 26 states have enacted or are debating further information privacy and security legislation during 2007.

1.4 Industry Standards Requiring or Affecting Application Security

Standards organizations such as the International Organization for Standardization (ISO), the National Institute of Standards and Technology (NIST), the Software Engineering Institute (SEI), the Open Web Application Security Project (OWASP), and others have been providing guidance and standards for application security for years. Some of these organizations (NIST, ISO) have the power to enforce the standards they publish, at least for a limited audience, whereas others simply attempt to provide guidance and assistance for those wishing to create more secure applications (OWASP). However, because most of the guidance provided by these organizations does not have the rule of law behind them, unlike those produced by a legislative or regulatory agency, the effect they have had on making applications more secure is difficult to accurately assess.

Perhaps the industry standard with the largest impact on application security is the Payment Card Industry Data Security Standard (PCI DSS). This standard, although its origins came from several different places, was brought about as a result of the increasing number of data security breaches affecting credit card information. In 2000, VISA initiated its Cardholder Information Security Program (CISP). MasterCard followed suit with its Site Data Protection (SDP) program in 2002. American Express and Discover also began development of their own data security guidelines around this time. In December 2004, CISP (VISA) and SDP (MasterCard) aligned as the PCI Data Security Standard (DSS). The first set of 12 high-level requirements was released as the PCI DSS version 1 in January 2005. Since that time, other major credit card consortiums including American Express, Discover, JCB, and Diner's Club have joined the PCI Security Standards Council.

The PCI DSS applies to two distinct groups:

■ Merchants who accept electronic credit card transactions
■ Service providers who store data or handle credit card transactions for merchants

This includes government agencies at the national, state, and local level who accept electronic credit card transactions for payments of all kinds. Compliance with the standards is enforced by the PCI Security Standards Council. There are three main components of compliance:

■ On-site audits by a qualified third party. These audits must be conducted annually, but are only required of the largest of merchants and service providers.
■ Security self-assessment. PCI compliance is primarily based upon this feature. The self-assessments must be conducted annually, and apply to the smaller merchants and service providers.

■ Network scans. These scans must be conducted quarterly by a qualified third party against all external-facing information resources and are required of all but the smallest of merchants.

Failure to comply with the standards can result in fines and other financial penalties, as well as a loss of the ability to accept credit cards electronically for payment. Imagine a major online retailer losing the ability to accept credit cards as payment. If the retailer could not accept payment via credit card for any significant time at all, that retailer would be out of business. The author is aware of one case where a local business lost the ability to take credit card payments electronically for a nine-month period due to a breach of its credit card payment system. This business lost 75 percent of its revenue stream during that timeframe, and only managed to stay in business because it was allowed to take credit card information over the telephone. It's very easy to see that failure to take the PCI DSS seriously can affect a company's ability to remain in business. Let's take a closer look at the standard itself to see how it affects the software development life cycle.

The standard is made up of 12 high-level requirements. These requirements include the following:

Requirement 1:   Install and maintain a firewall configuration to protect cardholder data.

Requirement 2:   Do not use vendor-supplied defaults for system passwords and other security parameters.

Requirement 3:   Protect stored cardholder data.

Requirement 4:   Encrypt transmission of cardholder data across open, public networks.

Requirement 5:   Use and regularly update anti-virus software.

Requirement 6:   Develop and maintain secure systems and applications.

Requirement 7:   Restrict access to cardholder data by business need-to-know.

Requirement 8:   Assign a unique ID to each person with computer access.

Requirement 9:   Restrict physical access to cardholder data.

Requirement 10: Track and monitor all access to network resources and cardholder data.

Requirement 11: Regularly test security systems and processes.

Requirement 12: Maintain a policy that addresses information security.

Let's look a bit closer at Requirement 6: Develop and maintain secure systems and applications. In September of 2006 version 1.1 of the DSS was released by the PCI Security Standards Council. This version beefed up a number of the requirements in the original standard, among them, Requirement 6. Here is a copy of Requirement 6 from DSS version 1.1.

Requirement 6: Develop and maintain secure systems and applications

Unscrupulous individuals use security vulnerabilities to gain privileged access to systems. Many of these vulnerabilities are fixed by vendor-provided security patches. All systems must have the most recently released, appropriate software patches to protect against exploitation by employees, external hackers, and viruses. Note: Appropriate software patches are those patches that have been evaluated and tested sufficiently to determine that the patches do not conflict with existing security configurations. For in-house developed applications, numerous vulnerabilities can be avoided by using standard system development processes and secure coding techniques.

6.1 Ensure that all system components and software have the latest vendor-supplied security patches installed. Install relevant security patches within one month of release.

6.2 Establish a process to identify newly discovered security vulnerabilities (for example, subscribe to alert services freely available on the Internet). Update standards to address new vulnerability issues.

6.3 Develop software applications based on industry best practices and incorporate information security throughout the software development life cycle.

    6.3.1 Testing of all security patches and system and software configuration changes before deployment

    6.3.2 Separate development, test, and production environments

    6.3.3 Separation of duties between development, test, and production environments

    6.3.4 Production data (live PANs) are not used for testing or development

    6.3.5 Removal of test data and accounts before production systems become active

    6.3.6 Removal of custom application accounts, usernames, and passwords before applications become active or are released to customers

    6.3.7 Review of custom code prior to release to production or customers in order to identify any potential coding vulnerability.

6.4 Follow change control procedures for all system and software configuration changes. The procedures must include the following:

    6.4.1 Documentation of impact

    6.4.2 Management sign-off by appropriate parties

6.4.3   Testing of operational functionality

6.4.4   Back-out procedures

6.5   Develop all Web applications based on secure coding guidelines such as the Open Web Application Security Project guidelines. Review custom application code to identify coding vulnerabilities. Cover prevention of common coding vulnerabilities in software development processes, to include the following:

6.5.1   Unvalidated input

6.5.2   Broken access control (for example, malicious use of user IDs)

6.5.3   Broken authentication and session management (use of account credentials and session cookies)

6.5.4   Cross-site scripting (XSS) attacks

6.5.5   Buffer overflows

6.5.6   Injection flaws (for example, structured query language (SQL) injection)

6.5.7   Improper error handling

6.5.8   Insecure storage

6.5.9   Denial of service

6.5.10 Insecure configuration management

6.6   Ensure that all Web-facing applications are protected against known attacks by applying either of the following methods:

Having all custom application code reviewed for common vulnerabilities by an organization that specializes in application security

Installing an application layer firewall in front of Web-facing applications.

Note: This method is considered a best practice until June 30, 2008, after which it becomes a requirement.

As you can see, Requirement 6 encompasses information security responsibilities and activities throughout the entire SDLC. The very fact that such language has been included in an industry standard carrying the potential consequences of the PCI DSS indicates that the responsibilities of securing applications is not just the job of network administration staff, information security staff, audit staff, and the chief information security officer, but it's also the job of application development staff as well.

As a former application developer, I always believed that it was the primary responsibility of the network administration staff to ensure that my applications were secure. I knew about firewalls, anti-malware programs, Intrusion Detection and Intrusion Prevention Software (IDS/IPS), and other safeguards, but they weren't my responsibility. My primary concern was that only those individuals who should have access to my applications and the data that they contained, did have access, and that as long as the network permissions were set up properly my applications would be secure. I felt that as long as I worked with the business analysts to develop a list of which users should have access to my applications, and passed those lists on to the network administration folks to create the proper network permissions for my applications and databases, then my part in securing applications was over. I couldn't have been more wrong.

Like many application developers, I had never been formally taught my role in securing applications through the code I was writing. I didn't know that unvalidated inputs, buffer overflows, injection flaws, and improper error-handling routines in my code were making my applications insecure. I also didn't realize that the code I wasn't writing (because I didn't realize I needed to prevent buffer overflows, unvalidated inputs, and injection flaws) was affecting the security of my applications and invalidating many of the controls that the network administration staff had put in place. In fact, some of the code that I wasn't writing was not only affecting the security of my own applications, but also the security of other applications and data housed on the same network segments as my application! In fact, because I was unaware of the risks involved with the code I was writing, I was opening up the network itself to attack from a number of different sources and invalidating a number of controls that the network administration staff spent many thousands of person-hours setting up and maintaining!

1.5   Risks Associated with Current Trends

It is evident from the increasing number of data breaches, along with the increasing number of standards published by legislative, regulatory, and industry standard bodies that we are not doing enough to secure our applications. Therefore we need to understand the risks involved in developing software that is not secure. In order to understand the risks involved, we need to understand how to discover risks, how to measure the impact of those risks upon our software development efforts, and finally how to eliminate or reduce those risks. This process is known as *risk assessment* (discovering and measuring impact) and *risk management* (elimination or reduction of risk).

The concept of risk—"the net negative impact of the exercise of a vulnerability or weakness, considering both the probability and the impact of occurrence" [1]—is a concept that is hundreds of years old. Even the concepts of measuring and weighing business risks have been around for a long time. Insurance companies calculate risks every day and use the calculations to set rates for life, health, and property coverage.

Software development is often a constant balancing act among functional requirements, funding, deadlines, limited resources, risk, and flexibility. Many of the current major software development life cycles treat security simply as just one more nonfunctional requirement [2] and do not cover the topic of information security or address it in any detail. The result is often that security remains a non-functional requirement during the software development process. During the software engineering process, when resources, budgets, and schedules become tight, trade-offs must be made as some requirements must be dropped. This trade-off process introduces risk into the software development process. This is not to imply that security is always an important requirement of every software development effort. However, if confidentiality, integrity, and availability of the software or the information it stores, transmits, processes, or displays is important, then security should be considered an important requirement.

When risk is introduced into the software development process where confidentiality, integrity, and availability of the software or its information are important, then the result may be that the resulting software is not as secure as it needs to be. Earlier in this chapter we have seen that data security breaches continue to plague applications. In addition, the General Accounting Office estimates $38 billion per year [3] in U.S. losses due to costs associated with computer software security lapses. How can we resolve this problem?

One solution is to apply information security risk assessment practices to the SDLC. Information security risk assessment is a practice used to ensure that computing networks and systems are secure. By applying these methods to the SDLC, we can actively reduce the number of known vulnerabilities in software as it is developed. For those vulnerabilities that we cannot or choose not to mitigate, we at least become aware of the risks involved as software development proceeds. The remainder of this book focuses on how to apply simple risk assessment techniques to the SDLC process.

But before we can learn risk assessment and risk management techniques, we need some working definition terms that are used in the risk assessment and risk management processes, particularly as they apply to SDLC processes. In addition, it is helpful to understand the relationships between these terms. Therefore, let's look at some definitions we use throughout the book.

- *Risk:* The possibility of suffering harm or loss. It is the potential for realizing unwanted negative consequences of an event. It refers to a situation in which a person or process could do something undesirable or a natural occurrence could cause an undesirable outcome, resulting in a negative impact or consequence.
- *Asset:* Something of value to an organization. It can be a person or person(s), information, a proprietary formula, software, hardware, a building, or a facility.
- *Threat:* Something that is a source of danger to an asset.

- *Vulnerability:* A weakness in the controls protecting an asset that could be exploited by a threat to gain unauthorized access to information or disrupt critical processing.
- *Control:* A mechanism designed to protect an asset. Controls can be physical (i.e., walls, locks, guards, fire alarms, security cameras, etc.), administrative (policies, procedures, standards, and guidelines), or technological (firewalls, anti-virus software, intrusion detection/prevention software, etc.) in nature.

In order to understand the relationship among these concepts, please examine the diagram in Figure 1.1.

An asset is something that we want to protect. For example, an asset might be the credit card number of an online customer. We protect that asset by placing controls (i.e., firewalls, use of encryption software, identification and authorization mechanisms, use of anti-virus software, patch management, etc.) to prevent a malicious individual (our threat is someone who wants to steal our customer's identity) from gaining access to the asset. Some of the controls we may already have in place, for example, a patch management program which ensures that patches are applied to operating system software in order to prevent known vulnerabilities (weaknesses in operating system software) from being exploited by that malicious individual (who could be either external or internal to our operations) to gain access to the customer's credit card number.

However, there may be other vulnerabilities or weaknesses in our applications design of which we are unaware. Consider Figure 1.2. This figure provides an example of how the design of our application may be vulnerable to a type of attack

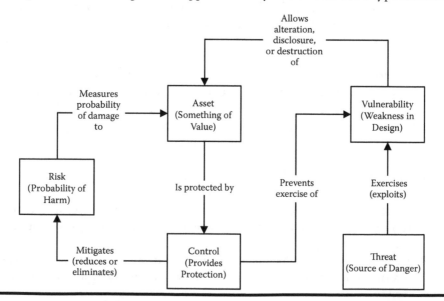

FIGURE 1.1   Relationship among risk concepts

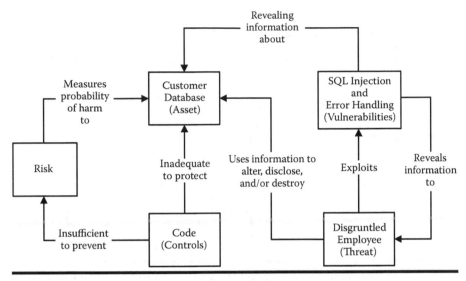

FIGURE 1.2   Risk exists: threats use vulnerabilities to damage assets

known as a Structured Query Language (SQL) injection that could allow our malicious individual (threat) to get the credit card number of our customer despite the other controls we already have in place (patch management, firewalls, encryption, etc.). But how likely is our attacker to discover our SQL injection vulnerability and actually exploit that vulnerability in order to gain the credit card numbers of our customers? What damage would such a breach do not only financially, but also to the reputation of our company? And finally, how can we discover this vulnerability and prevent it from being exploited by the malicious user in the first place?

These are all questions that can be answered through the process of risk management which includes: risk assessment, risk mitigation, and continuous evaluation and improvement in risk assessment and risk mitigation processes. The remainder of this book attempts to teach the basic principles of risk assessment and risk management as it applies to the SDLC. First, we examine how to assess risks during software development including selecting a risk management methodology, identifying assets, identifying threats to those assets, identifying vulnerabilities that might allow a threat to harm an asset, and finally assessing a relative level of risk associated with the threat–vulnerability pair. Next, we look at ways of reducing the relative level of risk through a process known as risk mitigation. During risk mitigation, the attempt is to transfer or eliminate all or part of the risk associated with a threat–vulnerability pair. Consider Figure 1.3, which is a graphical representation of what may happen if additional controls are used to mitigate the risk in our previous example, preventing the threat–vulnerability pair from doing any harm to the asset.

Once we have examined methods of risk mitigation, we turn towards looking at where some of the steps within the risk management process can be

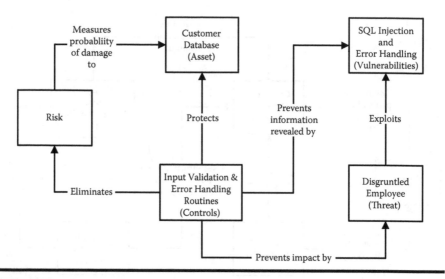

FIGURE 1.3   Risk mitigated: threats are blocked by controls from damaging assets

conducted in a typical software development life cycle. The risk management process outlined in this book consists of ten distinct steps, however, not all of the steps can or should be conducted in any one phase of the software development life cycle. Figure 1.4 outlines this ten-step process, and shows important inputs, as well as outputs from each step. The final step is preparing a risk management plan that:

- Summarizes risks discovered during the risk assessment
- Summarizes the risk mitigation strategies selected
- Provides action plans with timelines for risk mitigation efforts
- Provides plans for continuous evaluation, assessment, and improvement of all risk management activities

1.6   Introduction to Test Case That Relates to Current Trends

The concepts within this book are generally not difficult to understand. But in order to better illustrate the concepts of the book, we apply them to a test case, which is based upon the real-life experiences of the author. As each new concept is developed throughout the course of this book, those concepts are applied to the test case, to help illustrate how such concepts may be used in your situation. With that in mind, let's take a look at the test case.

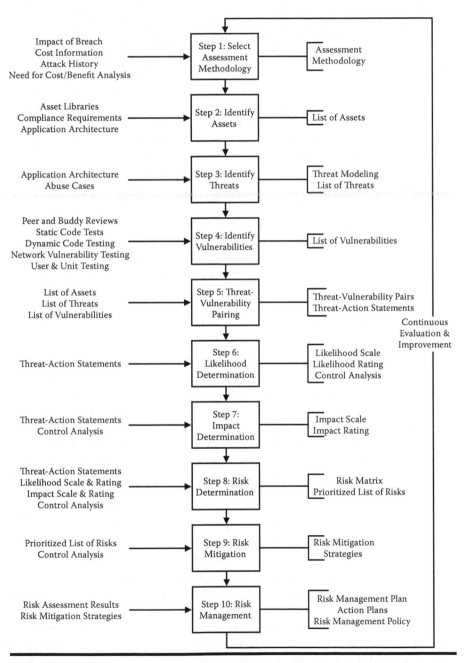

FIGURE 1.4 Risk management process showing inputs and outputs of each step

Imagine that you are a part of a software development team working for a Fortune 500 company in the financial services industry. The company is a publicly traded corporation, and a leader in providing group life and health insurance, as well as retirement services to small- and medium-sized business. The company is a large company with a large and diverse workforce. The company sells numerous retirement plans, each of which can be customized to a large extent. Customers of these plans may have anywhere between ten and several thousand employees.

Your team has been assigned the task of building an application to calculate retirement benefits for the vast majority of retirement plans your company sells. Many of the retirement plans sold by your company allow customers (i.e., employers who provide a retirement plan to their employees through your company) to make additional contributions to their retirement plan at the end of their fiscal year, in order to reduce corporate income tax liabilities. The business rules associated with the calculation of the retirement plan benefits are extremely complex, especially those business rules required by the Internal Revenue Service (IRS) for tax purposes.

Many of the monetary and age limitations imposed upon the IRS business rules may change from year to year, and the application must be able to handle these changes without the need for additional programming changes each year. The IRS also requires that any additional contributions to a retirement plan must be made within two and one half months following the end of the company's fiscal year. Because the majority (90 percent) of your organization's customers synchronize their fiscal year with the calendar year, this means that the majority of calculations conducted by the application you are developing will be processed between January 1st and March 15th of each year. And because the majority of customers make their decisions during the last two weeks of the period (generally because their end-of-year financials are not available before this time period), the majority of the application's use will be during the first two weeks of March each year.

This was one of the primary driving business reasons for developing the application, as prior to this development effort, there was no automated method for calculating retirement benefits associated with a year-end contribution by an employer. Retirement plan administrators used a number of different spreadsheets to calculate the benefits by hand. Some retirement plan administrators understood the complex business rules well, and could correctly calculate the benefits. But the vast majority of retirement plan administrators did not understand how to apply the business rules correctly, with the result that calculations were often completed incorrectly, and the results provided to customers were inconsistent at best.

Whenever a calculation was made incorrectly, the retirement plan company was required to make restitution in order to correct the calculation, regardless of how much time had passed between when the mistake was made, and when it was noticed by any party. Usually, this wasn't a great amount of money, but in some instances could result in large sums. For example, in one particular instance, an IRS audit of a customer revealed that an incorrect limit was applied to a calculation done five years previously. The corporation not only had to pay the IRS penalties and interest fees associated with the incorrect tax deduction its client took, it also had to pay back interest and earnings on the money that would have been invested in individual retirement plan accounts of the employees of that customer and would have earned additional interest over that time period.

The basic requirements of this application include the following.

- It must be Web-based.
- The application must be usable by your company's employees who administer retirement plans for the company's customers.
- The application must also be usable by your company's sales force who will use the calculated results of the application to sell retirement plans to new customers.
- The results of the calculations must be viewable over the Internet by retirement plan customers.
- All Internal Revenue Service (IRS) rules must be followed when calculating benefits. Some of these rules describe limits that may be legally contributed to pension plans which may change from year to year.
- Proprietary business rules created by your company must be used when calculating benefits for certain types of plans.
- The results of the application's calculated benefits must be viewable on screen, printable, and must also be available to be e-mailed to a client in a format that the client cannot change.
- Because a large number of user inputs are required in order to use the application, all user inputs must have the ability to be saved and retrieved at a later time.
- The data required to calculate the benefits must come from current pension plan member databases already established. Such data includes information about individual members of a pension plan including:
  - Names
  - Dates of birth
  - Salaries
  - Identification numbers
  - Amounts contributed to the pension plan
  - Dates of employment/termination

Because members of the company's sales force will use the application for the purpose of selling new pension plans to customers, they must be able to:

- Import datasets provided by potential customers.
- Create dummy datasets on the fly for illustration purposes.
- Utilize dummy datasets created and stored in the application data base.
- The results of all calculations must be saved and archived for a given period of time.

Although these are by no means all of the requirements the application must meet, they do represent enough of the major requirements required to illustrate the concepts of this book. Throughout the remainder of this book, at the end of each chapter, we apply the lessons learned in that chapter to this test case. It is hoped that by the end of the book, you will understand the concepts of risk assessment and risk management as they apply to the information security risks inherent in all software development efforts.

1.7   Conclusion

In this introductory chapter we have laid the foundation for a need for more secure application development processes. We looked at some of the data security breaches that have appeared in recent headlines, and we have looked at some of the most recent legislative and compliance initiatives that require increasing levels of application security. We have also looked at how some of these compliance issues are coming not from legislative or compliance agencies, but from within industry itself, such as the PCI DSS.

From there, we looked at how the recent trends represent a level of risk to organizations and their software development efforts. We also looked at the need for understanding the concepts associated with risk and developed a working definition of risk as it applies to software development efforts. A brief outline of the risk management process was included. Finally, we were introduced to a test case, based upon the real-life experiences of the author, which is utilized to demonstrate each of the steps associated with the risk management process. In the next chapter, we turn to the first step of the risk management process: the selection of a risk assessment methodology.

References

[1] Petersen, Gunnar. Phasing security into the SDLC – A Comparison of Approaches. *Risk Management.* January 10, 2006. http://1raindrop.typepad.com/1_raindrop/2006/01/phasing_securit.html.
[2] Improving security across the software development lifecycle – Task force report. *National Cyber Security Partnership.* April 1, 2004. http://www.cyberpartnership.org/SDLCFULL.pdf.
[3] Lavenhar, Steven and Petersen, Gunnar. Architectural risk assessment. *Cigital Inc.* September 28, 2005. https://buildsecurityin.us-cert.gov/portal/article/bestpractices/architectural_risk_analysis/architectural_risk_assessment.xml.

Chapter 2

Security Risk Assessment Methodologies

The first step in the risk management process is the selection of a risk assessment methodology. Figure 2.1 illustrates the some of the inputs and outputs associated with this step of the risk management process.

There are two ways of measuring risk, quantitative and qualitative. *Quantitative* analysis assigns real dollar values to the loss of an asset. *Qualitative* risk analyses are all about identifying and relating risks relative to each other. The perceived impact of loss is determined rather than the actual dollars associated with the loss. Quantitative risk measurement is the standard in many industries, particularly the insurance and finance industries. However, quantitative risk analysis is typically not used to measure the risk associated with information system assets. Why? Because it is difficult to accurately assign a value to information assets, and also because there is a lack of statistical information making it possible to determine how often threats materialize. For example, how do you assign a value to the loss in public confidence in the services an organization provides? How often will spam attacks be directed against an organization? When will the next new exploit for a specific application be discovered and how quickly will that exploit find its way into malicious code? It's improbable to expect to be able to answer these types of questions with any degree of certainty.

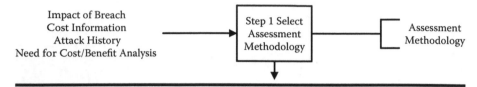

FIGURE 2.1   Inputs and outputs associated with selecting a risk assessment methodology

2.1   Definitions

Before we can compare the two methods of measuring risk, we need some good working definitions of each type of method.

- *Quantitative* risk assessment practices are numerical approaches that assign real dollar values to the amount of damage an organization may sustain when assets are altered, destroyed, disclosed, or made unavailable by threats that exploit vulnerabilities in the controls or safeguards which protect those assets. Quantitative methods estimate the numerical frequency or probability that an asset may be compromised by a threat–vulnerability pair.
- *Qualitative* risk assessment practices identify risks and rate them in relation to each other, or to a defined rating scale based upon the perceived impact an organization may sustain when assets are altered, destroyed, disclosed, or made unavailable by threats that exploit vulnerabilities in the controls or safeguards which protect those assets. Qualitative methods use subjective means and relative rating scales to estimate the frequency or probability that an asset may be compromised by a threat–vulnerability pair.

As you can see from the definitions, although both methods attempt to measure the amount of damage that might be sustained by an organization when assets are altered, destroyed, disclosed, or made unavailable, the way they go about it is very different. Quantitative methods attempt to assign an actual dollar amount to the damage caused, whereas qualitative methods use subjective ratings rather than an actual dollar amount. Each method has pros and cons, and either method will produce a tangible result. Because each method is different in nature, it may be difficult to choose between the two. We are then left with the question: which methodology should be used in a given situation? Before we can answer that, we need to look more closely at each of the methodologies involved, including their benefits and liabilities.

2.2 Quantitative Risk Assessment Methodologies

As we've already seen, quantitative methodologies assign real dollar values to the amount of damage sustained by an organization when its assets are altered, destroyed, disclosed, or otherwise made unavailable. But how are these dollar values assigned? Basically the dollar values are assigned using five standard equations:

- Calculation of exposure factors
- Calculation of a single loss expectancy
- Calculation of an annualized rate of occurrence
- Calculation of annualized loss expectancy
- Cost-benefit analysis

Let's examine each of these equations in detail.

2.2.1 Exposure Factor

An *Exposure Factor* (*EF*) represents the percentage of asset loss caused by an identified threat. It represents a number between 0 and 100 percent. As an example, our asset is a database containing the credit card information of our customers. If an attacker (threat) destroys that database, and we have no backup copies of the database available, then the EF is 100 percent. If however, an attacker is only able to destroy about half the database before the attacker is discovered, then the EF is 50 percent. There are a number of methods that may be used to calculate the EF, some of which are subjective in nature and some of which are objective in nature. Either method of calculating the EF includes looking at the records of historical attacks and determining on average how much of an asset is lost when an attack on that asset occurs. Often these methods also involve determining how quickly attacks on assets are discovered, as well as how quickly attacks are blocked. Objective methods will actually calculate statistical averages utilizing this type of information to arrive at a final figure for the EF, whereas subjective methods will utilize generalizations based upon a review of this data, for example, typically 50 percent of a database is lost when an attack of one type occurs, while only 25 percent is lost when a different type of attack occurs.

2.2.2 Single Loss Expectancy

Single Loss Expectancy (*SLE*) represents the dollar amount caused during a single loss from a given cause. It is calculated by multiplying the Value of the Asset (AV) by the EF.

$$SLE = AV \times EF$$

Continuing our example from above, let's assume that our exposure factor is 50 percent and that the value of the database is $100,000.00. In this instance the SLE would be:

$$SLE = AV \times EF = \$100,000.00\ (AV) \times 0.5\ (EF) = \$50,000.00.$$

Of course it is important to understand the value of the asset in order to calculate this value. Unfortunately, it isn't always easy to determine the value of a specific asset. For example, how much is the data within a database worth? If the data within a database consists of account numbers, access codes for those accounts, and amounts of funds contained in those accounts, the data may be worth the combined total of funds in all of the accounts. However, what about a database that contains customer names and addresses? How much is that information worth? Is it worth the amount of money paid to the sales staff to generate the leads associated with the list of customers? Or is it worth some other amount? How much would it be worth to a competitor? These questions aren't always so easy to answer. What about intangible assets such as corporate reputation? What value can be placed upon an organization's reputation if that corporation suffers a public data breach of confidential information? Is it the amount the stock goes down when such a breach is announced? Is it the amount of revenue lost when customers leave? But what about lost revenue in the form of potential customers who might have considered purchasing from the company before a breach, but who take their business elsewhere afterwards? Again, these intangible questions are not always easy to answer.

2.2.3 Annualized Rate of Occurrence

Annualized Rate of Occurrence (ARO) represents the estimated frequency with which the threat will occur in the period of one year. If we expect the threat to occur only once every five years, then the ARO is 0.2; that is, 1 threat/5 years = 1/5 = 0.2. Likewise if we expect the threat to occur quarterly, then the ARO is 4; that is, 4 threats/1 year = 4/1 = 4.

ARO = number of times a threat will occur in a one year time span.

Although ARO seems like a straightforward number to calculate, it is often difficult to determine. How often will an organization be hit with a computer virus that the corporate anti-virus solution cannot handle in the next year? How often will a tornado destroy a data center? How often will an employee erroneously enter data used to make critical calculations? Calculations of ARO are often based upon statistical analysis methods of the same type used to calculate insurance rates. It is possible to look at histories of similar threats to determine the likelihood that they will occur. For example, there is plenty of data available through anti-virus software vendors on the number of virus threats that affect specific platforms, including information on current trends. Likewise, insurance companies have statistical analyses that can provide data on how often a typical organization suffers damage due to severe weather or other environmental threats. And internal audit organizations may have information on how many errors and omissions are discovered within the organization in a given year.

2.2.4 Annualized Loss Expectancy

The *Annualized Loss Expectancy (ALE)* represents the dollar loss that can be expected in a given year for a particular threat. ALE is calculated by multiplying the SLE by the ARO.

$$ALE = SLE \times ARO$$

Again, let's continue the example we started above. We assume that an attacker will get through our defenses and destroy our customer database once every five years. Therefore our ARO is 0.2 (1 event/5 years = 0.2 events/year). Because we already determined that our SLE would be $50,000.00, our ALE then becomes:

$$ALE = SLE \times ARO = \$50,000.00 \; (SLE) \times 0.2 \; (ARO) = \$10,000.00.$$

When calculating ALE it is important to understand that the ALE is only as reliable as the SLE and the ARO. Because both of these values can often be difficult to accurately determine, an analyst must be careful when considering the accuracy of any ALE calculation.

2.2.5 Cost-Benefit Analysis

Finally, we can conduct a *cost-benefit analysis* for any potential controls or safeguards we planned in order to prevent the threat from destroying our customer database. Let's assume that we can put in place intrusion detection software that will detect any attempt to destroy our customer database and allow us to stop such an attempt earlier in the process. Instead of 50 percent of the database being destroyed, only 10 percent of the database would be destroyed. Therefore our new EF would be 0.1. Let's apply all of the formulas again using this new EF.

$$SLE = AV \times EF = \$100,000.00 \; (AV) \times 0.1 \; (EF) = \$10,000.00$$

The software won't change the number of times we are attacked, so our ARO is still 0.2. Therefore ALE is:

$$ALE = SLE \times ARO = \$10,000.00 \; (SLE) \times 0.2 \; (ARO) = \$2,000.00.$$

So the loss we could expect before we installed the new intrusion detection software is \$10,000.00/year where the loss we could expect after we installed the new intrusion detection software is \$2,000.00/year. It certainly appears that the intrusion detection software is a worthwhile purchase and we should automatically put it in place, right? This isn't necessarily the case. We first must consider the cost of the intrusion detection software itself.

Let's assume that the cost of the intrusion detection software is \$10,000.00 per year. But that's simply the cost of the software. To do a true cost-benefit analysis, we need to know the *value* of the intrusion detection software to the company. To calculate that, we use the following equation:

VALUE (of a control) = *ALE* (before the control is implemented)
– *ALE* (after the control is implemented) – *Annual cost of the control.*

Using our example the value of the intrusion detection software then becomes:

Value = \$10,000.00 (ALE before implementation) – \$2,000.00 (ALE after implementation) – \$10,000.00 (annual cost of the software) = –\$2,000.00.

In this case, the value to the company is a negative number. Therefore, even though we would suffer less due to any single loss of the database, we would end up costing the company more in the long run. If the value of the intrusion detection software is only \$5000.00, then the value to the company becomes:

Value = \$10,000.00 (ALE before) – \$2,000.00 (ALE after) –
\$5,000.00 (annual cost) = \$3,000.00.

In this case the value to the company is a positive number and therefore implementing the intrusion detection software will save the company money in the long run.

As you can see, the formulas used to perform quantitative risk analyses are not complicated at all. Although there may be some art in determining the exact value of assets, the exact exposure factor, and the annualized rate of occurrence, specific values for these terms can be determined based upon historical and statistical records and other factors. The bottom line is that concrete numbers can be calculated to determine the value to the company of any specific control that may be implemented. That's the greatest strength of a quantitative risk analysis: concrete dollar amounts can be assigned, so that budgets can be built wisely with a full understanding of all risks involved. Because all decisions resulting from quantitative analysis are based upon actual dollar amounts, consensus is often easier to achieve. In addition, it is often easier to obtain budget dollars for information security controls and safeguards when cost-benefit analysis can provide the value of those safeguards to management. It is also easier to set priorities among competing projects when the value of those projects is clearly understood against the bottom line. Finally, because the end results of all controls and safeguards can be easily related to the company's financial objectives, it is easier all around to obtain funding for such controls.

However, although there are a number of powerful benefits to using quantitative risk analysis methods, there are also some liabilities involved. First, while the calculations themselves within a quantitative analysis aren't difficult to understand or to calculate, some of the individual values can be difficult to determine. For example, how much is a customer database worth? Is it worth the annual profit provided by those customers to a company? Is it worth the amount of advertising spent in order to develop the leads that led to the database? Or is it worth some other amount? What about reputation? What is the cost of a loss in reputation for a company who has had a public breach of data security? Or what about the cost in lives if a military troop movement database was hacked into? Sometimes it's not easy to come up with exact dollar figures for these amounts.

And what about EF and ARO? Both of these values represent the probability or likelihood that an event will occur, or how severe the damage will be if it does occur. Although historical data can give you some sense of how often an event has occurred in the past, or how much damage was caused when the event did occur, it is not a 100 percent accurate barometer of how often such an event will occur in the future, or the amount of damage that might be caused by such an event. This is especially true in today's environment where the interval between vulnerability and exploit is rapidly decreasing

Perhaps the biggest drawback to quantitative risk assessment methodologies is the amount of information that must be gathered. ALE both before and after implementation of controls and safeguards must be determined for each combination of asset, threat, and vulnerability. Depending upon the scope of the risk assessment, this can lead to hundreds, if not thousands or even tens of thousands, of calculations.

So how do we determine if a quantitative risk analysis is the right methodology to use? Before answering, we need to understand the benefits and liabilities of qualitative risk assessments.

2.3 Qualitative Risk Assessment Methodologies

Whereas quantitative risk assessment methodologies rely on assigning probabilities and dollar values to the loss that can be expected when a threat exploits a vulnerability to attack an asset, qualitative risk analysis focuses on the perceived damage a threat could cause to an asset, and ranks those perceived risks against each other, or against a pre-defined scale. Typically, qualitative risk analysis is based upon three factors: likelihood of occurrence, impact of occurrence, and risk level.

2.3.1   Likelihood of Occurrence

Likelihood of occurrence represents the likelihood that a threat will exploit a vulnerability to affect an asset. It is typically represented by a subjective term such as high, medium, or low instead of an actual value, as is the case in a quantitative risk analysis. Typically, before a risk analysis process begins, once the scope of the analysis has been set, a scale for likelihood of occurrence is created. Such scales can be based upon how often an event may occur, the motivation of the threat, or what controls or safeguards are already in place to prevent vulnerabilities from being exploited. A simple example of a likelihood of occurrence scale based upon how often an event may occur is shown below:.

- *Low likelihood* occurs when vulnerabilities are exploited by threats less than once a year.
- *Medium likelihood* occurs when vulnerabilities are exploited by threats more than once a year, but less than once a month.
- *High likelihood* occurs when vulnerabilities are exploited by threats more than once a month.

Likelihood scales may also be based upon such things as:

- Whether a threat has the motive or means to exploit vulnerabilities
- Whether current controls or safeguards are effective in preventing a threat from exercising vulnerabilities
- Combinations of all of the above

An example of a scale based upon the motive and means of the threat might be:

- *Low likelihood* occurs when the threat has neither the motive, nor the means necessary to exploit vulnerabilities.
- *Medium likelihood* occurs when the threat has either the motive or the means necessary to exploit vulnerabilities, but not both.
- *High likelihood* occurs when the threat has both the motive and the means necessary to exploit vulnerabilities.

An example of a scale based upon the effectiveness of controls might be:

■ *Low likelihood* occurs whenever current controls and safeguards are completely effective in preventing threats from exercising vulnerabilities.
■ *Medium likelihood* occurs whenever current controls and safeguards are partially effective in preventing threats from exercising vulnerabilities.
■ *High likelihood* occurs whenever current controls and safeguards are totally ineffective in preventing threats from exercising vulnerabilities.

Finally, an example of a combined scale might be:

■ *Low likelihood* occurs whenever the following conditions are met:
  – Controls are completely effective against threats.
  – Threats have neither motive nor means.
■ *Medium likelihood* occurs whenever:
  – Controls are partly effective against threats.
  – Threats have motive or means but not both.
■ *High likelihood* occurs whenever:
  – Controls are completely ineffective against threats.
  – Threats have both motive and means.

As you can see, these scales are very subjective in nature. The exact nature of the scale used can vary widely depending upon the scope and requirements of the assessment. Numeric scales of 0–10, 1–5, and so on can be used instead, as can scales using subjective terms such terms as negligible, very low, low, medium, high, very high, and so on.

2.3.2   Magnitude of Impact

Magnitude of impact is an attempt to measure the damage to an organization if the threat is able to exploit vulnerabilities and cause damage to assets. Again, it is represented in qualitative risk analysis methodologies as a subjective scale that is often determined when the scope and requirements of the risk assessment are determined. An example of a simple impact scale follows:

■ *Low impact* occurs when there is the loss of some assets or some resources must be utilized to clean up or repair the loss. There is no noticeable impact upon the organization's mission, reputation, or interests from such a loss.
■ *Medium impact* occurs when there is a costly loss of assets or resources, or a considerable number of resources must be utilized to clean up or repair the loss. There is a noticeable impact upon the organization's mission, reputation, or interests from such a loss.
■ *High impact* occurs when a death or human injury results, or there is a significant loss of assets and resources, or a significant cost to clean up or repair the

loss. There is a substantial impact upon the organization's mission, reputation, and interests from such a loss.

Again, this is a very subjective listing. As with the likelihood of occurrence scales, varying scales can be used. Additionally, it is possible to assign dollar values using this methodology. A scale utilizing dollar values might look something like the following:

■ *Low impact* occurs whenever the damage to an asset or the amount of resources needed to clean up from a loss is $10,000.00 or less.
■ *Medium impact* occurs whenever the damage to an asset or the cost to clean up from a loss is more than $10,000.00 but less than $100,000.00.
■ *High impact* occurs whenever the damage to an asset or the cost to clean up from a loss is greater than $100,000.00.

2.3.3   Risk Level

Risk level in a qualitative risk analysis represents a relative assessment of the overall risk involved dependent upon the likelihood of occurrence and the impact of the threat. It is typically based upon cross-referencing likelihood of occurrence with impact of the threat in a table that is created at the time the scope and requirements of the risk assessment were established. An example of such a table is found in Table 2.1.

Let's return to the example of a malicious individual destroying a customer database we used in our quantitative risk analysis and determine a risk level. We use the following likelihood and impact scales in our analysis:

■ *Low likelihood* if the threat occurs less than once a year
■ *Medium likelihood* if the threat occurs more than once a year but less than once a month
■ *High likelihood* if the threat occurs more than once a month
■ *Low impact* if the damage is $10,000.00 or less

Table 2.1   Risk Level

Threat Likelihood	Impact		
	Low	*Medium*	*High*
Low	Low Risk	Low Risk	Medium Risk
Medium	Low Risk	Medium Risk	Medium Risk
High	Medium Risk	Medium Risk	High Risk

- *Medium impact* if the damage is more than $10,000.00 and less than $100,000.00
- *High impact* if the damage is $100,000.00 or more

If you remember in our previous example, we determined that such an attack was likely to happen only once every five years. Therefore in our qualitative analysis our likelihood of occurrence is *Low*. The single loss expectancy from our quantitative example was $50,000.00, therefore in our quantitative analysis our impact is *Medium*. Cross-indexing a *Low* likelihood with a *Medium* impact in Table 2.1 we see that the risk level is *Medium*. In a typical qualitative risk analysis we would then perform the same analysis for all potential threat–vulnerability–asset pairings. All high risks would be grouped together, all medium risks would be grouped together, and all low risks would be grouped together. Resources would then be assigned to address the high risks first, then the medium risks, and finally the low risks, if any resources remained.

Cost-benefit analysis can also be performed using qualitative analysis, however, the results of such an analysis are not as conclusive as those produced using a quantitative analysis. Continuing using our quantitative analysis example, we found that the SLE after the installation of an intrusion detection safeguard was $10,000.00. Therefore the impact level in our qualitative analysis is now *Low*. Cross-indexing a *Low* impact with a *Low* likelihood in Table 2.1 we see that our risk level is now *Low*. Our cost-benefit analysis would then tell us that our risk level has been reduced from *Medium* to *Low* by implementing the intrusion detection safeguard. However, that's as far as we can go with a qualitative cost-benefit analysis. Our quantitative analysis was able to distinguish if the intrusion detection safeguard was of value to our organization or not based upon the annual cost of the safeguard. The best that a qualitative analysis can due is to compare the cost of the proposed safeguard with the change in impact level.

For example, if the cost of the safeguard was $10,000.00 and the impact level changed from medium to low, we would have a potential savings of between $0.00 and $90,000.00 a year. If we suspected that our potential savings was only going to be $0.00 we may have concluded that the cost was too high and would not have spent the money on the safeguard. However, if we suspected that our savings were going to be on the high end, we may well have suspected that the safeguard at $10,000.00 was a good value to the company. However, if you remember our quantitative analysis, we determined that the value to the company of a $10,000.00 intrusion detection system would actually end up costing us $2000.00 a year!

If qualitative risk assessments cannot provide us with accurate numbers to base our decisions on, then why would anyone ever use a qualitative risk analysis? There are a number of reasons to use qualitative risk analyses. In fact, within the information security field, qualitative risk analysis is probably used more often than quantitative methods. First and foremost, qualitative risk analyses are easier to conduct than quantitative methods, at least without a large database that provides historical data on the value of assets, the cost to clean up after events, and the probability and frequency of events occurring.

Secondly, and perhaps more important, is that it is often difficult to assign the values required in a quantitative risk analysis. For example, how do you assign a value to the loss in public confidence in the services an organization provides? How often will spam attacks be directed against an organization? When will the next new exploit for a specific application be discovered and how quickly will that exploit find its way into malicious code? It's improbable to expect to be able to answer these types of questions with any degree of certainty. It is much easier to assign a subjective label to these values than an actual value. And assigning the wrong value to an asset or to an exposure factor or annualized rate of occurrence can lead to the conclusion that the cost of a safeguard is worthwhile when it actually isn't.

Let's return to the example we began in our look at quantitative analysis. Let's assume that we wrongly assigned a value of 0.5 instead of 0.2 to our annualized rate of occurrence or ARO before we implement any additional safeguards. That is, we expect to see the threat happen every other year, instead of only once every five years. This now means that our ALE is $25,000.00 (i.e., *ALE = SLE × ARO* = $50,000.00 × 0.5 = $25,000.00). Now if we apply our cost-benefit analysis to the $10,000.00/year intrusion detection safeguard we get a value to the company of $5000.00/year (i.e., *Value = ALE* (before control) – *ALE* (after control) – annual cost of control = $25,000.00 – $10,000.00 – $10,000.00 = $5000.00). We would come to the conclusion that implementing the $10,000.00 intrusion detection safeguard would save the company $5000.00 a year when in reality it would actually cost the company $2000.00 per year, all because we did not accurately determine an ARO. Because we often do not have accurate values for AV, ARO, and EF, or because they may be impossible to determine, the results of a quantitative analysis may not prove to be any more accurate than the results from our qualitative analysis.

However, without any numeric cost-benefit numbers, it may prove difficult, if not impossible to convince management to spend limited resources on additional controls or safeguards. In addition, when losses do occur, it may be difficult to quantify how additional controls or safeguards can effectively reduce those losses to an acceptable level.

Understanding the differences between quantitative and qualitative risk assessments is the first step to choosing a risk assessment methodology. However, there are numerous published risk assessment methodologies and automated tools for performing both quantitative and qualitative risk analysis. Choosing from among these published methodologies and tools is not an easy task. Before selecting a risk assessment methodology for our test case, we examine a couple of these published methodologies and tools in more detail.

2.4   Published Methodologies

2.4.1   *Software Engineering Institute's OCTAVE*

OCTAVE stands for Operationally Critical Threat, Asset, and Vulnerability Evaluation. It was developed by the Computer Engineering Institute (CEI) at Carnegie-Mellon University. It is a qualitative risk analysis methodology. It relies on small teams of individuals from both the business units of an organization and from the IT function within an organization to work together in addressing the security needs of the organization. OCTAVE relies on the knowledge of many different individuals to define what security safeguards are already in place, identify critical assets, and then identify threats to those assets. From this knowledge a security strategy that reduces or eliminates the threats to those assets can be developed.

OCTAVE was designed to be flexible and uses a three-phased approach. First, critical assets and the threats to those assets are identified. Next vulnerabilities, both organizational and technical, that expose the assets to the threats are identified. Finally, risk mitigation strategies are developed to reduce or eliminate the threats to those assets. All of these activities are supported by a catalog of known practices, as well as surveys and worksheets designed to facilitate the discussion and capture of information. Although OCTAVE was designed for large organizations (300 or more employees) there are other versions, including OCTAVE-S and OCTAVE Allegro that have been designed for smaller organizations.

There are numerous publications describing the OCTAVE methodology in detail and training is also available should you choose OCTAVE for your methodology.

2.4.2   *STRIDE*

Stride is a methodology used primarily for the identification of threats. It was fathered by Microsoft and is based on six basic types of threat category. These threat categories spell out the acronym STRIDE and include:

- *Spoofing:* Where a user attempts to become another user or assume some of the attributes of another user. One simple example of spoofing is a user who obtains the log-in credentials of another user through techniques such as shoulder surfing, keystroke logging, or finding the yellow sticky note with a password left behind by the user of a system, and logging in as a different individual who may have different privileges.
- *Tampering of data:* Where users can change information provided to them by an application and return that changed information in order to manipulate the validation routines, or lack thereof, utilized by the application. Example: In an e-commerce site, the price of an object is embedded in the HTML code used to display the shopping cart. An attacker alters the price by altering the

underlying HTML code and returns a price that is lower than it should be, and which is not validated by the application.

▪ *Repudiation:* Where users of an application can claim that they didn't make a transaction when there are insufficient auditing controls in place. Example: If account transfers are not properly logged in an audit file, or if the audit file is not sufficiently protected such that it can be altered, then it may become impossible to determine who or what process transferred money from one account to another.

▪ *Information disclosure:* Where information provided by a user to an application, such as a bank account number, password, or credit card number is intercepted and revealed by an attacker. Example: Data left in hidden fields, HTTP headers, or other system caches is found and revealed by an attacker.

▪ *Denial of service:* Where the use of large files, complex calculations, or large and complex queries can be used to tie up system resources for a significant amount of time.

▪ *Elevation of privilege:* Where users are able to gain additional rights and privileges that are normally associated with administration accounts.

STRIDE is easy to understand and apply and addresses key application security threats.

2.4.3   DREAD

DREAD is a methodology also fathered by Microsoft. However, the focus of DREAD is not on the identification of threats, but rather the impact associated with a risk. DREAD is an algorithm and also an acronym. The DREAD acronym stands for:

▪ Damage potential
▪ Reproducibility
▪ Exploitability
▪ Affected Users
▪ Discoverability

It is a quantifiable analysis based upon the following algorithm:

$$RISK = (Damage + Reproducibility + Exploitability + Affected\ Users + Discoverability) / 5.$$

This algorithm produces a number between 0 and 10, and the greater the number the greater the potential risk. It works using a series of scales that assign number values to each of the DREAD categories.

- *Damage potential* is the amount of damage potentially caused by a threat ranked on the following scale:
  - 0 = No damage.
  - 5 = Individual user data is affected.
  - 10 = Complete system or data destruction.
- *Reproducibility* represents how easy it is to reproduce the attack:
  - 0 = Very hard or impossible.
  - 5 = Only one or two steps are required, perhaps authentication and authorization.
  - 10 = Nothing more is required other than a browser and address bar.
- *Exploitability* represents the knowledge necessary to exploit a threat:
  - 0 = Advanced programming and network knowledge and advanced or custom attack tools.
  - 5 = Published exploit instructions are available on the Internet, or an exploit is easily performed using available attack tools.
  - 10 = Just a Web browser.
- *Affected users* represents the number of users affected by a possible exploit:
  - 0 = None.
  - 5 = Some users but not all.
  - 10 = All users.
- *Discoverability* represents how easy it is to discover the threat:
  - 0 = Very difficult or nearly impossible, at least not without source code or administrative access.
  - 5 = Monitoring network traffic will allow an attacker to figure it out.
  - 9 = Details of the fault are in the public domain.
  - 10 = Information is visible in the Web browser address bar or in a Web form.

DREAD represents more of a business impact threat model than a true risk analysis methodology.

2.4.4 TRIKE

TRIKE is a methodology sponsored by the open-source community. It is a risk-based approach with models for:

- Requirements
- Implementation
- Threats
- Risks

But TRIKE differs from STRIDE and DREAD in its focus on stakeholders, on the communications with those stakeholders, and empowering those stakeholders to make informed decisions based upon their understanding of the risks associated with a development effort.

2.4.5 Australian/New Zealand Standard 4360:2004

AS/NZ 4360 is one of the first formal standards for documenting and managing risk. It is a five-step process that is flexible and iterative in nature. The five steps of this process include:

- *Establishing context:* That is, which assets or systems are important?
- *Identifying risks:* Which specific risks are apparent?
- *Analyze risks:* Look at the risk and determine if any controls or safeguards are already in place.
- *Evaluate the risk:* Does any residual risk remain after the controls or safeguards have been taken into account?
- *Treat the risk:* Devise strategies for mitigating any residual risk.

2.4.6 Common Vulnerability Scoring System (CVSS)

CVSS was developed by the U.S. Department of Homeland Security as a method of scoring the vulnerabilities that allow a threat to access assets. CVSS receives input from a number of different and well-known organizations and corporations including:

- Cisco Systems
- Symantec
- ISS
- Qualys
- Microsoft
- The Computer Emergency Response Team Coordination Center (CERT/CC)
- eBay

CVSS can be used to assist in the relative ranking of risks based upon how easy a vulnerability is to exploit.

2.5 Automated Risk Assessment Tools

There are a number of commercially available and freeware tools to help automate the process of collecting information for either a qualitative or quantitative risk assessment methodology. Some of these tools include: RiskWatch®, Acertus™, and others. One of the freeware tools available to assist in risk management is the Automated Security Self-Evaluation Tool (ASSET) developed by the National Institute of Science and Technology. Asset is a qualitative risk assessment methodology based upon NIST's Self Assessment Guide for IT systems. Although ASSET is no longer supported due to the NIST adoption of a new self assessment methodology by NIST, it is still available through the NIST Web site at: http://csrc.nist.gov/archive/asset/ and can provide a good starting point for any individual getting started with risk analysis.

The power that most automated risk assessment tools bring to any project lies in their ability to:

■ Help in the data-gathering process
■ Identify and quantify risks by using the relationships among asset, threats, loss probability, and vulnerability
■ Assess baseline compliance against requirements
■ Identify current threat and vulnerability levels
■ Provide recommendations for remediation of risks
■ Help in repeating risk assessment activities
■ Provide metrics and trends between current and past risk assessment results

These automated risk assessment tools allow organizations to develop strong risk management programs by helping establish repeatable risk gathering, assessment, and mitigation processes.

2.6 Tips in Selecting a Methodology

OCTAVE, STRIDE, DREAD, TRIKE, AS/NZ 4360, CVSS, and ASSET represent a very small sampling of the published risk assessment methodologies and tools available to use when performing a risk assessment. Selecting a published methodology or toolset can greatly assist in getting consistent results from an assessment. However, following a published methodology or using a commercial or freeware risk assessment tool is not required in order to actually conduct a risk assessment. Both quantitative and qualitative risk assessments can be conducted without utilizing a published methodology or using risk assessment software.

The first step in conducting any information security risk assessment for a software development project is in choosing either a quantitative method or a qualitative method. The key lies in determining which method is best for a given software development effort. There are some key factors that are helpful in determining which methodology should be utilized.

Quantitative risk assessment practices are numerical approaches that assign real dollar values to assets, and numerical values to probabilities of occurrence. Therefore in order to use a quantitative risk analysis we need to know or identify:

- The real dollar value of all assets involved
- The dollar values associated with the loss, damage, disclosure, or delay in availability of those assets
- All potential threat sources to our assets
- The vulnerabilities or attack routes that those threats can use to gain access to those assets
- The probability that those assets will be damaged by a threat exercising a vulnerability

How does any organization know what these values are? There are a number of ways this information may be gathered. The value of assets may be what was paid to obtain them, or what it would cost in the current market to replace them. Damage to data and systems can be gathered by an analysis of past attacks and understanding the costs required to repair, replace, and restore systems to their pre-attack status. Past attack histories can provide us with the frequency, severity, and likelihood of attack. Newer organizations that may not have historical repositories of attacks, their severity, frequency, and costs, can look to institutions such as the Computer Security Institute (CSI), Federal Bureau of Investigation (FBI), and other organizations that publish statistics on data security breaches and their frequency, severity, and associated costs in order to obtain this information.

However, simply having the statistical information on assets, threats, and vulnerabilities required to perform a quantitative risk analysis does not mean that an organization should automatically use a quantitative risk analysis. There are other factors to take into consideration. For example, how much time is required to perform the analysis? Typically, unless large databases of cost and probability are already in place, quantitative analysis will usually take longer than qualitative analysis, particularly when used in conjunction with software development efforts. When using rapid software development methodologies, quantitative risk analysis may not be practical. Another consideration is cost-benefit analysis. As we have seen from the examples in this chapter, qualitative analysis may not provide enough information to justify increased costs associated with longer development cycles, or additional safeguards built into a software development project. Likewise, if the costs or probabilities used in performing a quantitative risk analysis are not completely accurate a risk exists that any additional safeguards selected for our software development may not be cost effective and may actually increase the cost of the software development effort without making that effort any safer or less risky.

Selecting a methodology should always depend upon the sensitivity and criticality of the information being stored and utilized by the software development effort. Quantitative methods are generally preferred where the data stored, displayed, modified, and transmitted by the software development effort is extremely sensitive or critical. However, the more sensitive and critical the data is, the more important it is to have accurate cost and probability numbers required to perform a quantitative risk analysis.

2.7   Selecting a Methodology for the Test Case

Which methodology, quantitative or qualitative, should be used for the test case established in Chapter 1? A review of the requirements of the test case reveals a complex application for the calculation of retirement benefits which is:

■ Web-based
■ Used by internal employees of a specific division within the organization
■ Used by company sales force
■ Used by customers to review results
■ Driven by IRS business rules
■ Driven by proprietary business rules
■ Used to display results over the Internet to customers
■ Used to store and recall inputs used in calculations
■ Used to display critical and sensitive personally identifiable information about customer employees

A simple review of the requirements does not provide some of the information required to make a decision between quantitative and qualitative methods. Additional information is required. For example, does accurate cost information for all assets exist? How critical and sensitive is the information used by the application? What is the cost in confidence lost by customers if the application is used to alter, destroy, or disclose the information used by the application? Does the company have an accurate database for predicting the frequency and probability of attacks on Internet-based applications and the costs associated with cleaning up and restoring operations after an attack? Does management require a cost-benefit analysis before making decisions on software development efforts? These are just some of the many questions it is necessary to ask in order to determine if a quantitative or qualitative risk assessment method should be applied to the software development effort.

The answers for these questions for the test case are as follows:.

Q: Does accurate cost information for all assets exist?
A: No. Although accurate cost information for most assets exists, the proprietary business rules were developed through a trial-and-error process over many months and no information exists on how much it cost to develop those business rules.
Q: How critical and sensitive is the PII to be used in the application?

A: Fairly sensitive, because Social Security numbers, names, and salaries are all used by the application. However, the availability of the application is only critical during tax preparation system when it is very critical, but other times of the year the application has little or no criticality.

Q: What is the cost in lost customer confidence if information is altered, destroyed, disclosed, or made unavailable?

A:. Unknown. Although some data is available on losses caused by not investing money within a given time period, no statistics have been gathered by the company on customer confidence.

Q: Does the company have a historical database for predicting the frequency and probability of attacks made upon its computing infrastructure and the cost to clean up after an attack?

A: Yes and no. The company does have a database for predicting the frequency and probability of certain types of attack such as computer viruses and malware and the cost of cleaning up from those events. However, it does not have a database for attacks of other types.

Q: Does management require a cost-benefit analysis before making decisions on software development efforts?

A: No. A cost-benefit analysis can always accompany any software development effort, but is not required in order to proceed with development efforts.

Conducting an analysis of the reasons both for and against each method reveals the arguments both for and against using each method within the test case, reveals the following.

2.7.1 Arguments for Using a Quantitative Risk Analysis Method in the Test Case

The sensitivity of the application is high, while the criticality of the application is only high during a given period. Therefore there is little to argue for the use of a quantitative method in the test case.

2.7.2 Arguments against Using a Quantitative Risk Analysis Method in the Test Case

There are several arguments against using a quantitative method, including:

■ Accurate cost information is not available for all assets.
■ Accurate cost information is not available to determine the costs associated with cleaning up after a threat has damaged an asset.

■ No reliable data exists for determining the frequency of attacks from the Internet upon the test application.

2.7.3 Arguments for Using a Qualitative Risk Analysis Method in the Test Case

There are several arguments for using a qualitative risk analysis method, including:

■ Accurate cost information is not available for all assets.
■ Accurate cost information is not available to determine the costs associated with cleaning up after a threat has damaged an asset.
■ No reliable data exists for determining the frequency of attacks from the Internet upon the test application.

2.7.4 Arguments against Using a Qualitative Risk Analysis Method in the Test Case

While the sensitivity of the application is high, there is little else to recommend against the use of a qualitative risk analysis.

Granted this is a fairly simplistic method for selecting between quantitative and qualitative risk analysis techniques. However for the test case, primarily because no accurate cost or probability information exists for a number of factors, a qualitative analysis is used. In the author's experience, generally the data to support a true quantitative risk analysis, especially for software development efforts does not exist, and therefore qualitative risk analysis is more often used. Quantitative methods may often yield better results, but only if the data to support the analysis is available.

2.8 Checklist for Deciding on a Security Risk Assessment Methodology

☐ If the confidentiality, integrity, or the availability of the application under development or its data were to be breached, would there be a substantial impact upon the organization's mission, reputation, and interests from such a breach?

☐ Is accurate cost information available for all assets involved in a software development effort?

☐ Is accurate information available for determining the cost of any data breach?

☐ Is accurate information available concerning the probability or likelihood of any given avenue of attack for the information system under development?

☐ Does management require an accurate cost-benefit analysis before making decisions on changes to software development schedules, requirements, or resources?

If you can answer yes to at least four out of these five questions, then a quantitative analysis should probably be used. Otherwise, a qualitative analysis will probably be the best bet.

2.9 Conclusions

Quantitative and qualitative risk analysis techniques are both fairly easy to understand and apply. There are numerous published methodologies of both types available for use and adoption for use in software development life cycles. Software is available to assist in gathering data and calculating risks using both quantitative and qualitative methods. The key lies in determining which type of methodology, quantitative or qualitative, to use for a given software development effort. Quantitative methods can often provide a clearer picture of the risks associated with software development, especially when used with risk assessment software. However, accurate data on the cost of assets, the cost to repair data breaches, and the probability and frequency of attacks is essential to a good quantitative analysis. Because accurate data on costs and the probability and frequency of attacks is seldom known, especially in software development efforts that are introducing new technologies, a qualitative analysis is more often utilized.

Throughout the remainder of this book, a simple qualitative analysis that can be utilized with any software development effort is developed. It is the author's sincere desire that if this analysis is applied to your software development efforts, the resulting software that is deployed will be more secure. The next step after selecting a risk assessment methodology is to understand the threats to your software development effort, which is the topic of the next chapter.

Chapter 3

Identifying Assets

Picture the following scene: Footsteps leading up to a darkened door. There is a sense of unease in the air, a sense that something is wrong or out of place. A hand with a key reaches for the lock, only to find that the door is already open, although only slightly ajar. Hesitantly, the hand with the key pushes the door open and there is a pause for breath, listening for some sign that whoever might have opened the door is still there. However, there is no noise above the heartbeat of the individual at the door. With great hesitancy the door is pushed open and a step inside is taken. Another pause is taken to listen. There is no noise. The hand with the key reaches out and flips the light switch and suddenly the room beyond is flooded with light.

The sight that is revealed brings a heavy gasp from the person at the door and the keys fall to the floor with a heavy thud. The camera backs out to reveal a room that has been ransacked. Furniture has been overturned. Lamps and other ceramic items have been knocked over and smashed. The glass in picture frames has been broken. The stuffing has been pulled from furniture. Every drawer in every piece of furniture has been opened, the contents spilled across the floor, and then the empty drawer tossed aside. The scene is the same throughout every room in the house. The house has been thoroughly tossed and by the looks of it, by some very professional people.

The scene switches to a later time period. The house is swarming with police, and cameras flash, taking photographs of the carnage. Other personnel are attempting to take fingerprints from various surfaces throughout the room. The detectives are questioning the homeowner. "Has anything been taken? Do you know who might want to do this to you? What were the thieves looking for?" The homeowner, who is obviously in shock, answers that he doesn't know if anything is missing, he can't understand why anyone would want to do this to him, and that he doesn't have anything worth stealing.

We've all seen scenes such as the one just described in our favorite television crime shows or read them in mystery novels. Someone was after something valuable and they were willing to tear apart a house in order to get it. Sometimes the criminals get caught in the act and beat a hasty retreat as the homeowner enters the house. In this case, the criminals always seem to get away, and come back later to try to retrieve the item of value again. Whatever the case, usually by the end of the TV show, the movie, or the novel, we understand what the object of value was, and why someone was trying to steal it.

In the real world, much as at the beginning of a crime story, it is often difficult to grasp all of the items of value an organization has that thieves would want to steal. Without a clear understanding of those items within an organization that have value—an organization's assets—it is impossible to design adequate safeguards to protect those assets. In this chapter we perform a little detective work in order to try to uncover what assets are and why identification of assets is a step in the risk management process. Figure 3.1 represents some of the inputs and some of the outputs associated with this step in the risk management process.

3.1 Definition

Understanding and recognizing *assets*, something of value to an organization, is one of the most difficult concepts of the risk assessment process. Assets can be obvious things such as money, artwork, commodities (gold, silver, oil, etc.), buildings, people, or computers. But assets can also consist of things that aren't so easy to quantify, such as knowledge, information, trade secrets, software, proprietary formulas, and reputation. Consider the case of Arthur Andersen LLP. Prior to the Enron and other accounting scandals, Arthur Andersen LLP was one of the "Big Five" international accounting firms. Its reputation alone brought in a large amount of business. As a result of the indictments it received for these accounting scandals, almost all of Arthur Andersen's clients took their business elsewhere. Although the firm has yet to declare bankruptcy or go out of business, it remains to be seen if the company can rebuild itself to the point it was at prior to the accounting scandals.

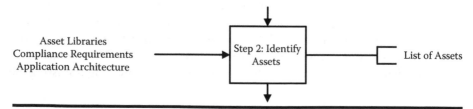

FIGURE 3.1   Inputs and outputs associated with the identification of assets

It is important to understand what an asset is in order to be able to put proper safeguards in place to protect it. If an organization does not recognize all of the assets that it has, then inevitably someone who does recognize the value will come along and attempt to steal it. And unlike the homeowner in the detective story who experiences a ransacked house when someone comes to steal something of value, an organization may not realize that its assets have been stolen, particularly when the thief is a hacker who steals from the organization electronically, leaving no trace of his passing. Take, for example, the case of TJ Maxx or TJX. In 2006, TJX reported the theft of more than 45.8 million credit card records. Evidence would reveal that the theft had been taking place for more than two years and went undiscovered for some time before the theft was discovered. If TJX found it so difficult to protect an asset it recognized as an asset (credit card numbers), how much more difficult would it be to adequately protect something that was not recognized as an asset in the first place?

For any software development effort *typical* assets will be the sensitive or business critical information that the application displays, stores, processes, modifies, or transmits. However, assets in a software development effort may also include such items as business rules, external databases, encryption keys, authentication processes, passwords, or methods used in the secure transmission of data.

3.2 Types of Assets Typically Found in Software Development

There are a number of different types of assets that may typically be found in a software development project. These types of assets include but are not limited to the following:

- Information assets
- Business rules
- Services or functions
- Software
- Proprietary formulas
- Encryption methods and keys
- Databases
- People, or specifically the knowledge or skillset possessed by individuals
- Accounts and the funds associated with those accounts
- Transactions

3.2.1   Information Assets

Information assets typically represent pieces of sensitive or business critical information stored, transmitted, displayed, or modified by the application being developed. Most Personally Identifiable Information (PII) such as names, addresses, Social Security numbers, credit card numbers, account numbers, dependent names, telephone numbers, and similar information is considered sensitive and is protected by legislation such as HIPAA, SB1386, and other privacy legislation. But other information an organization may hold, such as interest rates, overhead rates, quantity discount rates, loan information, financial information, and account numbers may be just as important to an organization as PII, if not more so. Take for example, an application developed to record stock trades. Information about the specific trade such as the market price of the stock in question at the time of the trade, the amount of the stock purchased, the portfolio or account of the purchaser (i.e., who will be the new owner of the stock), and the source of the funds used to purchase the stock are all very important pieces of information and are critical to the success of the organization using the stock trading application.

The information used by a five-axis milling machine in order to mass produce a specific part, the GPS coordinates used to navigate a ship or an airplane, the automated formulas utilized by a production line to assemble computers or automobiles, or the list of ingredients and steps used by an automated assembly line that produces candy, all represent types of information that may be critical to a company. Customer lists, inventories, and previous orders made by customers may all represent business critical data.

Likewise, employee data such as timesheets, reprimands, termination dates, awards, training and development plans and records, and performance reviews may all be business critical data. If timesheet data is not recorded properly or lost, then employees may not get paid on time, or might not get paid the right amount. Similarly, if the employee is a consultant who works billable hours for a customer and timesheet information is not recorded properly, then the customer may not receive the correct billing for services received. Likewise, if an employee is to be terminated on a given date, and this information is lost or misplaced, the employee's access to sensitive information or other assets may not be terminated in a timely manner.

Of course not all information held by an organization is critical to the business of the organization. But all sources of information that may be used or consulted by a given application should be *considered* when developing a list of assets for the risk assessment process.

3.2.2   External Databases

Many software development efforts rely on data that comes from external sources, such as databases, which are not controlled directly by the software development effort. Consider for a moment, a billing application used by a hospital or clinic to send bills to patients. Any given hospital or clinic may have agreements in place to receive standard fees for given services. These agreements may vary between different insurance providers. For any given patient, it may be that the hospital's billing application needs to retrieve data from a given insurer on how much that insurer will pay for the service received, before it can know how much, if any amount, has not been paid by the insurance company and needs to be billed to the patient. How much an insurer will pay for a given service is critical to billing for the correct amount, but the tables referred to by the hospital's application may belong to the insurer.

Another example concerns large corporations with many different business units. Consider a large financial services corporation that may offer individual and group life insurance products, individual and group health insurance products, and retirement plans and annuities. Typically each separate business unit, Individual Insurance Products, Group Insurance Products, and Retirement Plans maintains its own databases of customers and members of group insurance plans or retirement plans.

What if a new division of the company, say for instance a virtual bank, were to be opened up by the company? Because the new division would be a virtual bank (i.e., all transactions would take place electronically or over the telephone; no branch offices or automated teller machines would be created), it would need to market its services to potential customers in a unique way. What if a marketing campaign were based upon the customers of its individual insurance products, group insurance products, or members of the retirement plans the company's other divisions sell? For example, a customer who had her 401k money invested with the company's retirement business unit might receive a discounted rate on a loan. Or perhaps a customer who had both life insurance and a retirement plan would qualify for a higher interest rate for the first six months to a year if he opened a new checking or savings account.

In each of these instances, a banking application used to set up new accounts would need access to the customer databases from the other divisions of the corporation in order to know when to apply these discounted or increased rates. In this instance, the banks' application development staff may be granted access to views or copies of the customer databases from the other business units with the company, but they would not have direct control over those databases themselves. In such an instance, especially if direct access were granted from the banking application to the other database, it is important for the banks' development staff to understand how much the other business units value these customer databases so that the links between the bank application and the customer databases can be appropriately protected.

3.2.3   Business Rules

Often, there are complex business rules that must govern the calculations a given application must utilize. Take, for example, the business rules associated by an application used to calculate income tax and file taxes and request refunds electronically. Everyone who has ever filled out an income tax form, other than perhaps the 1040 EZ knows that there are literally hundreds if not thousands of business rules that may be applied to determine how much income tax an individual owes to the government. When state and local income tax rates are included, the amount of business rules involved in calculating the correct amounts is staggering! Although the business rules involved in an income tax application are public knowledge, when translated into programming code, the business rules may become proprietary in nature. There are many other types of business rules including chemical or mathematical formulas, retirement benefit formulas, or actuarial formulas that may represent business critical assets to a given organization.

3.2.4   Services and Functions

Computer software relies on many different services and functions in order to work properly. Messaging services, encryption services, translators, gateways, and transmission services are all examples of types of services and functions that code within an application can call on in order for the application to function as intended. At one point, client/server or Web-based applications could not directly interface with mainframe-based applications. But services now exist that allow client/server or Web-based applications to directly interface with mainframe-based applications. These services are now widespread and available to most organizations with a need to use them. However, new services are always under development, and can represent a significant investment in time and resources to create and therefore become proprietary to a given organization. In this instance, such services and functions may represent an asset to the organization who developed them.

3.2.5   Software

Software itself can be an asset to an organization. Organizations often have large sums invested in all kinds of off-the-shelf software from operating system and office productivity software to specialized applications to assist those organizations with a host of different business needs. Many organizations also build their own custom applications in order to meet specific business needs or service the needs of their customers.

Often, software development efforts may rely upon other software either purchased or already developed to provide a particular function. As an illustration, consider the virtual bank discussed earlier in this chapter. The software development staff at the new banking business unit of the financial services company is charged with developing a custom application to serve its new customers, in this instance an enrollment application that will allow a customer to create a new savings or checking account via a Web site.

For marketing purposes, the company wants all of its customers who do business over the Web to reach the company via a company portal on one specific Web page. The company has already developed, at great cost, a custom Web portal from which its retirement services and insurance customers may reach their respective accounts. In addition, the company does not want customers who may have more than one product with the company (e.g., both individual life and group health insurance) to have to log on to each Web site separately. Therefore, a customer must first enter through the custom Web portal and be identified and authenticated by that Web portal, before being passed through to the bank's Web portal. In this instance, the company's Web portal can be considered an asset to the custom application being built by the banking business unit.

3.2.6 Proprietary Formulas

Many organizations hold trade secrets in the form of proprietary formulas. These formulas can range from the secret formula for a soft drink, or a formula for a biodiesel fuel, to the formulas used to navigate pilotless aircraft utilizing terrain-avoidance software. These proprietary formulas often only hold their value as long as they are kept secret. They often represent some of the biggest assets a company holds. Take, for example, the formula for a popular soft drink. As long as the formula for creating the soft drink remains a secret, then the company who owns the formula can continue to reap a profit from selling it. However, if the formula were to become public knowledge, then other soft drink companies could market the same drink and the increased competition could cut into not only the original company's market share, but drive down the price per unit that could be gained by selling the soft drink.

Not all proprietary formulas will end up being utilized in a software development effort, but they may. Consider the business rules associated with the calculation of retirement benefits. Although federal law requires that all employees covered by a given retirement plan receive the same minimum benefit paid for by their employer, under certain circumstances, key employees under a given plan can receive extra benefits beyond the minimum given to the rank-and-file members of the plan. The key to calculating the correct benefits for these key members is often proprietary in nature. Therefore, software designed to calculate those benefits may require that the calculation formulas are embedded within the software. In this instance, the software itself then becomes an asset to the organization.

3.2.7 Encryption Software and Encryption Keys

Most encryption methodologies are freely published for anyone to examine. The reason for this is so that organizations can try to break the encryption methodology or otherwise prove the ineffectiveness of the methodology. The more the individuals try to break the encryption scheme, the stronger the resulting methodology will be. And although the methodology, or formula, used to encrypt data is almost always public knowledge, the software used to apply that methodology is almost always proprietary in nature. Encryption formulas represent complex mathematical functions based upon the factoring of large prime numbers (often numbers with more than 300 digits). Applying those formulas within software, especially when trying to speed up the calculation process, is a challenging process and therefore most encryption software is proprietary in nature and often will be considered an asset for most organizations.

Of course not all encryption software is proprietary in nature and freeware encryption software is available for use in software development efforts. In these cases, the encryption software may not represent an asset for the software development effort. However, the encryption keys may be considered an asset. An encryption key is a parameter that controls the operation of the encryption methodology. It is used by the encryption algorithm to convert plaintext into ciphertext or vice versa during the encryption and decryption processes. Encryption keys, especially those used in Public Key Infrastructures (PKIs) can also represent a significant investment for an organization even beyond the value encryption keys hold in keeping data secret.

3.2.8 People

People are an often overlooked asset. Although most organizations value their employees as a general rule, they often do not understand that the specific knowledge that certain employees possess can often be an asset. As an illustration, consider the following. As an organization matures, many processes that were once done manually, such as enrolling employees in a benefit plan, or calculating the benefits an employee will receive upon retirement, become automated. Where once it was important for individual employees to understand how to calculate employee benefits, now an automated program performs all of the calculations, and it only becomes necessary for employees to understand how to use the automated program, without needing to understand how the benefits are actually calculated. As the organization continues to mature, employee turnover and attrition will reduce the number of employees who understand how to calculate the benefits manually. Soon, there may be only one or two key individuals with the knowledge of how to calculate the benefits manually. If it ever becomes necessary at a future date to revise the application that calculates benefits, the organization may have already lost the corporate knowledge of how the new calculations need to mesh with the older ones if nobody is left within the organization who knows how to calculate the benefits manually.

3.2.9   Accounts, Transactions, and Calculations

Software is often used to transfer funds from one account to another, or from one institution or organization or another. The funds that sit in those accounts represent a very tangible asset which is very easy to identify. However, the methods used to transfer those funds electronically from one location to another, or the method used to apply a specific interest rate, transaction fee, or commission to a given transaction is often not recognized as a potential asset. For example, how the price of a stock is calculated at the moment that a transaction is made to purchase or sell the stock can represent a great deal of money if incorrectly calculated for a large transaction based upon hundreds of thousands of shares of stock sold or purchased. And if no electronic record of a specific transaction is available within an audit trail, then it may prove impossible to understand who made a transfer of funds and how that transfer of funds was authorized. In this instance, the transaction audit log itself is a valuable asset, because without such a log, funds may disappear, or at least may be transferred into other accounts and become unretrievable by legal means.

3.3   How to Identify Assets in Application Development

With so many different types of assets to consider, how then does a software development team identify the assets involved in any software development effort? Although there is no sure-fire method that can be used to uncover all assets involved in a software development effort, there are a number of methods that can be used to identify assets.

3.3.1   Business and User Management Involvement

In any quest to uncover assets, it is important to look to management, especially the management of the business areas of an organization. Typically business management is in the best position to understand what information or other assets are essential to the mission and goals of the development effort as it relates to supporting the business objectives of the organization. Business management is also in the best position to identify the business impact of the failure to protect critical information or other assets.

One method of determining assets lies in gathering members of management from the business areas of the organization that will either use or be supported by the application under development. Through a guided process controlled by a facilitator, the key members of the organization are all asked to brainstorm a list of potential assets. It is important in this process that all members participate in the process and that all ideas brought forth are recorded. Once a brainstormed list of assets has been created, then a smaller team of key management personnel supported by IT staff can then prioritize the brainstormed list, creating a smaller list of key assets to be considered in the risk assessment process for the given software development element.

3.3.2 Review of Organizational Documentation

Assets can also be identified by looking at an organization's policies and procedures. Often it is possible to discover assets through a review of the organization's policies and procedures to determine what types of information and processes the policies and procedures are designed to protect. For example, a password policy may require that passwords are always encrypted and that they are never transmitted in cleartext. From this policy, it is clear that passwords are assets requiring protection, in this case through encryption. A further example might be a data classification policy. Such a policy might require that all customer information that could directly identify a customer (i.e., name, address, customer ID, etc.) must be considered confidential. If a software development effort were to use or process any of this information, then that information could be considered an asset.

Other documents an organization produces can also reveal items that organization considers assets. Advertising materials, corporate Web sites, and annual reports can often highlight items that an organization considers important. For example, if a company values its reputation highly, it may advertise that fact heavily in its advertising materials and on its corporate Web site. Likewise if an organization feels that it has an edge over its competition, it is likely to advertise that fact.

3.3.3 Other Methods of Identifying Assets

There are many methods of identifying assets. Some of these methods include:

- Consulting lists of assets developed during previous risk assessments
- Utilizing lists of common assets that may be found on security-related Web sites
- A review of legislative, regulatory, and compliance initiatives
- A review of the architecture associated with a development effort
- A review of current headlines covering data security breaches

3.3.3.1   Lists of Assets Found during Previous Risk Assessments

Each risk assessment performed by an organization should contain a well-documented list of assets that were uncovered during the risk assessment process. These asset lists should be combined and placed in an asset library that the organization can then use to identify potential assets in new development projects, and can also serve as a repository for custom software and other code that has been developed by the organization and which could be reused in subsequent development efforts.

3.3.3.2   Lists of Common Assets Found on Information Security Web Sites

There are many organizations that routinely publish lists of assets, or methodologies for uncovering assets associated with application development projects. These organizations include such well-known entities as:

■ The Open Web Application Security Project (OWASP)
■ The National Institute of Science and Technology (NIST)
■ The Software Engineering Institute (SEI)
■ The SysAdmin, Audit, Security, Network (SANS) Institute

3.3.3.3   Review of Legislative, Regulatory, or Compliance Initiatives

A simple review of legislation or other regulatory processes that require the protection of data can often reveal other potential assets. The Health Insurance Portability and Accountability Act of 1996 (HIPAA) requires organizations to protect all Personal Health Information (PHI) held by that organization electronically. Gramm–Leach–Bliley (GLB) and SB 1386 and other similar legislation passed by various states protect financial information and other PII such as Social Security numbers. Finally, Sarbanes–Oxley requires organizations to protect accounting and other financial records as well as protect the processes used to gather, record, and modify that information. If legislation or other regulatory agencies require protection for specific pieces of information, or processes used to collect, modify, and record that information, then that information could easily be an asset to a given organization.

3.3.3.4   Review of System Architecture

Yet another method requires utilizing the architecture to be used within a software development effort. By studying the architectural design for an application it is possible to determine where information used by the application will be read, written, modified, or monitored by the application. Data flows will reveal where information is stored in databases or other files. Examining the software architecture will also reveal other processes used to display or transmit the information. The processes used to store, modify, transmit, or display data and the data itself may all be assets that need to be protected properly, as may audit trails and logs that can provide nonrepudiation of transactions inasmuch as it is often important to understand who initiated a transaction along with additional information including: amounts, account numbers, dates, times, and other pertinent information.

3.3.3.5 Review of Current Headlines

But there may be an even easier method to uncover assets, those items of value that a thief wants to steal, destroy, alter, or disclose: look at the headlines. Nearly every day, some data breach or break-in is reported in the press. Web sites such as the Privacy Rights Clearinghouse (http://www.privacyrights.org) and Attrition. org (http://attrition.org) maintain lists of reported data breaches. A review of these breeches can often reveal items that were obviously important to a hacker or other criminal, but may not be obvious. Examples include: the details of some 1.6 million job seekers on Monster.com stolen in August 2007, college applications stolen from the Louisiana Office of Student Financial Assistance in October 2007, membership forms stolen from a Blockbuster Video store in Sarasota, Florida in October 2007, or urology records stolen from a Swedish urology group.

3.4 Determining Assets for the Test Case

What are the assets in the test case? A review of the requirements of the test case reveals a complex application for the calculation of retirement benefits which is:

- Web-based
- Used by internal employees of a specific division
- Used by company sales force
- Used by customers to review results
- Driven by IRS business rules
- Driven by proprietary business rules
- Used to display results over the Internet to customers
- Used to store and recall inputs used in calculations
- Used to display critical and sensitive PII about customer employees

A cursory glance at the requirements reveals the following items that could be considered assets include: critical and sensitive PII about customer employees, and proprietary business rules. Because the PII utilized by the application contains fairly sensitive information about individuals in a given retirement plan, such as names, ages, Social Security numbers, account numbers, salaries, and contributions to retirement plans it is easy to recognize the information as an asset, especially when you consider the requirements of legislation such as SB 1386 and GLB.

Likewise, the proprietary business rules to be utilized by the application are easy to identify as assets. Proprietary business rules provide an edge that one organization holds over its competition. Therefore they are assets that require appropriate protection.

What about the other requirements for the test case? Do any of the other requirements clearly reveal an asset? What do the individual requirements reveal in terms of other assets that may be a part of the software development effort outlined in the test case?

The application must be Web-based. This statement by itself does not reveal any assets for test application. However, when taken in context with some of the other requirements, a potential asset may be revealed. One of the other requirements reveals that the results of the calculations performed by the application must be viewable by customers external to the organization over the Internet. How will these external customers gain access to these calculations? If the application will e-mail the results to the customer, or if a Web portal will be built as a part of the application development process to allow the customer to view the results, then there may be no further assets to uncover from these two requirements. However, in this instance, the application will make use of a Web portal already built by the organization to communicate with customers. Is this Web portal an asset? It might be, depending upon the effort required to build and maintain the Web portal. At this point, it would be best to involve the retirement plan administration business management to determine if the Web portal should indeed be considered an asset. For the purposes of this book, we consider the Web portal, which was built at great expense by the company, to be an asset.

The application will be utilized by internal employees of the organization to actually calculate the benefits associated with a given retirement plan. What does this statement reveal about the application that may reveal an asset? Typically when an application is utilized only by the internal employees of an organization the protections that are in place for the data utilized by that application are different from those utilized for applications which are accessible by external customers. This might mean that the data utilized by an internal application is not encrypted, whereas data utilized by an external application will be encrypted, because it is transmitted over a public network. In this particular instance, the data utilized by the application is not encrypted, nor is it necessary to encrypt the results of the calculations that will be accessed through the Web portal because of the protections in place with that Web portal. Hence there are no further assets revealed by this specific requirement.

The application will be utilized by the organization's sales force. Because the sales force of the organization will not utilize "live" data but rather datasets designed specifically to reveal the strengths of a particular retirement plan, this requirement reveals no additional assets involved with the application development effort.

The application will be driven by IRS business rules. These business rules are not proprietary in nature and are freely available to the public. Nevertheless, because the business rules are very complex, they can require a significant effort to program within an application. The architecture involved with how the business rules will be applied can end up being proprietary in nature. Due to the effort involved in understanding and programming these business rules, they are considered an asset for the test case.

A review of the assets uncovered for the test case so far includes:

- PII utilized by the application to calculate retirement benefits
- The proprietary business rules used within the application to calculate retirement benefits
- The Web portal used by external customers to access and view the results of a retirement benefit calculation
- The application of IRS business rules as they apply to the calculation of retirement benefits

Are there other assets that should be considered? What about the database that holds the PII necessary to calculate the retirement benefits? If such a database belonged to another organization or another business unit within our organization, the database itself could be considered to be an asset. However, in this particular instance, because the database is not owned by an outside organization, it is not considered an asset separate from the PII it contains that we have already considered should be an asset.

A review of corporate policy reveals the following: "Authentication methods include the use of user IDs and passwords and that all passwords must be encrypted during transmission." A review of proposed architecture for the application reveals that internal users of the application must be authenticated to ensure that they may have access to the PII used by the application. After all, even though the application will be used by internal employees, it is not necessary to allow all employees within the company to view sensitive PII. Only employees assigned to administrate a given retirement plan (and their managers of course) need to have access to the PII for that plan. Therefore, passwords can be considered an asset for our test case.

What about other potential assets? What about corporate reputation? If the results of the calculations, or the data used to calculate the retirement benefits, or even the fact that a given company had a retirement plan for its executives were to be revealed to the public, or to another customer by mistake, or the PII itself were to be unintentionally modified or destroyed, what would the damage be to corporate reputation? Depending upon the customer and who the information was revealed to, or the specific damage done to the PII, the resulting damage to corporate reputation could prove to be devastating. Therefore corporate reputation is considered as an asset for the test case.

The business rules involved in calculating the retirement benefits for some of the plans sold by the corporation in the test case are very complex. So complex that only three individuals within the corporation know and understand how to apply the business rules and the IRS rules to correctly calculate the retirement benefits for certain types of plans. Therefore, these individuals and their collective knowledge are considered assets for the test case.

A review of the final list of assets for the test case includes the following:

- PII utilized by the application to calculate retirement benefits
- The proprietary business rules used within the application to calculate retirement benefits
- The Web portal used by external customers to access and view the results of a retirement benefit calculation
- The application of IRS business rules as they apply to the calculation of retirement benefits
- The passwords utilized by internal employees to access the PII used by the application
- Corporate reputation
- The collective knowledge of the only business analysts within the organization who understand the complexity of the calculations involved

Although it would be possible to come up with yet other assets for the test case such as the assets held by the retirement plan and the investment selections made by individual members of the retirement plans, the list developed so far is adequate for the illustration purposes of this book.

3.5   Asset Checklist

In determining assets associated with a specific software development effort consider the following sources of assets:.

- ☐ Common assets including:
    - ☐ Sensitive or business critical information such as PII or PHI
    - ☐ External data sources
    - ☐ Business rules
    - ☐ Functions and services
    - ☐ Software
    - ☐ Proprietary formulas
    - ☐ Encryption software and encryption keys

     ☐ People
     ☐ Accounts
     ☐ Transactions
  ☐ Consulting business area management
     ☐ Items important to business managers/brainstorming
     ☐ Understanding the consequences of failing to protect management
  ☐ Reviewing corporate documentation
     ☐ Policy and procedure review including:
        ☐ IT policies and procedures
        ☐ HR policies and procedures
     ☐ Review of corporate advertising, corporate Web pages, and annual reports
  ☐ Creating and consulting asset libraries from earlier development efforts
  ☐ Consulting IT security Web sites and organizations including:
     ☐ OWASP
     ☐ NIST
     ☐ SEI
     ☐ SANS Institute
     ☐ PrivacyRights.org
  ☐ Reviewing legislation, regulatory, or other compliance requirements including:
     ☐ HIPAA
     ☐ SOX
     ☐ GLB
     ☐ SR 1386
     ☐ PCI DSS
     ☐ Others
  ☐ Reviewing application architecture to determine
     ☐ Data flows
     ☐ Authentication processes
     ☐ Transmission protocols
     ☐ Other services

3.6 Summary

Although it may not be evident at first glance, software development efforts have a lot in common with a good crime story. Just as every crime story has an object of value that the criminal wishes to steal, destroy, alter, or reveal, every software development effort has assets associated with it that must be protected from theft, destruction, alteration, or disclosure. As is the case at the start of a crime story or a software development effort it may not be readily apparent what the item of value or asset is. However, it is ultimately important that the item of value or asset be discovered, if adequate safeguards are to be put in place in order to protect it.

In order to prevent our software development efforts from resulting in a break-in such as that described at the start of this chapter it is important that we uncover all of the assets the software development effort will utilize, so that adequate safeguards can be built into the application at the start of the software development effort, rather than after the software has been implemented. This chapter has examined a number of ways to reveal the assets within our applications including comparing requirements versus a list of common software development assets, consulting with business unit management to identify assets, reviewing corporate documentation for possible sources of assets, consulting asset libraries developed from previous software development efforts, consulting IT security and development Web site organizations, reviewing legislation and regulatory requirements, and reviewing the proposed architecture of the software development effort itself.

The ultimate goal is to provide a secure application that protects the assets used or touched by our application from theft, destruction, alteration, or disclosure. We want the footsteps approaching the house to feel secure, to find the door securely locked, and when the light switch is flipped on to find everything within the house exactly as it was left. However, in order to protect the house properly, we need to do some investigative work to make sure that we have identified all of the valuables stored within the house. Without such knowledge, it is difficult, if not impossible, to provide the proper security controls at the perimeter that will keep potential thieves out of the house. The goal is to provide a proper balance between the amounts spent on protective measures for the house, with the value of the items we are protecting within the house. It isn't an effective use of resources to protect an aging house that only contains the sentimental personal possessions of its owner with armed guards, guard dogs, alarms, camera systems, and safes. Likewise, it isn't wise to leave the doors unlocked or windows left open in a home that is full of valuable artwork, jewelry, cash, and other easily stolen goods.

Chapter 4

Identifying Security Threats

Picture the scene of the crime from the previous chapters. The house has been put back in order after the break-in. A number of individuals sit uncomfortably on chairs and couches, or lean against walls or other pieces of furniture. Still other individuals pace uncomfortably up and down across the floor, pausing only occasionally to glance at a clock or consult a wristwatch. No one in the room dares to make eye contact with anyone else. Everyone looks uneasy, and it is obvious that everyone is quickly losing patience with the situation. Someone decides he has had enough, and gets up to leave, but is unable to get past the policeman at the door, and so he returns to his spot.

Finally the great detective enters the room. The detective apologizes for being late, but takes his time removing his coat and retrieving his notepad from a pocket, or perhaps lights up a pipe or cigarette. The detective deliberately takes his time, making the others in the room continue to build up their frustrations. It's all a game to the detective, he knows that the criminal is in the room, and he's playing on the nerves of the criminal. Someone gets frustrated and tries to leave the room again. The detective starts with that individual.

Slowly, the detective weaves a masterful tale, spinning together the clues of the crime and recreating the scene. One by one the detective confronts the individuals in the room, pointing out how each one of them had the motive, means, or both to commit the crime. He's relying on the tension building up in the room between the suspects to bring out that last little clue he needs to wrap up the case. He knows who committed the crime; he just can't quite prove it, not until the criminal slips up and reveals something that he shouldn't have known.

In the end, the criminal slips up and reveals something only the criminal could have known, and is revealed to the group at large. The police enter the room and make the arrest. The detective is triumphant, knowing that he's solved yet another crime. Yet not every crime story ends with just one criminal. Sometimes there is more than one individual involved, whereas at other times, we find that nobody was to blame: there is no crime; it was all an accident, no matter how it might otherwise appear.

If the assets in our software development effort are represented by the item of value stolen, destroyed, altered, or disclosed in a crime story, then a threat to our software development is represented by the thief or criminal. And just as in a lot of different detective stories, we often find that there is no criminal, but rather the crime was the result of an accident, or of negligence on someone's part. However, that doesn't mean that we don't need to know who the usual suspects are.

Just as in the detective story, in software development there is a need to understand who the "usual suspects" or threats are to development projects. And like the detective, it is not enough to simply know who the "usual suspects" are, but it is also important to understand the motivation of those suspects. Once this potential impact is understood, then measures or safeguards that protect the software from the threat may be identified and implemented. The earlier such controls are identified within the SDLC the easier they may be incorporated into the design. Studies show that including new features during the implementation phase can cost up to 100 times the amount it would have cost if the feature were introduced during the design phase.

This chapter discusses the methods of identifying threats that are associated with software development efforts. Figure 4.1 represents some of the inputs and outputs associated with the threat identification step of the risk management process.

4.1   Definition

What is a threat? For the purposes of this book, a *threat* is considered a source of danger to an application development project as that project will be implemented. In order to truly understand the nature of threats to software development, it is

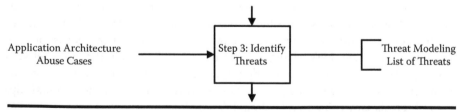

FIGURE 4.1   Typical inputs and outputs of the threat identification step

necessary to review some of the "usual suspects" and describe how they affect the confidentiality, integrity, and availability of applications and associated data.

There are a number of ways that threats may be categorized including:

- *Business threats* are threats to underlying business functions and may not be readily apparent.
- *System threats* are typically more direct threats aimed at software applications or the platforms upon which they are deployed.

Likewise threats may be broken down into more logical categories such as:

- Natural threats including floods, earthquakes, tornadoes, and other acts of nature.
- Human threats which can range from the unintentional to deliberate.
- Environmental threats which can include such items as long-term power failure, water leaks, chemical spills, and fire.

4.2 Information Security Threats to Software Development

4.2.1 Business Threats

In a typical software development effort there are two types of threats to consider, business threats and system threats. *Business threats* are threats to the business function that may cause disruption in or damage to the business function or supporting business process and resources. For example, consider the payroll function in most businesses. If an employee timesheet application is unavailable to report the number of hours that employees have worked, then the payroll function may be affected because there would be no basis on which to measure how many hours each employee has worked. Business threats are often overlooked during software development because it is easy to get lost in the focus of meeting the requirements of the design process, without realizing that additional business functions may be affected.

Failure to recognize business threats during the risk assessment process can result in a failure to add the proper safeguards during the design phase when they would cost relatively little in comparison to adding those same safeguards after the implementation phase. For example, consider a human resources application. During requirements gathering for the application, we find that the application is to record performance review information, disciplinary documentation, and achievement awards. An application is designed to process and store the required information, and access is limited to the appropriate personnel. However, it is easy to forget that we must also consider the business functions the application must fulfill. One of these functions is that if disciplinary documentation is not issued on a timely basis, it could result in delayed termination of an undesirable employee. Therefore the threat becomes a disgruntled employee who is not terminated in a timely manner, because disciplinary documentation was not issued to the employee in a timely manner.

4.2.2 System Threats

System threats are usually much easier to recognize during software development efforts. A system threat is a direct threat to an application or one of its subsystems. For example, simple data entry errors represent a system threat. In a timesheet application, if an incorrect number of hours is entered for a given employee, then that employee may be overpaid or underpaid. If, in a human resource application, an incorrect employee identification number is entered, an employee who does not deserve an award or a reprimand may receive an award or a reprimand by mistake.

System threats are typically categorized much as are suspects in a detective story: based upon their means (capabilities), motive (intentions), and opportunity. When classified based upon their capabilities, intentions, and opportunities, software development threats can be classified as follows:.

- Human Threats
  - Unintentional
    - From outside an organization
    - From within an organization
  - Intentional
    - From outside an organization
    - From within an organization
- Technical Threats
  - Nonmalicious
  - Malicious
    - Targeted at a specific asset, vulnerability or system
    - Nontargeted
- Natural Threats
- Environmental Threats

Typical threats that affect software development from each category are identified and described below, along with their impact upon confidentiality, integrity, and availability. This is not an exhaustive list of threats by any means, but is intended to supply a list of the "usual suspects" that often affect software development projects.

4.2.3   Human Threats

Human threats represent threats to systems based upon the behavior of individuals. The intent behind the human threat is not always malicious in nature, but can be based on curiosity or simple error. Likewise, human threats can come from inside an organization and its trusted computing zone, or from outside an organization. Human threats include the following.

4.2.3.1   Curiosity

Curiosity may represent authorized users abusing access privileges and rights or curiosity may represent unauthorized users attempting to access unauthorized information. Take, for example, an authorized user within a company who has celebrity clients. The individual user may have access to the company systems, but have no need to view the details of a particular celebrity client's file. Curiosity about the celebrity may cause the employee to attempt to access the celebrity's file. Conversely an external user who is curious as to the safeguards in place upon a given Web site may attempt to run scripts against the site to determine what vulnerabilities are in place. This may be done either maliciously, in an attempt to deface a Web site or bring it down, or nonmaliciously in an attempt to discover the weaknesses in a Web site and bring them to the attention of the Web site owner. Internal threats generally affect the confidentiality of information, whereas external threats generally affect the availability of information.

4.2.3.2   Data Entry Errors and Omissions

Data entry errors and omissions represent mistakes in data entry. Such mistakes could affect system resources or the safeguards that protect other system resources. For example, entering incorrect values such as the number of hours in a timesheet application could affect how much an employee was paid. Entering incorrect or inconsistent abbreviations for addresses (i.e., Blvd or Bvd instead of Boulevard) could make accurate reporting or standard searches of address data difficult if not impossible. This type of threat generally affects data integrity, although in the case of inconsistent abbreviations making standard searches impossible it could affect the availability of data as well.

4.2.3.3   Espionage

Espionage is the act of spying utilizing various means including: bugs, wiretaps, copying, photographing, following, bribing, and interception to obtain information that will provide a competitive edge. Espionage is not utilized just by foreign governments, but is also used by one corporation against its competitors, or one corporation against a government agency. For example, a business agreement between two corporations may allow for on-site liaison personnel who may in reality be spying for their parent organization in order to provide a competitive edge. Espionage typically affects the confidentiality of information, but in conjunction with other threats could also affect the integrity and availability of information.

4.2.3.4   Fraud

Fraud occurs when authorized users abuse their access rights in order to gain additional information, access rights, or system privileges beyond what they should have. Take, for example, an employee who accesses a customer database to gain names and addresses in order to market his own personal services to those customers. In conjunction with other threats, such as impersonation, a user could access a customer database to gain Social Security numbers and use those numbers to commit identity theft. Because fraud involves abuse of access rights, it could significantly affect the confidentiality, integrity, and availability of data.

4.2.3.5   Improper Disposal of Sensitive Information

Improper disposal of sensitive information can lead to the compromise of that information. Residual data left over in a computer that is disposed of can be read. This can be particularly devastating if home computers are used to allow access to sensitive work systems and the home computer is not disposed of properly. Readable data can also be removed from hard copies, magnetic tapes, or CDs that are thrown in the trash. This type of threat primarily affects the confidentiality of data, but in conjunction with other threats could also affect the integrity and availability of data.

4.2.3.6   Inadvertent Acts or Carelessness

Inadvertent acts or carelessness generally represent unintentional acts such as programming, synchronization, and development errors. For example, if error-handling routines within an application are not programmed correctly, it is possible that information could be provided to an attacker which would allow that attacker to compromise the application or the system on which the application was deployed. Or, if the clock in a stock trading application is not synchronized correctly, the price of a stock transaction could be affected. This type of threat can affect the confidentiality, integrity, and availability of data.

4.2.3.7 Misrepresentation of Identity

Misrepresentation of identity threats allows assumption of the identity of someone else through the use of stolen or falsified identification including: ID Cards, key cards, PIN numbers, or passwords. Examples include: using a keystroke logger to capture passwords or PIN numbers allowing a user to authenticate using someone else's identity; stealing an employee access badge allowing physical access to restricted areas within an organization; or tricking users into revealing information such as passwords, account numbers, names, or phone numbers using social engineering techniques. This type of threat typically affects the confidentiality of data, although it could also affect the integrity and availability of data depending upon the specifics of an attack.

4.2.3.8 Policy Violations

Policy violations represent the act of not following organizational policies and procedures, either intentionally or unintentionally. For example, failure to conduct acceptance testing to meet release dates for a new product or service can result in the deployment of an application that could compromise safeguards and other services running on the same infrastructure. Likewise failure to properly reboot a computer as required by policy may result in anti-virus definitions or other software patches not being properly installed and therefore allow an attacker to bypass security protections that may have otherwise been in place. This type of threat primarily affects the availability of information, but in conjunction with other threats could also affect the confidentiality and integrity of information as well.

4.2.3.9 Shoulder Surfing

Shoulder surfing is the act of attempting to gain knowledge through simple observation. For example, cleaning staff or visitors could view information visible on computer monitors when employees leave such devices unattended. Shoulder surfing could also lead to impersonation if an unauthorized individual is able to view authentication processes. Shoulder surfing is especially important to consider in instances where remote access to systems is used to allow employees to work from home or other less secure locations. Shoulder surfing primarily affects only the confidentiality of data, but in conjunction with other threats such as impersonation, could affect integrity and availability as well.

4.2.3.10 Theft or Vandalism

Theft or vandalism is a deliberate act designed to cause the damage or destruction of information or information systems. Logic bombs planted by disgruntled employees are one example of this threat. Defacement of a corporate Web site by a malicious individual is another example of this type of threat. This type of threat primarily affects the integrity and availability of data, although it could affect the confidentiality of data as well.

4.2.3.11   Other Human Threats

There are a number of other possible human threats including:

■ Labor unrest or strikes
■ Riots or civil disorders
■ Terrorism
■ Arson

These threats generally affect the physical infrastructure that software applications depend upon to work. Generally, physical security is beyond the scope of the types of threats considered during software development, primarily because software development teams don't have any control over physical security. However, these threats are mentioned here because they can affect the service provided by an application. Most organizations have physical security measures and policies in place and are covered by data backup solutions and disaster recovery/business continuity plans. In any software development effort it pays to know and understand what physical security, data backup, and disaster recovery/business continuity protections are in place in order to ensure that the service the software under development will provide will continue, despite those threats.

4.2.4   Technical Threats

Technical threats represent threats to systems based upon the behavior of systems or applications. The intent behind a technical threat is not always malicious in nature, but can be based on simple error. Likewise, technical threats can be directed against a specific target or be completely random. Technical threats include the following.

4.2.4.1   Compromising Emanations

Compromising emanations represent unauthorized interception or interruption of signals that can either intentionally or unintentionally cause damage, disclosure, or destruction of information or of information systems. Take, for example, an application using wireless access points in a large warehouse to conduct inventory and routing of packages. Interference from other systems could intercept or interfere with the signals sent by the application and result in inaccurate inventories or misrouted packages. Although compromising emanations primarily affect the hardware instead of the software involved in such a system, the decisions to use such a wireless system are typically made during the design phase of the application and should be considered during the software development effort. Typically this type of threat affects the integrity and availability of information, but may also affect confidentiality as well.

4.2.4.2   Corruption by System Failures

Corruption by system failures represents the corruption of data caused when other systems that may affect system operation fail. For example, take a simple Web application to authorize payment of a bill. If during the process to authorize a credit card payment the Web server housing the application crashes, it may be that the payment is authorized, yet the user does not realize this fact. The user may try to repay the bill once the Web server is up and running again only to have her credit card charged a second time because the application did not complete all processes required to validate the credit card payment. Threats of this type could affect the confidentiality, integrity, and availability of information and information systems.

4.2.4.3   Data Contamination

Data contamination occurs when data values that stray from their field descriptions and business rules are allowed to intermix. For example, multiple account numbers for the same entity could allow unauthorized access to data. Likewise corrupted strings of data placed in an error log could contain sensitive information to which the log administrator should not have access, or file fragments containing sensitive information could be scattered across a hard drive instead of within an encrypted sector where the data would be protected. This type of treat affects the confidentiality of information, and to a lesser extent the integrity and availability of information.

4.2.4.4   Eavesdropping

Eavesdropping is an intentional attempt to gain information through the use of listening devices or programs. Keystroke monitoring, where a program logs the keystrokes of a user is an example of this type of threat. Trojan horse programs can also be utilized to capture user or system activity. Network sniffers can monitor and intercept packets that are sent between computer systems and can compromise unencrypted data. This type of threat generally affects the confidentiality of data, but in conjunction with other threats, can also affect the integrity and availability of data.

4.2.4.5   Failures and Intrusions Not Properly Logged

Failures and intrusions not properly logged represent improper logging and auditing of system and application errors. Take, for example, a banking application. If transaction logs are not properly configured and maintained then a system failure could result in duplicate transactions that are impossible to reconstruct, or worse: it could allow an unauthorized intrusion to take place with no knowledge of the event. Similarly the design of an application allows an audit log to remove the oldest data in order to preserve space and if the audit logs reach their maximum threshold, then an attack may go unnoticed. This type of threat typically affects the integrity and availability of information.

4.2.4.6   Installation Errors

Installation errors often occur when poor installation procedures accompany the implementation of new software. If the installation procedures for software do not specify certain hardware or operating system software settings, then built-in security features in the application being implemented may not function properly. In addition, installation programs used to install new software could modify system initialization scripts already in place to protect a system and change the configuration of that system allowing unauthorized access to systems and data. Therefore, during software development it is important to develop and document installation instructions and installation scripts. Threats of this type affect the confidentiality, integrity, and availability of information.

4.2.4.7   Intrusion

Intrusion represents gaining unauthorized access to a system. An example of this type of threat is the backdoor attack, where a programmer places a backdoor into code that allows the programmer to bypass normal identification, authentication, and authorization processes. This type of threat can significantly compromise the confidentiality, integrity, and availability of data.

4.2.4.8   Malicious Code

Malicious code includes viruses, worms, logic bombs, Trojan horses, spam, SpyWare, and backdoors. Through the use of malicious code a user or system can conduct denial-of-service attacks against a Web sever, application server, or e-mail server. Logic bombs and backdoors can allow users to gain unauthorized access to systems that can alter or destroy data. Although some of these threats such as spam and backdoors may have a specific target, others including viruses and worms can cause widespread damage without having a specific target. Threats of this type can affect the confidentiality, integrity, and availability of data.

4.2.4.9   Misrepresentation of Identity

Misrepresentation of identity represents assuming the identity of another individual or another system through the use of stolen or falsified credentials. An example is the man-in-the-middle attack, in which an attacker tricks John into believing he's Tom, and tricks Tom into believing he's John, thus gaining access to all messages in both directions. Another example is a pharming attack, where a link from an e-mail or Web page is used to lure a user to a Web site that appears to be the legitimate Web site, such as a banking Web site, but is in actuality a copy of the actual Web site. The user is prompted to use his credentials to log on to the Web site, and the fake site records the log-on information supplied by the user and sends the user directly to the real Web site. At some future point, the log-on credentials are used to access the real Web site and commit identity theft. This threat primarily affects the confidentiality of data, but could also affect the integrity and availability of data.

4.2.4.10   Misuse of Known Weaknesses

Misuse of known weaknesses is the deliberate act of bypassing security controls for the purpose of gaining additional information or additional privileges. For example, many known software applications come with root or administrator passwords set to a default parameter. Many of these root passwords and administrator IDs are well known and well published. Failure to delete or reset these passwords can lead to an attacker compromising a system. This type of threat affects the confidentiality, integrity, and availability of information and information systems.

4.2.4.11   Saturation of Resources

Saturation of resources represents threats such as Denial-of-Service (DoS) and Distributed-Denial-of-Service (DDoS) attacks designed to overwhelm the capacity of a Web site by using up all of its available bandwidth. Another example of this type of threat includes buffer overflow attacks that can allow a system compromise at the root level. This type of threat is common in software development efforts. Take, for an example, a shopping cart application. Users can browse a list of items for sale, and place them in a shopping cart. Users can alter the amount of a specific item by changing a "quantity" field on the Web page. If the development team assigns a variable type of "integer" rather than "long" to the variable that holds the quantity and a user enters a value for quantity greater than an integer may hold and appropriate safeguards are not in place to either validate the user's input, or to handle the resulting exceptions properly, then an attacker who has entered a large number may be able to gain access at the root level. This type of threat affects the integrity and availability of information.

4.2.4.12 Takeover of Authorized Sessions

Takeover of authorized sessions occurs when an unauthorized individual assumes the access rights of an authorized party. For example, if a workstation is left unattended and is not locked out, then another individual who is not authorized could use the system. Likewise, database communications made in the clear could be captured, modified, and then sent on to the original destination. This type of threat primarily affects the confidentiality of information, but could also affect the integrity and availability of information.

4.2.4.13 Tampering

Tampering represents unauthorized acts designed to cause the damage or destruction of information or information systems. Examples of this type of threat include: scripts designed to deface a Web site or disable Web server functionality, or Domain Name Service (DNS) hacks that prevent authorized users from properly accessing system resources. This type of threat typically affects the integrity and availability of information.

4.2.5 Environmental Threats

Environmental threats represent danger to information or information systems based upon the environment surrounding the information system. The intent behind a purely environmental threat is almost always not malicious in nature, but coupled with human threats such as arson, can result from a malicious threat. Typically, environmental threats are physical in nature and therefore don't affect application development directly. However, environmental threats do affect data backup policies and processes as well as disaster recovery and business continuity plans, which should all be considered during an application's design phase. Consider, for example, an application that records stock trades. How often should the data associated with the stock trade application be backed up? If the application development team does not ask this question, and simply assumes that the server is adequately backed up in a timely manner, costly programming errors could occur. What if:

■ The server is only backed up daily.

- The backup system used by the organization cannot back up the data more frequently due to bandwidth or other constraints.
- To avoid costly litigation associated with dropped or missed transactions, a backup of each and every transaction is required.
- The development team never inquired how often backups were made, and what the backup capability of the current system was and the new application was implemented without knowing the answers to these questions.

The result is that either a potentially costly new backup solution would have to be purchased by the organization, or that design changes would need to be made to the application after the application was implemented to save the data to multiple backup locations for purposes of redundancy. However, if the development team had considered data backup frequency during the design phase, then perhaps the design could have been built with the required redundancy up front.

For these types of reasons, it is just as important for software development teams to understand environmental and natural threats, as it is for them to understand human and technical threats. Environmental threats include the following.

4.2.5.1 Cable Cuts

Cable cuts are physical cuts in the cabling that provides power or network connectivity between information systems. A cut in the network cabling between a Web server and its associated data server could prevent data from being displayed or retrieved by an application. Cable cuts primarily affect the availability of information systems.

4.2.5.2 Electromagnetic Interference

Electromagnetic interference represents the threat to an information system from the proximity of an electromagnetic source such as a generator, transformer, or high-powered transmission line. For example, it may not be wise to place a server room or network cabling next to the emergency generator for a facility. The electromagnetic interference given off by the generator while in operation could affect the transmissions going through the cabling resulting in dropped or damaged packets if the cabling is not properly shielded. This type of threat affects the integrity and availability of information systems.

4.2.5.3 Environmental Conditions

Environmental conditions represent the climate in which an information system is found. Most computer systems only operate efficiently in a relatively small range of humidity and temperatures. Conditions that are too dry are just as hazardous to computer systems as conditions that are too humid. The same goes for temperature. Failures in heating and cooling systems can cause data centers to be shut down. This type of threat affects the availability of information systems.

4.2.5.4 Hazardous Materials

Hazardous materials such as chemical spills are a threat to both information systems and their users. Chemical spills or threats of such a spill can cause the evacuation of a building and cause systems to be unavailable for extended periods of time. Therefore this type of threat affects the availability of information systems.

4.2.5.5 Power Fluctuations

Power fluctuations include spikes, surges, faults, brownouts, and blackouts. Each of these types of fluctuation can affect the availability of information systems if the systems are not protected by surge suppressors, uninterruptible power supplies, or backup generators.

4.2.5.6 Secondary Disasters

Secondary disasters represent disasters caused indirectly due to another type of threat. For example, a fire could set off a sprinkler system that could affect the availability of workstations used by the staff of a call center. Although the call center's servers may be protected in a server room which is protected by an FM 200 or other system, the workstations for the call center may be in an open room only protected by sprinkler systems that, if set off, could damage the workstations.

4.2.6 Natural Threats

Natural threats represent danger to information or information systems from a natural event such as a flood, tornado, avalanche, or hurricane. The intent behind a natural threat is not malicious in nature. Typically natural threats are physical in nature and therefore don't affect application development directly. However, as with environmental threats, natural threats do affect data backup policies and processes as well as disaster recovery and business continuity plans, which should all be considered during an application's design phase.

4.3 How to Identify Security Threats

A list of the "usual suspects" as provided in this chapter is a good starting point for discovering the threats associated with a software development project. However, there are many other potential threats that may affect a software development effort. Although it is not practical to uncover all potential threats to a software development project during a risk assessment, all probable threats should be considered. How then can threats that may not be on the list of "usual suspects" be identified?

There are a number of methods of identifying threats. Some of these methods include:

- Reviews of attack histories
- Reviews of current headlines involving data breaches
- Reviews of Internet sites
- Threat modeling

4.3.1 Attack Histories

One of the easiest methods is to look at the attack history an organization has sustained. Reviewing incident response, help desk, and audit logs which most organizations maintain can provide insight into the threats that have already targeted the organization. Another method is to review the threats considered during risk assessments for similar software development projects within an organization, or even the threats uncovered during organizational risk assessments or audits.

4.3.2 Current Headlines

As with assets, one way to gain insight into current threats is to look at current headlines. What are the threats associated with the latest data breaches being reported? Many organizations such as the Privacy Rights Clearinghouse and Attrition.org, publish the latest reported data breaches on a daily basis, and provide regular updates as more information is revealed about the nature of the breach, including details about the threats involved. In addition, the Computer Security Institute (CSI) (http://www.gocsi.com/) publishes an annual computer crime survey conducted in conjunction with the Federal Bureau of Investigation (FBI). This annual report provides statistics on new and emerging threats and provides a good comprehensive look at the ever-changing threat landscape.

4.3.3 Internet Sites

The Internet is a wonderful source of information about new and upcoming threats. In addition to the sources listed above, there are numerous sites that deal with information security in general and many of these sites will have articles that describe the ever-changing threat landscape. Some are maintained by organizations dedicated to providing information on a wide variety of information security topics. However, there are others dedicated to dealing primarily with issues surrounding software development, including how to develop applications in a secure manner. One of the latter is the Open Web Application Security Project (OWASP) (http://www.owasp.org/).

According to their Web site, OWASP is "a worldwide free and open community focused on improving the security of application software." There is a wealth of good information on this Web site and it is an invaluable resource in developing applications in a secure manner. Although the site is primarily focused on Web-based applications, most of the techniques, tips, and tools provided on the site can be applied to client/server- and mainframe-based software development projects as well.

In addition to the many commercial and open source Web sites dealing with application security, the United States government also provides a number of Web sites that are helpful in understanding the risk management and threat identification process. Guidance is available from any number of U.S. government agencies including the following:

- *The Office of Management and Budget* (OMB) which published Circular A-130 "The Management of Federal Information Resources" governing the security of Federal automated information resources.
- *The Centers for Medicare and Medicaid Services* (CMS) which published the HIPAA privacy and security standards and also publishes a number of information security guidelines and standards required for organizations that provide Medicare and Medicaid services.
- *The Department of Defense* (DoD) which publishes a number of application security standards including the DoD Information Assurance Certification and Accreditation Process (DIACAP) which establishes the requirements for certifying and accrediting new systems within the DoD.
- *The National Institute of Standards and Technology* (NIST) which provides guidance in securing all Federal IT systems. NIST maintains a Computer Resource Security Center (CSRC) which provides a wealth of information on how to secure systems. A host of information on how to create secure application architectures including new technologies and services can be found on the NIST Web site (http://www.csrc.nist.gov/).

4.3.4   *Threat Modeling*

In addition to learning about threats from attack histories, headlines, and sources available on the Internet, there are some techniques that can be utilized during the application development process to uncover potential threats. Perhaps the most powerful of these techniques is *threat modeling*. Threat modeling is a technique used to look at the potential attacks that can be applied to a given software development by breaking down the software into its most basic components. Threat modeling has become an integral part of Microsoft's Security Development Lifecycle (SDL) process.

The threat modeling process begins during the requirements phase of the SDLC. It is important to begin with the identification of the following:

- Business objectives of the development effort
- User roles that will react with the application
- Data the application will manipulate or display
- Use cases for operating on the data that will be handled by the application

Once these items have been identified, the application's architecture can be modeled, including:

- Application components
- Service roles
- External dependencies
- Calls among the roles, components, external dependencies, and data sources

Once the calls have been modeled, then it is possible to examine the threats to those calls on a case-by-case basis considering the following general types of threat:

- Human Threats
  - Unintentional
    - From outside the organization
    - From within the organization
  - Intentional
    - From outside the organization
    - From within the organization
- Technical Threats
  - Nonmalicious
  - Malicious
    - Nonspecific target
    - Specific target

Natural and environmental threats do not affect software development projects directly, but rather indirectly through the effects that they have upon the systems supporting the software. Typically these threats are considered alongside technical threats during the threat modeling process.

STRIDE is a good example of a threat modeling methodology. STRIDE is based on six basic types of threat category. These threat categories spell out the acronym STRIDE and include the following:

- *Spoofing:* where a user attempts to become another user or assume some of the attributes of another user. One simple example of spoofing is a user who obtains the log-in credentials of another user through techniques such as shoulder surfing, keystroke logging, or finding the yellow sticky note with a password left behind by the user of a system, and logging in as a different individual who may have different privileges.
- *Tampering of data:* where users can change information provided to them by an application and return that changed information in order to manipulate the validation routines, or lack thereof, utilized by the application. Example: In an E-commerce site, the price of an object is embedded in the HTML code used to display the shopping cart. An attacker alters the price by altering the underlying HTML code and returns a price that is lower than it should be, and which is not validated by the application.
- *Repudiation:* where users of an application can claim that they didn't make a transaction when there are insufficient auditing controls in place. Example: If account transfers are not properly logged in an audit file, or if the audit file is not sufficiently protected such that it can be altered, then it may become impossible to determine who or what process transferred money from one account to another.
- *Information disclosure:* where information provided by a user to an application, such as a bank account number, password, or credit card number is intercepted and revealed by an attacker. Example: Data left in hidden fields, HTTP headers, or other system caches is found and revealed by an attacker.
- *Denial-of-service:* where the use of large files, complex calculations, or large and complex queries can be used to tie up system resources for a significant amount of time.
- *Elevation of privilege:* where users are able to gain additional rights and privileges that are normally associated with administration accounts.

Under STRIDE all threats are considered to be one of the six types identified above. Therefore it is easy to apply because there are only six threats to consider.

4.4   Test Case Threats

Understanding the concept of threat modeling is not an easy process. Applying threat modeling techniques to the test case established in this book will highlight the basics of this process. First, the business objectives of the test case must be identified. A review of the requirements of that test case is provided here.

Your team has been assigned the task of building an application to calculate retirement benefits for the vast majority of retirement plans your company sells. Many of the retirement plans sold by your company allow customers (i.e., companies or corporations) to make additional contributions to their plan at the end of their fiscal year, for tax purposes. The requirements of this application include the following.

- It must be Web-based.
- The application must be usable by your company's employees who administer retirement plans for the company's customers.
- The application must also be usable by your company's sales force who will use the calculated results of the application to sell retirement plans to new customers.
- The results of the calculations must be viewable over the Internet by retirement plan customers.
- All Internal Revenue Service (IRS) rules must be followed when calculating benefits. Some of these rules describe monetary and/or age limits that may be legally contributed to retirement plans which may change from year to year.
- Proprietary business rules created by your company must be used when calculating benefits for certain types of plans.
- The results of the application's calculated benefits must be viewable on screen, printable, and must also be available to be e-mailed to a client in a format that the client cannot change.
- Because a large number of user inputs are required in order to use the application, all user inputs must have the ability to be saved and retrieved at a later time.
- The data required to calculate the benefits must come from current retirement plan member databases already established. Such data includes information about individual members of a retirement plan including:
  - Names
  - Dates of birth
  - Salaries
  - Identification numbers
  - Amounts contributed to the retirement plan
  - Dates of employment/termination
- Because members of the company's sales force will use the application for the purpose of selling new retirement plans to customers, they must be able to:

- Import datasets provided by potential customers
- Create dummy datasets on the fly for illustration purposes
- Utilize dummy datasets created and stored in the application database
■ The results of all calculations must be saved and archived for a given period of time.

NOTE: The focus of this book is upon risk assessment activities and applying those risk assessment activities to the SDLC with the purpose of providing more secure applications. It is not intended to be a primer on the basic principles of software development. However, in order to understand some of the principles involved in risk assessment as it applies to the SDLC such as threat modeling, it is necessary to understand the software architecture of the test case, and some of the decisions involved in that test case. The remainder of this chapter describes many of the decisions made by the actual design team during the development of the application described in the test case.

4.4.1 Test Case Business Objectives

Three primary business objectives associated with the test case are as follows:

1. Calculation of retirement benefits for retirement plans at the end of a fiscal year.
2. Illustration of the benefits of the various retirement plan products sold by the organization.
3. Review and approval of the calculations by external customers.

4.4.2 Test Case User Roles

From these three business objectives the major user roles associated with the application can be determined as follows:

1. *Retirement plan administrator.* An employee of our organization who administers retirement plans for external clients/customers. This role uses the application to calculate the retirement benefits based upon the specific requirements of the plan and the requirements of the customer (i.e., how much of a year-end contribution the customer wants to make).
2. *Sales force.* An employee of our organization who is responsible for selling retirement plans. This role uses the application to illustrate the benefits of specific retirement plans to different prospective customers.
3. *Authorized customer representative.* An employee (usually from the human resources staff) of a company who has purchased a retirement plan administered by our company. This role uses the application to view the results of the

retirement benefit calculation and then provide direction to the retirement plan administrator on whether the customer will choose to make an additional contribution to the plan.

The data to be manipulated by the application has already been outlined in the requirements and includes elements of PII of individual eligible participants in a retirement plan. This includes names, SSNs, dates of birth, salaries, and current-year contributions made by the participant to the retirement plan. In the case of the sales force, either a "dummy" dataset designed to represent the employees of varying size companies is used, an extract from a potential customer's files is imported into the application, or the sales force creates the dataset on the fly.

4.4.3 Test Case Use Cases

The major use cases for operating on the data used by this application are shown in Figure 4.2. Each use case is described in detail below.

4.4.3.1 Use Case 1: Calculate Retirement Benefits

This use case allows a retirement plan administrator who has the proper access rights to calculate the retirement benefits for a specific retirement plan, for a specific fiscal year. It also allows an authorized member of the sales staff to calculate

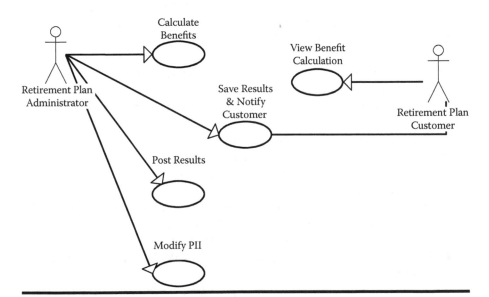

FIGURE 4.2   Test case use cases

retirement benefits based either upon a dummy dataset selected by the sales force member, or an extract from a potential customer's employee records supplied by the potential customer to the sales staff member.

> *Pre-Conditions:* The application is available and the administrator has the proper access rights to the information contained in the records for the customer in question.
>
> *Post-Conditions:* Details required for the calculation of the retirement benefits have been entered and all calculations have completed successfully.

Inputs for this use case include details about the specific benefit calculation that is to be made, including:

- The customer's retirement plan identification number
- The fiscal year-end date for which the calculation is to be made
- The amount of additional contribution that is to be made to the retirement plan
- The type of retirement plan for which the calculation is to be made
- The formula used by the retirement plan in question to calculate benefits

Processing requires that all fields will have to have valid data entered.

Outputs for this use case include the calculated results of the retirement benefits for the given plan and given fiscal year organized for each eligible participant within the retirement plan. An explanation must be given for why any plan participant does not receive a calculated benefit amount for the fiscal year in question.

Figure 4.3 is a depiction of the data flow for this use case. The data flow follows a step-by-step process as follows:

- Step 1: The retirement plan administrator chooses to calculate retirement benefits for a specific plan.
- Step 2: The application makes a request to the mainframe service to gather the PII required for calculating benefits.
- Step 3: The mainframe service requests the PII from the Plan Database.
- Step 4: The mainframe service gathers the PII from the Plan Database.
- Step 5: The mainframe service places the PII in the Retirement Calculation DB2 Database.
- Step 6: The mainframe service informs the application where to find the PII within the Retirement Calculation DB2 Database.
- Step 7: The application queries the DB2 Database for the PII.
- Step 8: The PII is retrieved and used to calculate the retirement plan benefits.
- Step 9: The calculated benefit is displayed on the screen for the retirement plan administrator.

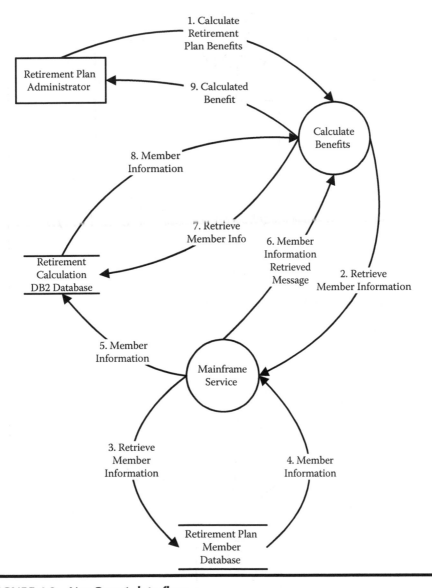

FIGURE 4.3   Use Case 1 data flow

Figure 4.4 is a representation of the sequence diagram for this use case. The sequence of events is as follows:.

- The retirement plan administrator enters authentication credentials and a plan ID number into the application.
- An authentication service authenticates the user. If there is a problem with the authentication credentials, the user must re-enter her authentication

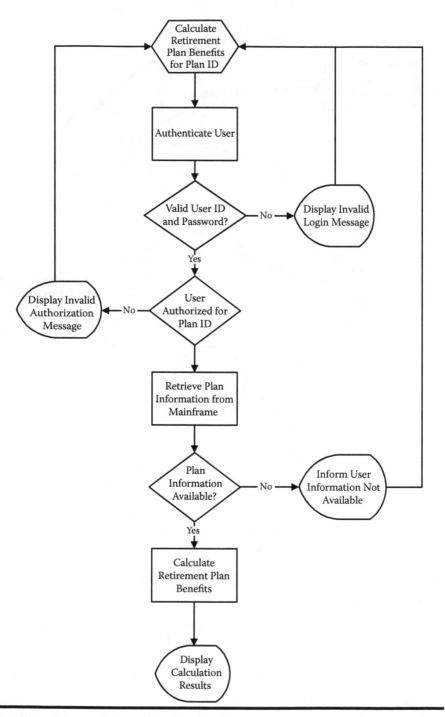

FIGURE 4.4   Use Case 1 sequence diagram

credentials. After three tries the credentials in question will be locked out and must be reset through the organization's help desk.

- If the user is authenticated, then the authentication service will indicate whether the user is authorized to see the particular plan information for the retirement plan ID entered. If not, then the user must enter another plan ID for which she is authorized before she can continue.
- Once the user is authenticated and authorized, the application places a call through the gateway to a mainframe service. The mainframe service will attempt to gather the data for the plan ID specified, as well as for the fiscal year end specified. If the data does not exist, or if the mainframe service is unavailable, then the user will be informed that the data does not exist or is not available at the current time. The user may then enter another plan ID, or another fiscal year end date.
- If the data is available, then the mainframe service will gather the data and place it in a DB2 table on the mainframe.
- The application will then retrieve the information from the DB2 table and perform the calculations.
- The results of the calculation are displayed on screen for the user.

4.4.3.2 Use Case 2: Save Calculated Results and Notify Customer

This use case allows a retirement plan administrator or a member of the sales force to save the results of a benefit calculation and notify the customer that the results of the calculation are ready for review.

Pre-Conditions: Use Case 1.

Post-Conditions: The inputs made by the retirement plan administrator have been saved to a database, as well as the results of the calculations. The customer has been notified via e-mail that the results of the calculation are ready for the customers' review.

Inputs to this use case include:

- The e-mail address of the customer representative authorized to review the calculation and authorize the contribution of funds.
- Notes about the specific calculation. For example, some customers, when considering how much they may contribute to the retirement plan at the end of the fiscal year, may wish to review the results of several calculations, each utilizing a different contribution amount. The notes field allows the retirement plan administrator to distinguish among these various calculations for a given retirement plan and fiscal year combination.

Outputs for this use case include:

■ A saved dataset containing the retirement plan administrator's inputs to use case 1
■ A saved result set containing the results of the calculation
■ An e-mail that has been delivered to the authorized customer representative

Figure 4.5 represents the data flow for this use case. The data flow follows a step-by-step process as follows.

■ Step 1: The retirement plan administrator chooses to save the calculation he is viewing on the screen and notify the customer.
■ Step 2: The results of the calculation are saved within the DB2 table.
■ Step 3: A PDF file of the calculated results is created and saved to the Customer Web Portal.
■ Step 4: An e-mail is generated and sent to the external customer informing the customer to check her mailbox on the Customer Web Portal to view the results of the calculation.

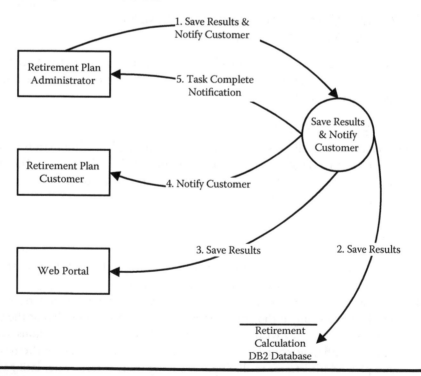

FIGURE 4.5   Use Case 2 data flow

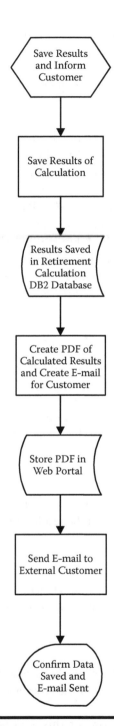

FIGURE 4.6   Use Case 2 sequence diagram

- Step 5: The retirement plan administrator is informed that the information is saved and that a notification has been made.

Figure 4.6 is a representation of the sequence diagram for this use case. The sequence of events is as follows:

- The retirement plan administrator (who has already been authenticated) chooses to save the results of the calculation.
- The application saves the results of the calculations to the DB2 database.
- The application then creates a PDF file of the results of the calculation and stores that PDF within the Customer Web Portal Database.
- The application then creates and sends an e-mail to the external customer informing that customer to check her mailbox through the Customer Web Portal in order to view the results of the benefit calculation.
- Finally, the application confirms to the retirement plan administrator that the information has been saved, and the customer has been notified.

4.4.3.3   Use Case 3: Customer Review of Calculations

This use case allows an authorized customer representative to log in to a secure portal and view the results of the calculation provided by the retirement plan administrator. Strictly speaking, this is not a use case that must be programmed, because the Customer Web Portal already exists and is in use by external customers. However, it is included here for the sake of being thorough and to provide the reader with a thorough understanding of the entire process.

Pre-Conditions: Use Cases 1 and 2.
Post-Conditions: The authorized customer representative has been authenticated to the secure portal and has reviewed the results of the calculation.

Inputs to this use case include:

- The identification and authentication credentials supplied by the authorized customer representative to the secure Web portal

Outputs to this use case include:

- The results of any retirement plan benefit calculations made by the retirement plan administrator on the behalf of the customer

Figure 4.7 represents the data flow for this use case. The data flow follows a step-by-step process as follows:

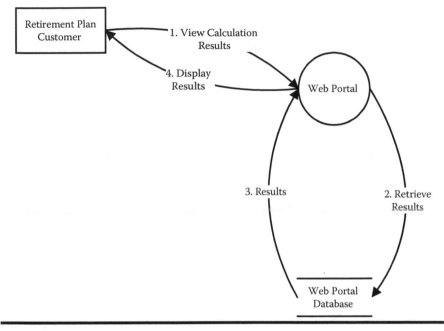

FIGURE 4.7 Use Case 3 data flow

- Step 1: The customer requests the Web portal to display the results of the calculation.
- Step 2: The Web portal application queries the Web portal database for the required information.
- Step 3: The Web portal database returns the required PDF file.
- Step 4: The PDF is displayed for the customer.

Figure 4.8 is a representation of the sequence diagram for this use case. The sequence of events is as follows:

- The customer enters his authentication credentials into the Customer Web Portal.
- The Web portal attempts to authenticate the user.
- If the user cannot be authenticated the user will be asked to re-enter his authentication credentials. The user may do this up to three times before he will be automatically locked out of the Web portal and then must deal with customer service to have his authentication credentials re-established.
- If the user is authenticated then the Web portal will query the Web portal database for the PDF in question.
- The PDF is then displayed on screen for the customer.

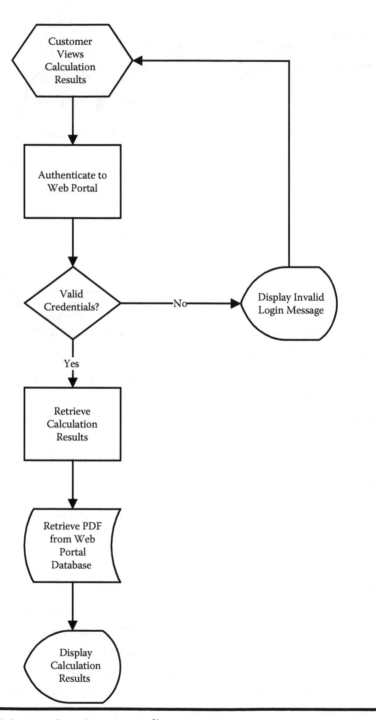

FIGURE 4.8 Use Case 3 sequence diagram

4.4.3.4   Use Case 4: Posting Retirement Plan Benefits to Member Accounts

This use case allows the retirement plan administrator to post the results of a retirement benefit calculation to the individual accounts of the individual participants in the plan. A retirement plan benefit calculation represents an additional contribution to a retirement plan made by an employer to the plan, and this additional contribution must be split equitably among the members of the plan based upon such things as length of service, age, vesting requirements, salary, key employee status, and so on. The calculation represents an additional benefit that will be added to the individual retirement accounts of each employee who is an eligible member of the plan. If the calculation is approved by the customer, the customer will deposit the required funds in a specific account set up for the plan. The funds in that account will then be split among the eligible plan members and transferred to their individual retirement plan accounts. This use case describes that process.

Pre-Conditions: Use cases 1, 2, 3, the approval of the authorized customer representative, and a source of funds

Post-Conditions: Distribution of funds into the individual accounts of retirement plan participants

Inputs to this use case include:

■ Identification of the specific saved results set (from Use Case 2) to be used for distribution of funds into individual accounts.

■ Identification of the account that holds the funds which are to be distributed.

Outputs to this use case include:

■ Distributed funds in the individual accounts of individual participants of the given retirement plan.

Figure 4.9 represents the data flow for this use case. The data flow follows a step-by-step process as follows.

■ Step 1: The retirement plan administrator requests the application to post the results of a calculation that has already been made by the application, and saved, to the individual member accounts.

■ Step 2: The application queries the DB2 database for the results of the calculation.

■ Step 3: The results of the calculation are retrieved from the DB2 database.

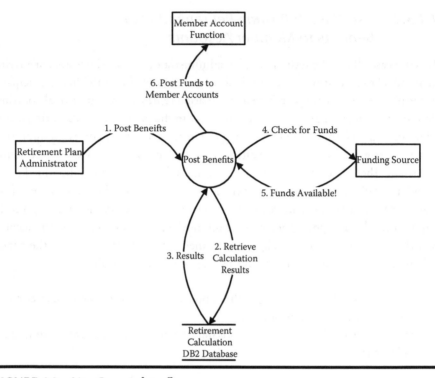

FIGURE 4.9   Use Case 4 data flow

- Step 4: The application requests the mainframe service to check to see whether the plan account has the necessary funds to cover all of the calculated benefits.
- Step 5: The mainframe service supplies a response about the amount of funds available within the account.
- Step 6: The application creates a special file and submits it to a batch processing program that, during the next nightly cycle, will transfer the funds out of the plan account, and into the individual members' accounts according to their investment selections.

Figure 4.10 is a representation of the sequence diagram for this use case. The sequence of events is as follows:

- The pension plan administrator enters her authentication credentials and a plan ID into the application.
- The authentication service will attempt to authenticate the user. If the user is not authenticated, the user will be allowed to re-enter authentication credentials. If invalid authentication credentials are supplied three times in a row,

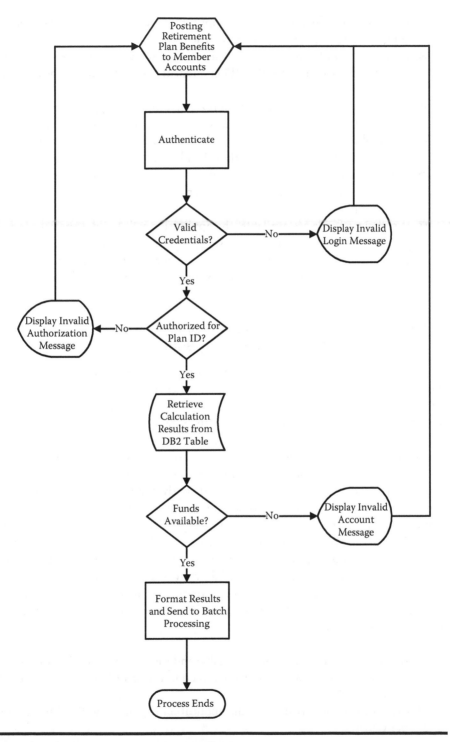

FIGURE 4.10   Use Case 4 sequence diagram

the user will be locked out of the application and will be forced to reset her application credentials by contacting the help desk.

- If the user is authenticated, the authentication service will check to see if the user is authorized for the plan ID entered. If not, the user will be asked to enter a different plan ID.
- If the user is authorized for the plan ID in question, the application will query the DB2 database for the saved results of the calculation in question.
- The application will then query the mainframe service to determine if the correct amounts of funds are within the plan account.
- If not, then the user will be informed that insufficient funds are available for this transaction and allow the user to enter a different plan ID or different calculation result.
- If sufficient funds are available, the application will build a special file and pass it to a mainframe batch processing program that, during the next nightly cycle, will transfer the funds from the plan account to the individual investment selections within each member's individual retirement plan account.

4.4.3.5   Use Case 5: Modification of PII Used to Calculate Retirement Plan Benefits

This use case allows the retirement plan administrator to modify the PII used in calculating the retirement plan benefit in cases where the PII was incorrectly entered or incorrectly reported by the customer. Because data about individual members of retirement plans is supplied and entered by the external customer, mistakes such as an invalid salary, date of birth, date of employment, date of termination, and the like can often find their way into the organization's records. There are processes in place to make corrections to these amounts so that they may be made current, but these processes cannot be made instantaneously, but rather must be made during the course of a night's batch processing on the mainframe. Due to the IRS limits of when contributions must be made to pension plans, often there is a rush on making a calculation (Use Case 1) and posting the results of that calculation to member accounts (Use Case 4) that cannot wait for nightly batch processing cycles to correct the information required for the calculation to be accurate. In such an instance, it is necessary to allow the retirement plan administrator to change the data used by the application to calculate the benefits on the fly. This use case describes that process.

> *Pre-Conditions:* The application is available and the administrator has the proper access rights to the information contained in the records for the customer in question.
> *Post-Conditions:* The PII used by the application has been modified to the correct values.

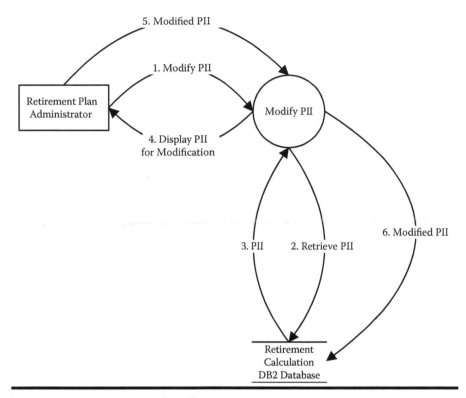

FIGURE 4.11   Use Case 5 data flow

Inputs to this use case include:

■ The customer's retirement plan identification number.
■ The fiscal year for which the calculation is to be made.
■ The specific change(s) to be made to the PII used in the calculation. Example: John Smith's salary for 2007 was originally reported by the customer as $25,700.00 but in actuality is $27,500.00.

Outputs to this use case include:

■ Saved corrections to the PII required to correctly calculate the retirement benefits for a retirement plan for a given contribution amount and fiscal year.

Figure 4.11 represents the data flow for this use case. The data flow follows a step-by-step process as follows:

■ Step 1: The retirement plan administrator chooses to modify the PII used to make a calculation.

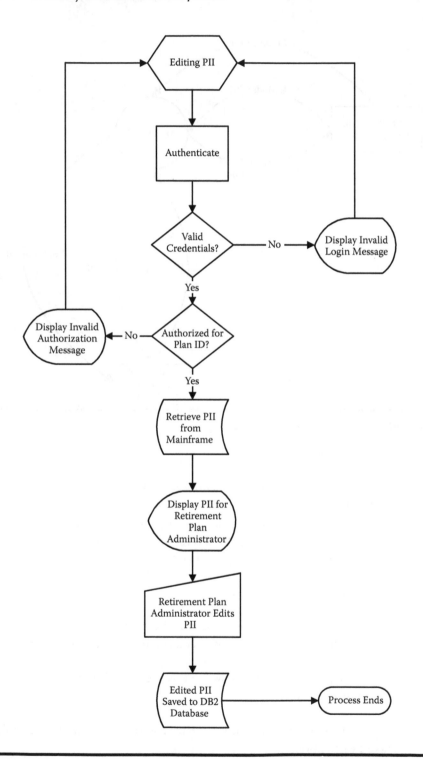

FIGURE 4.12 Use Case 5 sequence diagram

- Step 2: The application queries the DB2 database for the PII for the plan.
- Step 3: The DB2 database returns the PII to the application.
- Step 4: The PII is displayed on screen for the retirement plan administrator.
- Step 5: The retirement plan administrator manually edits the PII on screen and then chooses to save the modifications.
- Step 6: The modified PII is stored by the application in the DB2 database.

Figure 4.12 is a representation of the sequence diagram for this use case. The sequence of events is as follows:

- The retirement plan administrator enters authentication credentials and a plan ID number into the application.
- An authentication service authenticates the user. If there is a problem with the authentication credentials, the user must re-enter his authentication credentials. After three tries the credentials in question will be locked out and must be reset through the organization's help desk.
- If the user is authenticated, then the authentication service will indicate whether the user is authorized to see the particular plan information for the retirement plan ID entered. If not, then the user must enter another Plan ID for which he is authorized before he can continue.

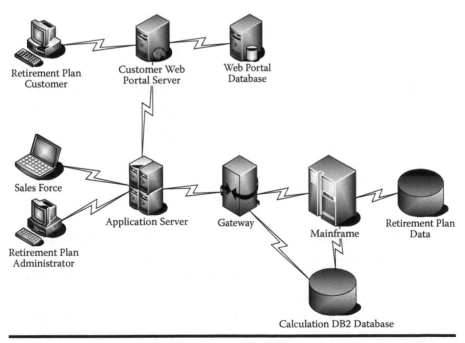

FIGURE 4.13　Test case hardware components

- Once the user is authenticated and authorized, the application retrieves the PII from the DB2 database.
- The PII is then displayed for the user on the screen.
- The user is allowed to manually edit the PII on the screen.
- The edited PII is saved by the application to the DB2 database.

4.4.4 Test Case Components

Figure 4.13 represents the hardware components utilized by the test case. The application itself sits on an application server within the organization's domain. Either the sales force or the retirement plan administrator accesses this information through the company's intranet. The application makes a number of calls to mainframe service(s) through a gateway device that allows for communication between the application server and the mainframe. The mainframe services do a number of things including:

- Authenticating the user
- Checking to see if the user is authorized for a specific plan ID
- Retrieving retirement plan data from VSAM records on the mainframe
- Placing retirement plan data into a DB2 database on the mainframe that can be accessed directly by the application server (through the gateway)
- Checking to see if sufficient funds exist in a plan account for distribution to individual member accounts
- Transferring the funds from the plan account to individual member investment choices within their individual accounts (via an overnight batch process)

The application server also can store saved calculation results to the DB2 database through the gateway. The application server also passes PDF files of calculated results to the Customer Web Portal server which in turn stores these results within its database server. Finally, the retirement plan customer interacts directly with the Customer Web Portal over the Internet.

Let's take a closer look at Use Case 3. The customer does not authenticate to the application being built, but rather to the secure customer service portal already built by our company and views the results of the calculation at that Web site. The customer portal represents an external dependency for our application—but how that customer portal operates is beyond the scope of our development effort—as long as our calculated results can be viewed through the customer portal. In this specific case, the customer portal holds "e-mails" and their attachments created by our application.

4.4.5 Test Case Architecture

Now that the use cases have been developed for the application, we can begin to develop the architecture of the application. Using object-oriented design techniques the following application components may be abstracted.

A *Plan* object that is designed to hold information about a specific retirement plan for which benefits will be calculated. Some of the properties of this object could include the following:

- A plan identification number
- A plan name
- A plan type (used to determine a type of benefit calculation)
- A plan formula (used in the calculation process)
- A collection of participants (individual employees who contribute to the retirement plan)
- A calculation (used to identify the set of inputs made when calculating specific benefits)
- An account number (used to identify the source of funds required for Use Case 4)
- A customer e-mail address (to satisfy the requirements of Use Cases 2 and 3)

Some of the methods for this object might include the following:

- Send notification method (used to satisfy the customer notification requirement of Use Case 2 and the requirements of Use Case 3).
- Post benefits method (used to satisfy the requirements of Use Case 4).

A *Participant* object designed to represent the individual participant within a retirement plan for whom benefits are being calculated. Some of the properties of this object could include the following:

- A plan identification number (to associate the participant with a given plan)
- A participant name
- A participant ID number (to associate the participant with his individual retirement accounts)
- A participant salary
- A participant date of birth (in order to calculate the participant's age as of the end of the fiscal year of the calculation, a requirement of IRS rules that allow for different contribution amounts depending upon age)
- A collection of the participant's contributions to the retirement plan for the fiscal year the calculation is made

- A participant date of employment (for eligibility and vesting purposes)
- Other PII necessary to fulfill the business rules of different plans
- A calculated benefit (to represent the calculated retirement benefit amount)

Methods for the Participant object might include the following:

- Retrieve data method (to retrieve the PII required in order to perform the calculation)
- Modify PII method (to fulfill the requirements of Use Case 5)
- Calculate eligibility (to determine if the member is eligible to receive a retirement benefit for the fiscal year in question)

A *Calculation* object designed to represent the business rules used in calculating retirement plan benefits given plan type, plan formula, contribution amount, and fiscal year. Some of the properties of this object include the following:

- A plan number (to associate the calculation results with a specific plan)
- A contribution amount (the amount to be contributed by the customer to the customers' retirement plan)
- A fiscal year end date (to determine which set of PII needs to be retrieved as well as to determine participant age and which IRS limitations and business rules to apply)

Some of the methods of the Calculation object might include the following:

- Retrieve IRS limitations (IRS business rules place different limitations on the amounts that may be contributed to a retirement plan. These limitations may vary depending upon the calendar year for which the retirement benefits are calculated. Because these limitations are continually changing, they are placed in a separate data file that is updated each time the IRS comes out with a new set of rules. This method will retrieve the correct set of IRS limitations for the year specified.)
- Calculate benefits (which calculates the retirement benefits to satisfy Use Case 1)
- Save results (to save the results of a calculation to satisfy Use Case 2)

What about other components of the application? The application must be Web-based, but what about the data? Where does the current information for the plan reside? Where is the data (PII) for the retirement plan participants stored? The company has been selling retirement plans for some time, and has a large data store of information for these retirement plans and their individual participants. The new application will tap into those sources of data to retrieve the information necessary to calculate the benefits for a specific plan for a specific fiscal year.

However, the new application must be Web-based, and the data stored about the individual plans and their participants is stored on the company's mainframe computer in a nonrelational format. How then, will the data necessary to achieve the business objectives of the development effort be retrieved? In this case, an application component will need to be developed. This component will consist of a mainframe component that can gather the necessary data and deposit it in a location which will be accessible by the Web-based components of the application.

An additional consideration is saving the inputs and results of the calculation required by Use Case 2. Both Use Case 2 and the mainframe component represent requirements to store data in a given location. It is easiest for the required mainframe component (which will gather the plan and participant data) to place this gathered data in a mainframe DB2 database. Therefore the same DB2 database on the mainframe will be used to store user inputs and the results of the benefit calculations required by Use Case 2.

Now that most of the application components have been defined, some of the service roles and external dependencies of the application can be defined. Some of these service roles and external dependencies include:

- A gateway service required for the Web-based portion of the application to communicate with the mainframe component of the application
- An e-mail service required to notify the authorized customer representative that the results of a benefit calculation are complete (Use Case 2)
- A service to send the results of a calculation to the secure customer service portal application so that the customer can log in to that application and view the results of the calculation (Use Case 3)
- An authentication service required to ensure that the user is authorized to view the plan and participant information required in order to calculate the retirement plan benefits

Now that most of the application components, service roles, and external dependencies of the application have been defined, we can begin to look at the calls required among these components, roles, and dependencies. For the purposes of this book, we concentrate on the calls made for Use Case 1, because it represents one of the more complicated use cases in the application.

Examining the pre-conditions for Use Case 1 we find that the application is available and the retirement plan administrator has the proper access rights to the information contained in the records for the customer in question. Therefore, the first call made by the application is from the application to the authentication service used by the application. The user will enter her authentication credentials as well as the Plan ID number for which the calculation is to be made. The application will then use the authentication service to ensure that the user's authentication credentials are accurate, and that the user is authorized to view sensitive information for the plan in question.

The authentication service will return several potential responses to the application, depending upon the situation. This call will attempt to answer the following questions.

1. Is the authentication service available? (Because the authentication service is an external dependency of our application, we need to know that the service is available for use.)
2. Are the user credentials (i.e., user ID and password) supplied to the authentication service valid?
3. Does the specific retirement plan identified by the user (by supplying a specific plan ID number) exist?
4. If the specific retirement plan identified exists and the user is an authenticated user, then is the user authorized to view the details of the specific plan in question?

Assuming that the user is authenticated and authorized to view the information of the specific plan, then the authentication service will supply some information to the application about the plan such as the plan name, plan type, and current fiscal year end date. At this point, the authenticated and authorized user must enter an additional piece of information: the fiscal year end date for which the calculation is to be made. Although this typically will be the current fiscal year end date, in some cases the calculation may be made for a previous fiscal year.

At this point, the second call is made. This call is to the mainframe service that will gather the PII stored within the mainframe and deposit it in the DB2 database. Once the mainframe program has gathered the required data and placed that data in the DB2 database, the mainframe program will return a response to the application depending upon the situation. The possible responses are:

1. Is the mainframe service available? Again, this is an external dependency of our application and we need to know that the service is available for use.
2. Does data exist for the specified plan, for the specified fiscal year?
3. If data exists for the specified plan and specified fiscal year, then the service will supply a count of the number of records copied to the DB2 database, along with an index number so that the correct data may be retrieved from the database.

Assuming that the data exists for the specified plan and fiscal year, the application will now make a call to the DB2 database to gather the PII necessary to make the calculations.

Once the application has gathered the necessary PII to complete the calculations, the user will be prompted for some additional information, such as the plan formula and the amount (if any) to be contributed. Once the entries have been made, the internal business rules of the application will be applied and the calculations will begin. At this point, only one additional call is made by the application, and that involves the "Retrieve IRS Limitations" method of the calculation object. The application will then retrieve the proper IRS limitations from the IRS limitation data file.

Now that the application has all of the information it needs to calculate the retirement benefits for the given plan for a given fiscal year, the application can apply the business rules within the application to calculate the retirement benefits. Once the calculations are complete, then the results of the calculations are displayed upon the screen for the user to view.

So far, we have identified a total of four calls:.

1. A call to the authentication service to ensure that the user is authenticated and authorized to view the information for the retirement plan in question
2. Calls to the mainframe service to gather the PII required for the calculation and place the data in the DB2 table
3. A call to the DB2 to gather the PII supplied by the mainframe service and to pull it into the application and populate our participant collection
4. A call to the IRS data file to gather the correct IRS limitations for the year the retirement benefits are to be calculated

4.4.6   Test Case Threats

At this point, threat modeling techniques can be applied to each of the specific calls. To begin, we examine each of the threat avenues to determine if they may potentially affect any of the calls. Let's recall the basic threat avenues identified in this chapter:

- Human Threats
  - Unintentional
    - From outside the organization
    - From within the organization
  - Intentional
    - From outside the organization
    - From within the organization
- Technical Threats
  - Nonmalicious
  - Malicious
    - Nonspecific target
    - Specific target

Taking each of these threat avenues one at a time, we can apply them to the calls to see if they may affect each of the calls. We begin with human threats which are unintentional from outside the organization. The roles for the test case are: Retirement Plan Administrator, Sales Force, and Authorized Customer Representative. However, the Retirement Plan Administrator and Sales Force roles are internal to our organization, not external. Only the Authorized Customer Representative is an external user. And we have already determined that this role does not actually interact with our application (other than via the receipt of an e-mail notification), but rather with the Secure Customer Portal which is an external dependency of our application. Therefore, we can eliminate human threats from external sources (either intentional or unintentional) from the potential threat avenues that may affect our calls. Or can we?

At this point, we only know that our application must be Web-based. We do not know how the application will be deployed. Will it be deployed on the Internet so that the sales force as well as retirement plan administrators working from home can access it? Or will it be deployed on the company's intranet so that only internal users can access the program? If it is deployed on the Internet, then we must first look at how it will be accessed by users before we can eliminate external human threats from our threat modeling. In this instance, we assume that the application will be deployed on the company intranet and that the company sales force will only access the application through the intranet. Therefore, we can eliminate human threats from external sources as potential avenues that may affect the calls made by the application.

Next we consider human threats from internal sources (either intentional or unintentional) to our calls. Do human threats from internal sources exist? The answer to this question is yes. A number of internal human threat avenues exist. What are some of these internal human threat avenues?

- Shoulder surfing could allow nonauthorized personnel to observe the authentication process.
- Impersonation could allow users with stolen identity credentials (i.e., a stolen user ID and password) to view information they are not authorized to see.
- Errors and omissions in updating the IRS limitation file could result in the application applying incorrect business rules to the calculation. Likewise errors and omissions in the entries made by the retirement plan administrator, such as the plan formula, fiscal year end date, or amount to be contributed could all result in an incorrect calculation.
- Inadvertent acts or carelessness could result in programming errors that do not apply the complex business rules properly, resulting in incorrect calculations or incorrect error handling or other potential vulnerabilities that could allow an attacker to gain access.

What about technical threats? Do any technical threats to our calls exist? The answer of course is yes; a number of technical threats to our calls exist. Nonmalicious threats include:

- Data contamination. The error log designed for this application placed all of the details associated with the error into an error log including sensitive information that the log administrator was not authorized to see.
- Corruption by system failures. If the mainframe service that gathers the PII required for the calculation is interrupted due to a mainframe system failure, the data placed in the DB2 tables could be garbled or corrupted. Or likewise the call to the DB2 table to pull the PII into the application could be corrupted by system failures such as the gateway to the mainframe, resulting in data that is garbled or corrupted.
- Failures and intrusions not properly logged. It is possible for the authentication service to determine that the user has not properly supplied log-in credentials, or is not authorized to view a specific pension plan. If these types of intrusions are not properly logged (i.e., the user is simply denied access to the information and no log entry is made) then no audit trail will exist that a user was attempting to view unauthorized information.
- Environmental and natural threats. The application will run on Web server located in the main data center for the company. This data center is also the home of the mainframe computer where all of the data files are stored. Therefore natural and environmental threats such as fire, flood, power fluctuations, tornadoes, and the like all could affect the operation of the application or its associated information.

Malicious threats with a nonspecific target include:

- Malicious code. Viruses, worms, or other malicious programs could attempt to alter or destroy the IRS limitations data file, or interrupt calls through the gateway between the Web-based application and the mainframe service or the mainframe DB2 database.
- Saturation of resources. DoS attacks aimed at the company Intranet could affect the availability of the application or of the mainframe service.

Malicious threats with a specific target include:

- Eavesdropping. Keystroke loggers could capture user IDs and passwords supplied to the authentication service. Network sniffers could detect, intercept, and corrupt or replace packets sent between the application and the gateway to the mainframe.
- Intrusion. Backdoors to the application could be programmed by the development staff.
- Takeover of authorized sessions. If an authorized retirement plan administrator left a workstation unattended and unlocked then it would be possible for an unauthorized individual to gain access to the information in the application.

4.5   Conclusion

Back at the scene of the crime, the great detective has examined all of the suspects in the case one by one. Using his knowledge of the suspect's motive and opportunity, he has eliminated the suspects who had neither the motive nor the opportunity to commit the crime. Now, only a handful of suspects remain. These suspects have both the motive and the opportunity for committing the crime. The detective now needs to examine the evidence to find out if the suspects have the means for committing the crime.

Software development teams are like the detective in this story. They need to protect the item of value or assets as discovered in the previous chapter. Unlike the detective, who is attempting to solve the crime in order to return the asset, the goal is to prevent the asset from theft in the first place. In order to accomplish this, software development teams need to understand who the suspects or threats to applications are. This chapter dealt with ways of determining who those suspects might be including:

- Lists of the "usual" threats involved in software development projects
- Examining current headlines to determine some of the current industry threats
- Consulting threat resources on the Internet
- Conducting threat modeling sessions

Once a list of threats to our assets has been determined, we can now go on to the next step in crime prevention: looking at the "means" or vulnerabilities associated with software development projects which allow the threats to compromise the assets. That is the subject of the next chapter.

4.6   Threat Identification Checklists

The following checklists are provided to assist software development teams in identifying the threats to their software development projects.

4.6.1   Typical Threats (the "Usual Suspects")

☐ Human Threats
  ☐ *Curiosity* may represent authorized users abusing access privileges and rights or curiosity may represent unauthorized users attempting to access unauthorized information.
  ☐ *Data entry errors and omissions* represent mistakes in data entry.

- [ ] *Espionage* is the act of spying utilizing various means including: bugs, wiretaps, copying, photographing, following, bribing, and interception to obtain information that will provide a competitive edge.
- [ ] *Fraud* occurs when authorized users abuse their access rights in order to gain additional information, access rights, or system privileges beyond what they should have.
- [ ] *Improper disposal of sensitive information* can lead to the compromise of that information.
- [ ] *Inadvertent acts or carelessness* generally represent unintentional acts such as programming, synchronization, and development errors.
- [ ] *Misrepresentation of identity* threats allow assumption of the identity of someone else through the use of stolen or falsified identification including: ID Cards, key cards, PIN numbers, or passwords.
- [ ] *Policy violations* represent the act of not following organizational policies and procedures, either intentionally or unintentionally.
- [ ] *Shoulder surfing* is the act of attempting to gain knowledge through simple observation.
- [ ] *Theft or vandalism* is a deliberate act designed to cause the damage or destruction of information or information systems.
- [ ] *Other* includes labor unrest/strikes, riots/civil disorders, and terrorism.
- [ ] Technical Threats
  - [ ] *Compromising emanations* represent unauthorized interception or interruption of signals that can either intentionally or unintentionally cause the damage or destruction of information or information systems.
  - [ ] *Corruption by system failures* represents the corruption of data caused when other systems that may affect system operation fail.
  - [ ] *Data contamination* occurs when data values that stray from their field descriptions and business rules are allowed to intermix.
  - [ ] *Eavesdropping* is an intentional attempt to gain information through the use of listening devices or programs.
  - [ ] *Failures and intrusions not properly logged* represent improper logging and auditing of system and application errors.
  - [ ] *Installation errors* often occur when poor installation procedures accompany the implementation of new software.
  - [ ] *Intrusion* represents gaining unauthorized access to a system.
  - [ ] *Malicious code* includes viruses, worms, logic bombs, Trojan horses, spam, SpyWare, and backdoors.
  - [ ] *Misrepresentation of identity* represents assuming the identity of another individual or another system through the use of stolen or falsified credentials.
  - [ ] *Misuse of known weaknesses* is the deliberate act of bypassing security controls for the purpose of gaining additional information or additional privileges.

☐ *Saturation of resources* represents threats such as Denial-of-Service (DoS) and Distributed-Denial-of-Service (DDoS) attacks designed to overwhelm the capacity of a Web site by using up all of its available bandwidth.

☐ *Takeover of authorized sessions* occurs when an unauthorized individual assumes the access rights of an authorized party.

☐ *Tampering* represents unauthorized acts designed to cause the damage or destruction of information or information systems.

☐ Environmental Threats

☐ *Cable cuts* which are physical cuts in the cabling that provides power or network connectivity between information systems.

☐ *Electromagnetic interference* represents the threat to an information system from the proximity of an electromagnetic source such as a generator, transformer, or high-powered transmission line.

☐ *Environmental conditions* represent the climate in which an information system is found.

☐ *Hazardous materials* such as chemical spills are a threat to both information systems and their users.

☐ *Power fluctuations* include spikes, surges, faults, brownouts, and blackouts.

☐ *Secondary disasters* represent disasters caused indirectly due to another type of threat.

☐ *Natural threats* represent danger to information or information systems from a natural event such as a flood, tornado, avalanche, or hurricane.

4.6.2 Sources of Threat Identification

☐ Current headlines
    ☐ Privacy Rights Clearinghouse
    ☐ Attrition.org
    ☐ Computer Security Institute (CSI)
☐ Internet sources
    ☐ Open Web Application Security Project (OWASP)
    ☐ The Office of Management and Budget (OMB)
    ☐ The Centers for Medicare and Medicaid Services (CMS)
    ☐ The Department of Defense (DoD)
    ☐ The National Institute of Standards and Technology (NIST)

4.6.3 Threat Modeling

☐ *Step One.* Identification of:
    ☐ Business objectives of the development effort
    ☐ User roles that will react with the application

☐ Data the application will manipulate or display
☐ Use cases for operating on the data that will be handled by the application
☐ *Step Two.* Model the application architecture including:
  ☐ Application components
  ☐ Service roles
  ☐ External dependencies
  ☐ Calls among the roles, components, external dependencies, and data sources
☐ *Step Three.* Examine the threat avenues open to each call based upon the threat tree:
  ☐ Human threats
    ☐ Unintentional
      ☐ From outside the organization
      ☐ From within the organization
    ☐ Intentional
      ☐ From outside the organization
      ☐ From within the organization
  ☐ Technical threats
    ☐ Nonmalicious
    ☐ Malicious
      ☐ Nonspecific target
      ☐ Specific target

Chapter 5

Identifying Vulnerabilities

Returning to the scene of the crime yet again, we go back in time to just after the discovery of the crime, as the crime scene investigation team begins its collection of evidence. Photographs are taken of the entire scene. Fingerprints are collected from relevant surfaces. Physical evidence such as hair, threads, suspicious fluids, or broken glass are collected and logged. Other evidence such as footprints, tool marks, tire marks, and the like are examined, collected, and logged. What the crime scene investigators are doing is collecting physical evidence that can lead to the identification of the criminal by providing evidence of the means used to commit the crime.

This chapter takes a look at some of the more common vulnerabilities that plague applications, in particular Web-based applications today, and provide information for development teams on where to go to learn more about these vulnerabilities. Figure 5.1 provides a list of the common inputs and outputs associated with the identification of vulnerabilities during the risk management process.

5.1 Definition

Vulnerabilities are weaknesses in design or in the safeguards put in place to protect an asset. At our crime scene the vulnerabilities might have been a door left unlocked, or a cheap lock that could be easily picked or forced. Perhaps the item of value or asset was left in plain sight or simply hidden underneath the mattress in the bedroom. If that was the case, the asset wasn't protected very well and almost anyone from off the street could have entered the house through the unlocked or cheaply locked door and ransacked the house for valuables. The problem is that

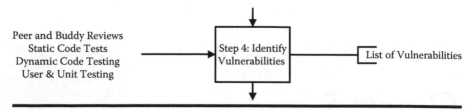

FIGURE 5.1   Common inputs and outputs of the vulnerability identification phase

often we don't understand or know about the vulnerabilities that make it possible for threats to access our assets.

Take, for example, a door lock: unless we're a lock specialist, most of us don't understand how much (or how little) protection an average door lock provides. We don't try to shoulder our way in past the lock, or pick up the garden tool left near the back door and see how easy it may be to force the locks open. We don't often see how tree branches can make it easy for an intruder to enter through an open second-story window. Or maybe we don't even think that it's possible for anyone to get inside our house, so valuable jewelry, artwork, electronics, or cash is simply left in plain sight. For the most part, we don't think as a thief would, so we often overlook potential weaknesses in the security of our homes that make it easy for a thief to enter the home and steal from us.

The same is true with software development teams. For the most part, software development teams concentrate upon meeting the business objectives of the development effort given the time, budget, and resources allotted. They aren't thinking like a hacker or cracker, and therefore don't always understand the vulnerabilities they build into their software development projects.

This chapter discusses how to identify vulnerabilities associated with software development projects. The discussion centers on both the inputs required to complete this step as well as the outputs that result from this step, as shown in Figure 5.1.

5.2   The Importance of Identifying Vulnerabilities

Why is it important to identify the vulnerabilities associated with software development projects? The answer is fairly simple: because all applications developed have coding defects or vulnerabilities within them. According to the Computer Emergency Readiness Team Coordination Center (CERT CC), over 90 percent of software security vulnerabilities are caused by known software defect types, and most software vulnerabilities arise from common causes. In fact the top ten causes account for about 75 percent of all vulnerabilities!

Why is this important? Consider the following example. If one design implementation defect is injected for every seven to ten lines of new and changed code produced (as benchmark tests suggest), and 99 percent of these are found before release, there would still be 1 to 1.5 design and implementation defects in every thousand lines of code produced! Yet despite this fact, software continues to be developed with the same vulnerabilities over and over again, producing software with the same vulnerabilities over and over again.

5.3   Identifying Vulnerabilities

How can these vulnerabilities be identified? One method is to review lists of the top 10 or top 20 design vulnerabilities monitored by third-party information security providers. Many organizations commonly publish lists of the top 10 or 20 design vulnerabilities discovered. Some of the more well-known sources of vulnerability lists include:

■ OWASP Top 10 (http://www.owasp.org/index.php/OWASP_Top_Ten_Project)
■ National Vulnerability Database (NIST) (http://nvd.nist.gov/nvd.cfm)
■ Common Vulnerabilities and Exposures (http://cve.mitre.org/index.html)
■ SANS Top 20 (http://www.sans.org/top20/)
■ U.S. Computer Emergency Readiness Team (US CERT) (http://www.us-cert. gov/cas/alldocs.html)

A review of the OWASP Top 10 list for 2007 reveals the following vulnerabilities:

■ Cross-site Scripting (XSS)
■ Injection flaws
■ Malicious file execution
■ Insecure direct object reference
■ Cross Site Request Forgery (CSRF)
■ Information leakage and improper error handling
■ Broken authentication and session management
■ Insecure cryptographic storage
■ Insecure communications
■ Failure to restrict URL access

The SANS Top 20 for 2007 reveals the following:

■ Server side vulnerabilities in:
   – Web applications
   – Windows services
   – UNIX and Mac OS services
   – Backup software
   – Anti-virus software

- – Management servers
- – Database software
- ■ Client-side vulnerabilities in:
  - – Web browsers
  - – Office software
  - – E-mail clients
  - – Media players
- ■ Security policy and personnel vulnerabilities including:
  - – Excessive user rights and unauthorized devices
  - – Phishing
  - – Unencrypted laptops and removable media
- ■ Application vulnerabilities including:
  - – Instant messaging applications
  - – Peer-to-peer sharing applications
- ■ Network device vulnerabilities including:
  - – VoIP servers and phones
- ■ Zero day attacks

As you can see, different organizations place different priorities on the vulnerabilities reported. The OWASP Top 10 represents a purely technical list of vulnerabilities associated with software development, whereas the SANS Top 20 includes vulnerabilities associated with the safeguards for those software development projects including policy and personnel vulnerabilities.

The problem is that most software development teams do not fully understand what these vulnerabilities are in most instances, or how to adequately protect their applications from these vulnerabilities, let alone have the ability to recognize whether their applications contain these vulnerabilities. The question then becomes: how are vulnerabilities associated with a specific software development project discovered?

Although there are a number of methods of discovering vulnerabilities within an application, including peer or buddy reviews, code scanning tools, application scanning tools, and vulnerability scanning tools, the key to preventing vulnerabilities from occurring over and over again is *education*. It is important that software developers, software testers, and software Quality Assurance (QA) analysts must understand what the most common vulnerabilities are, how to detect them, and how to eliminate them. Code reviews and scanning tools will never detect all software vulnerabilities within an application. Developers, testers, and QA analysts must become educated on what the common vulnerabilities in software are, how to detect them, and how to eliminate them.

5.4 Common Vulnerabilities

The scope of this book does not include an education regarding all common software vulnerabilities, nor would it be possible, because new vulnerabilities are constantly being discovered. However, because education is essential in preventing vulnerabilities from reoccurring, some of the most common vulnerabilities including how to prevent them are discussed below.

5.4.1 Buffer Overflows

Buffer overflows are perhaps the best known and best understood software security vulnerability. Yet despite this fact, buffer overflow vulnerabilities continue to be common in software development projects. Part of the reason for this is the number of different ways buffer overflows may occur. Another reason is that developers often have mistaken assumptions about the size or makeup of a piece of data. A simple example of this involves the assignment of variable types to hold user input. Take, for example, a Web-based shopping cart application. Users browse a Web site and select products they wish to purchase, placing them in an electronic shopping cart. At checkout time, users can update the quantities of items they wish to purchase. Assuming that shoppers are sane and reasonable (most of the time) a variable type of integer is typically assigned to hold the quantity value entered by the user. However, what if the user enters a value that is larger than an integer variable can hold? In most programming languages, this would trigger a buffer overflow. Whenever the limitations of a variable, call stack, memory module, or other parameter is exceeded, a buffer overflow may occur.

The main method of protecting from a buffer overflow in application development is through input validation. This means ensuring that all code which accepts inputs from users can handle arbitrarily large inputs.

5.4.2 Injection Flaws

Injection flaws are weaknesses in an application that allow input which subverts the otherwise legitimate use of a subsystem or interpreter. There are many different types of injection flaws, each dependent on the subsystem or interpreter involved. Some of the more common types of injection flaws include:

- SQL Injection which attempts to subvert relational database interpreters
- HTML Injection which attempts to subvert Web browsers
- Operating System Command Injection which attempts to subvert operating system software

Injection flaws occur when user-supplied data is sent to a subsystem or interpreter as a part of a command or query. The subsystem or interpreter is tricked into executing an unintended command via specially crafted data. Injection flaws can allow attackers to create, read, update, or delete data available to an application and can even allow an attacker to completely compromise the application and any system it resides upon, bypassing all perimeter controls.

For example, consider a standard retail sales Web site application. The application allows consumers to browse products for sale and select items for purchase. Items to be purchased are placed into an electronic shopping cart which the user can add to or empty as required before checking out by providing a method of electronic payment. We have all seen or used such sites before. Many of these Web sites offer the ability for consumers to provide opinions on the items for sale. Sometimes a user must have an account in order to record an opinion on one of the items for sale, but not always. Even when a user must have an account to record an opinion, often the user must only supply a name and an e-mail address in order to set up an account on the site. Injection attacks often make use of features such as the ability to provide user opinions.

Like a user who wishes to submit an opinion or review of a product the attacker selects the option to submit a review from the Web site. However, instead of submitting a product review, the attacker places a SQL statement or a code snippet into the space provided for the review and the application then saves the user review (i.e., SQL statement or code snippet) to a database. When the review is retrieved by the application so that it can be viewed on screen by a user the SQL statement or code will trigger.

In this instance, an attacker could craft code that will copy the information contained in a session cookie and to send that information to an anomalous Web site or e-mail account. Then all that the attacker has to do is await legitimate users to read the reviews for the product in question to trigger the code. At some later point in time, the attacker can go to his Web site or e-mail account and review the details of all of the session cookies that have been copied. If log-on credentials are stored within the session cookie, then the attacker now has log-on credentials for a number of different users that can then be used to enter the Web site and steal credit card or bank account information that the site may store to facilitate purchases by the users in question.

There are a number of methods for protecting against injection flaws. These methods include:

■ *Input validation.* All input data should be validated for length, type, syntax, and business rules before the data is accepted to be either stored in a database, or displayed in a Web browser. Use a "white-list" approach rather than a "black-list" approach; that is, accept only characters or values that are known to be good, rather than attempt to check to see if the characters or values match a description on a bad list.

- *Enforce least privilege when connecting to databases.* That means give the user no more privileges than required when connecting to a database. If the user only needs to view certain information in the database, then consider building a database view that contains only the information a user needs to see, and then only allowing the user read access to the database view.
- *Use parameterized stored procedures when developing SQL statements.* Parameterized stored procedures are compiled before user input is added therefore making it impossible for a hacker to modify the actual SQL statement.

There are numerous other methods for protecting against injection flaws, many of which are specific to the development language in use. Because injection flaws are common in Web applications, software design teams building Web applications should become familiar with injection flaws and ways of detecting and protecting against such flaws.

5.4.3 Information Leakage and Improper Error Handling

It is possible for applications to unintentionally leak information about their internal workings, usually through error or exception messages. Software developers are taught to handle all errors in order to avoid system crashes. As a result, error-handling routines are built to handle all potential errors. However, many of these error-handling routines include a "catchall" for unexpected errors (i.e., errors not uncovered in testing) and will often provide a wealth of information in the error message that is displayed to the user. Then when the user reports the error to the help desk, the error message can help the development staff debug the problem. The problem is that error messages by programming languages can often reveal valuable information back to an attacker including stack traces, failed SQL statements, and other debugging information.

Exception-handling messages may also unintentionally leak information about the internal workings of an application. For example, consider a simple authentication process, where a user must supply a user ID and a password. If a user supplies a user ID that does not exist, the application provides an exception message to the user. Likewise if the user supplies an incorrect password for a valid user ID the application provides an exception message to the user. If the user ID is valid and an invalid password is entered the exception message provided to the user should be the same regardless of what was entered as an invalid password. Unfortunately that is not the case with every system, and sometimes information about how the system operates can be leaked as a result.

There are a number of ways to protect applications from information leakage including the following:

- Ensuring that all software development teams within an organization share a common approach to handling errors and exceptions
- Ensuring that debug information is not supplied in an error message to the user, but rather that the debug information is stored in a log
- Ensuring that error messages from other layers of an application, such as the database layer are adequately checked and configured before being displayed to a user
- Creating a default error handler for use within an organization which returns appropriately sanitized error messages to the user

It is important that software developers, software testers, and QA analysts all become more educated on common vulnerabilities found in application development in order to prevent those vulnerabilities from affecting the confidentiality, integrity, and availability of the information systems they develop.

5.4.4 Cross-Site Scripting

Cross-Site Scripting (XSS) attacks are probably the most prevalent type of Web-based vulnerability today. In an XSS attack, the threat sends malicious code to a Web application in the form of browser side script to a different end user. XSS attacks use input supplied by a user that the application uses as output, without first validating or encoding the output. In this sense, it is similar to an injection flaw, because it utilizes input made by a user. An attacker using XSS can send malicious script to another unsuspecting user and that user's browser will have no way of knowing that the script should not be trusted and will therefore execute that script. This script can access cookies, session tokens, or any other sensitive information that is retained within the browser and used with that site, including the content of an HTML page.

There are two types of XSS attacks: stored and reflected. Stored attacks store the injected code permanently within the target servers, typically within a database in a user forum or comment field. Reflected attacks reflect the injected code off of the Web server in question in the form of an error message, search result, or other response that includes some or all of the input sent to the server as a request. The user then is tricked into clicking on a malicious link or submitting information in a specially crafted Web form which then travels to the Web server which reflects the attack back at the user's browser, which executes the code because it believes the code came from a trusted server.

The consequences of an XSS attack may involve the disclosure of a user's session cookie, allowing the attacker to hijack the user's session. Other potential consequences include:

- Installation of Trojan horse programs
- Redirecting users to other sites
- Modifying the content of a Web page

There are a number of ways of protecting an application from XSS attacks. One of the stronger methods is to validate all user input against a rigorous white-list of inputs that are allowed and expected.

5.4.5 Nontechnical Vulnerabilities

Not all vulnerabilities associated with application development are technical in nature. Some of the vulnerabilities may be physical or administrative in nature.

5.4.5.1 Physical Vulnerabilities

Physical vulnerabilities include such items as:

- *The lack of controls that may prevent visitors from walking unescorted through a building or facility.* Without proper physical controls for visitors, the architecture of an application displayed on a whiteboard could be revealed to a visitor, who could then devise an attack against that architecture.
- *Lack of fire suppression equipment in a facility.* A fire could destroy a critical asset involved with a software development effort such as the server farm the application is going to run on, or worse yet, it could cost the life of the only person in an organization who might understand the complex business rules that were to be applied within an application under development.
- *The layout of workstations within a facility.* In facilities with an open floor-plan it is difficult for strangers to go unnoticed, especially if they are attempting to perform actions such as shoulder surfing, or sitting down at an unoccupied workstation in an attempt to log on. In facilities that have cubicles with high walls and numerous access points, it is much easier for an individual to slip into an unoccupied desk and search that desk for written user IDs and passwords.
- *Exposed cabling.* In facilities where network cabling is not protected within a conduit, or inside walls, floors, or ceilings, it may become possible for a visitor to attach a device that can capture, record, or transmit data traveling over a trusted network that may not be encrypted.

5.4.5.2 Administrative Vulnerabilities

Similarly, policies and procedures—or more typically the lack thereof—could also represent vulnerabilities to an application development effort. Examples of administrative vulnerabilities include:

■ *Lack of a policy which requires that sensitive information must be shredded.* Printouts from an application that utilizes sensitive information that find their way into the trash bin represent a potential vulnerability.

■ *Lack of a policy that specifies the classification of data.* Without such a policy, it may be difficult to understand which data an application must use is sensitive or critical to business functions, and which is not.

■ *Lack of a policy that calls for the separation of duties (i.e., an individual should not be able to approve his own timesheet).* If such a policy is not considered during the design of a timesheet application, then safeguards may not be built into the application that would prevent an individual from being able to approve his own timesheet.

■ *Lack of a policy that requires an audit trail for transactions.* An application built to handle banking, stock trades, or other financial transactions must have an audit trail in order to provide evidence of nonrepudiation. An individual who authorizes that transaction should not be able to claim that she did not authorize that transaction. Without such audit trails and adequate safeguards for those audit trails, it may be difficult, if not impossible for an individual to provide evidence of who authorized a specific transaction, or even if the transaction actually took place!

5.5 Methods of Detecting Vulnerabilities during Software Development

Beyond the education of development staff on what vulnerabilities exist within their applications and the methods that can be used to protect applications against those vulnerabilities, there are a number of methods of detecting vulnerabilities during the SDLC including the following:

■ Review of current controls
■ Code/peer/buddy reviews
■ Testing
■ Static code scanning tools
■ Dynamic code scanning tools
■ Vulnerability scanning tools
■ Review of best practice standards

5.5.1 Review of Current Controls

A review of current controls or more precisely the lack of such controls, within a programming environment can often provide a clue to potential vulnerabilities for such an environment. Examples include:

- An organization not using intrusion detection or intrusion prevention controls is subject to vulnerabilities such as:
  - Privilege escalation
  - Unauthorized log-ins
  - Access to sensitive information
  - A susceptibility to malware
- An organization that does not have a policy which requires that all confidential information be shredded may find its confidential information in the trash where anyone could pick it up.

Although software development teams often do not have the power to ensure that these types of controls are implemented, they can take steps during the design of an application to ensure that the impact of some of these vulnerabilities is reduced.

Take, for example, the lack of a policy which requires that all confidential information should be shredded. In the absence of such a policy, there are several steps the application development team can take in order to reduce the impact of the vulnerability. First, unless printouts are a true business requirement, the application team can design the application such that the output of the application can only be viewed and not printed. If printouts are a business requirement, the software development team can design the application such that a warning is issued onscreen when a user chooses to print an application. This warning could warn the user that the printout created has confidential information and should be handled and destroyed properly. Finally, the printout itself could be created with statements in either the header or footer or both which state that the information on the printout is confidential in nature and should be handled and destroyed properly.

5.5.2 Code Reviews

Code reviews can search for code (or the absence of code) that might allow a vulnerability to exist within an application, but there are many possible mistakes to recognize, and code review can be a slow and expensive process. Still, code reviews often find and remove common vulnerabilities such as buffer overflows, improper error-handling routines, and lack of improper field validation rules. Other peer and buddy techniques such as pair programming where two authors develop code together at the same workstation can also reduce the probability that vulnerabilities will be introduced into software.

5.5.3 Testing

Testing can also be used to detect vulnerabilities. Common vulnerabilities such as buffer overflows, injection flaws, and information leakage can all be easily detected through testing. However, if the proper test scripts, scenarios, parameters, and syntaxes are not created and utilized, some vulnerabilities may be hard to detect.

5.5.4 Static Code Scanning

Static code scanning tools are available to crawl the code of the application line by line and look for vulnerabilities and inconsistencies within the style of the code. All of these scanners will point out potential vulnerabilities within an application. Most will also provide examples of how to fix the code to avoid the vulnerabilities, and some will even change the code to remove the vulnerability either automatically or on a case-by-case basis. Some also allow users to define their own rules for discovering vulnerabilities or enforcing code standards. Both open source and commercial products exist. Some of the open source products and the programming languages they support include:

- Lint (C)
- Bandera (Java)
- Checkstyle (Java)
- ClassCycle (Java)
- FindBugs (Java)
- Jlint (Java)
- PMD (Java)
- Soot (Java)
- CQual (C)
- Sparse (Linux)
- Splint (C language)
- Flawfinder (C++)
- Oink (C++)
- ftnchek (Fortran)
- JsLint (JavaScript)
- Perl::Critic (Perl)
- Pixy (PHP 4)
- PyChecker (Python)
- pylint (Python)
- Rough Auditing Tool for Security (RATS) (C, C++, Perl, PHP, and Python)

Although these tools are all useful in finding real bugs and they do help in identifying bugs, there are some problems associated with such tools. First, they will not find every bug or vulnerability within an application. Second, code scanning tools have false positives associated with them. It is often difficult to find the correct balance between finding the most bugs in a system and the fewest false positives. Too many false positives and developers have too much time wasted in tracking down the false positives. Too few false positives and the likelihood that bugs will go undetected increases. Finally, design bugs are not found by source code scanning tools. For example, a source code scanner will not detect a missed authentication step. Source code tools are useful, but only when used in conjunction with other secure software development practices.

5.5.5   Dynamic Code Scanning

Dynamic code scanning tools attempt to find vulnerabilities while the code is actually executing. Many of these tools operate from a virtual run-time environment and inject dynamic code snippets into programs to monitor such items as performance, call stack, execution trace, instantiated objects, and variables. The intent of dynamic analysis is to reveal how the software will behave when executed, and how it will interact with other processes and with the operating system itself. However, the problem with many of these tools is that it is difficult to trace back problems to documentation and the exact lines of code that may be causing the problem.

5.5.6   Web Application Scanning

Web application scanning tools provide an analysis of Web-based applications by "crawling" the Web pages associated with the application, investigating each Web page, input field, and link and finding vulnerabilities while attempting to "break" the application. Most of these tools will test applications both with and without authentication credentials. Both open source and commercial products exist. Two of the more well-known open source products are the following:

■ WebScarab
■ Paros Proxy

5.5.7   Network Vulnerability Scanning

Vulnerability scanning tools look for vulnerabilities and identify devices on an organization's network that are open to known vulnerabilities. These tools accomplish this process through different means and many look for different types of vulnerabilities. Some simply look for signs that a vulnerability may exist (i.e., check to see if a particular patch has been applied) whereas others may actually attempt to exploit a vulnerability to make sure that the patch has been applied correctly.

Vulnerability scanners are useful to software development teams by helping ensure that the servers (database, Web, and application), operating systems, and other services that applications rely upon are free from potential vulnerabilities. As with all of the other scanning tools, there are both open source and commercial vulnerability scanning products. Some of the open source tools include:

- Nessus
- Nmap
- Microsoft Baseline Security Analyzer
- HFNetChk
- NeWT
- Tripwire
- Nikto
- Whisker

The problem with most vulnerability scanners is the impact that they have upon the devices on which they are running. They can often eat up available network bandwidth and may also be intrusive enough to shut down or even damage network services and devices. It is important that the use of these tools is coordinated with network administration as well as business area management to ensure that the impact upon the network during prime business hours is minimized and that the proper personnel are on hand to restore network devices and services that may become disrupted by the scan.

5.5.8 Review of Best Practice Standards

One of the best ways of learning about potential vulnerabilities and how they may affect a software development effort lies in a review of industry "Best Practice" standards. These standards represent a code of practice for information security management. Through an analysis of the controls an organization has in place to enforce such standards (or an absence of such controls), a picture of the types of vulnerabilities that may threaten an organization may become clear. One of the most widely known and respected such standards is the International Standards Organization (ISO) 17799:2005 standard (now the ISO 27002 Series).

ISO 17799:2005 (now ISO 27002) is entitled *Information technology – Security techniques – Code of practice for information security management*. This standard consists of twelve main sections including:

- Risk assessment
- Security policy—management direction
- Organization of information security—governance of information security
- Asset management—inventory and classification of information assets

- Human resources security—security aspects for employees joining, moving, and leaving an organization
- Physical and environmental security—protection of the computer facilities
- Communications and operations management—management of technical security controls in systems and networks
- Access control—restriction of access rights to networks, systems, applications, functions, and data
- Information systems acquisition, development, and maintenance—building security into applications
- Information security incident management—anticipating and responding appropriately to information security breaches
- Business continuity management—protecting, maintaining, and recovering business-critical processes and systems
- Compliance—ensuring conformance with information security policies, standards, laws and regulations

A review of the standards contained within ISO 27002, which is one of the most comprehensive security standards available, and how these standards (or the lack of controls required by these standards) may represent potential vulnerabilities is worth understanding. Some of the vulnerabilities represented by the ISO 27002 standard include the following:

- *Risk assessment and risk management.* ISO 27002 requires that a risk assessment process and risk management policy and procedures are in place. As we are learning in this book, risk management and risk assessment practices are essential to understanding the risks associated with software development efforts.
- *Allocation of information security responsibilities.* Clear direction and management support are absolute essentials for the development of any lasting policy and procedure programs. In the absence of a specific management forum to provide this support, specific management responsibilities should be specified in a roles and responsibility policy that clearly outlines security responsibilities at each level of the organization.
- *Authorization process for information processing facilities.* Any new information processing facilities must be properly budgeted and duly authorized. Likewise, the purchase of all new software and hardware should be subjected to a proper procurement process. A documented process for the approval of all such facilities, software, and hardware should be developed.
- *Independent review of information security.* Periodic review of policies, procedures, standards, and guidelines is necessary to ensure that the documentation is in line with current infrastructure and organizational policies, missions, and goals. Whenever significant organizational or infrastructure changes take place, or at least every two years, all policies and procedures

should be reviewed to ensure that they are up to date. Minimum review periods of two years for all policies and procedures should be set, and this review period should be included within the policy and procedure review and approval process. Where possible, this review process should be conducted by a third party to ensure a nonbiased opinion.

■ *Identification of risks from third-party access.* Risks associated with third-party access (i.e., vendors who have access to network controls; contractors, volunteers, and interns with internal access to application systems; and external users and customers) should be identified and appropriate controls implemented. Types of accesses must be identified, classified, and reasons for access must be justified.

■ *Outsourcing.* Security requirements must be addressed in all contracts with third parties when an organization has outsourced the management and control of all or some of its information systems network or desktop environments. Contracts should address: how the legal requirements are to be met, how the security of the organization's assets are maintained and tested, right to audit, physical security issues, and how availability of the services is to be maintained in the event of disaster.

■ *Inventory of assets.* Policy and procedures for centralized asset tracking should be utilized rather than using multiple asset tracking systems. This process should provide detailed instructions on how assets can be added, removed, and changed.

■ *Classification guidelines.* An information classification scheme or guideline should be in place to assist in determining how information is to be classified, handled, and protected.

■ *Information handling and labeling.* Information labeling and handling procedures are important because they set the tone for how information should ultimately be protected not only in storage but during processing, and in transit as well.

■ *Including information security in job responsibilities.* Security roles and responsibilities for all levels of the organization should be spelled out in policy. In order for any organization to have good information security, all responsibilities should be laid out in policy and enforced from the top down.

■ *Confidentiality agreements.* Employees must be asked to sign a confidentiality or nondisclosure agreement as a part of their initial terms and conditions of employment. This agreement should cover the security of information processing facilities as well as organization assets.

■ *Employee transfers, promotions, and terminations.* Policies and procedures that outline the steps which must be taken whenever an employee is promoted, transferred to another position, or terminated must be developed. These policies and procedures should include checklists for reviewing and changing system and information access rights, keycard access, changing or returning keys, combinations, and so on.

- *Information security education and training.* All employees of the organization and third-party users must receive appropriate information security training and regular updates on organizational policies and procedures.
- *Responding to security incidents and malfunctions.* A formal reporting procedure should exist to require the reporting of security incidents through appropriate management channels as quickly as possible. Such a process should include mechanisms to record metrics on the types, volumes, and costs of incidents and malfunctions as well as a formal disciplinary process in place for employees who have violated organizational security policies and procedures. Such a process can act as a deterrent to employees who might otherwise be inclined to disregard security procedures.
- *Working in secure areas.* All access to information should be on a need-to-know basis. It is important to establish information ownership, along with information handling and classification policies and procedures to safeguard this process. An information ownership program should be instituted along with information classification and handling policies and procedures.
- *Equipment security.* There are a number of ISO standards relating to equipment security. Some of these standards include the following:
  - Equipment should be located in an appropriate place to minimize unnecessary access into work areas.
  - Items requiring special protection should be isolated to reduce the general level of protection required.
  - Controls to minimize risk from potential threats such as theft, fire, explosives, smoke, water, dust, vibration, chemical effects, electrical supply interfaces, electromagnetic radiation, and flood should be adopted.
  - A policy regarding eating, drinking, and smoking in proximity to information-processing services should be implemented.
  - The environmental conditions that would adversely affect information-processing facilities should be monitored.
  - Equipment should be protected from power failures by supplies such as multiple feeds, uninterruptible power supply, backup generators, and so on.
  - Power and telecommunications cables carrying data or supporting information services must be protected from interception or damage.

NOTE: It is often difficult to understand how a lack of these types of controls represents vulnerabilities to a software development project. However, all software runs on network equipment. If the network equipment is not protected properly, then it may be possible for attackers to place malicious code, keystroke loggers, Trojans, or eavesdropping devices on the network. If such devices have been placed within the network perimeter, then any assumption made during an application development effort that individuals outside the perimeter are not able to access an application is faulty and additional controls, such as encrypting all transmissions, even for transmission over local networks might be considered.

- *Secure disposal or reuse of equipment.* Storage devices containing sensitive information must be physically destroyed or securely overwritten. Otherwise, application data on a retired database server may still be recoverable by whoever comes in possession of the retired server.
- *Clear desk and clear screen policies.* Automatic computer screen locking should be enabled (i.e., all computer screens lock when the computer is left unattended for more than 15 minutes). Additionally, employees should be advised to leave any confidential material in the form of paper documents, media, and the like, in a secure container or room when left unattended. This includes printouts of confidential information. Too often, many organizations allow the printing of sensitive information to networked printers, and the individual who printed the material forgets that the information was printed, leaving the printout on the printer where any visitor could potentially pick it up.
- *Removal of property.* Equipment, information, or software should not be taken off site without appropriate authorization. Spot checks or regular audits should be conducted to detect unauthorized removal of property. Staff should be aware of these types of spot checks or regular audits.
- *Documented operating procedures.* It is very important that all operating procedures such as backup, equipment maintenance, and so on, are identified to ensure that no important processes are overlooked.
- *Operational change control.* All programs running on production systems must be subject to strict change control; that is, any change to be made to those production programs needs to go through change control authorization. Audit logs must be maintained for any change made to production programs.
- *Incident management procedures.* Incident management procedures should exist to handle security incidents. These procedures should address: incident management responsibilities; orderly and quick response to security incidents; and different types of incidents ranging from denial-of-service to breach of confidentiality, and so on, and ways to handle them. Audit trails and logs relating to incidents must be maintained and proactive action taken to ensure that incidents do not reoccur.
- *Segregation of duties.* Segregation of duties is a basic, key internal control and one of the most difficult to achieve. It is used to ensure that errors or irregularities are prevented or detected on a timely basis by employees in the normal course of business. Segregation of duties provides two benefits: a deliberate fraud is more difficult because it requires collusion of two or more persons, and it is much more likely that innocent errors will be found. At the most basic level it means that no single individual should have control over two or more phases of a transaction or operation. Policies and procedures where

management must assign responsibilities to ensure a crosscheck of duties should be developed.

■ *Separation of development and operational facilities.* Develop policies and procedures that make it clear which systems and hardware will run development environments and which systems and hardware will carry production environments. Clearly outline the types of processes and access procedures that are allowed in each environment. This is a key element of any data integrity program.

■ *External facilities management.* If an external company or contractor (third party) manages any information-processing capacity of the organization, then the risk associated with such management should be determined and discussed in advance with the third party, and appropriate controls incorporated into the contract.

■ *Capacity planning.* Capacity demands are monitored and projections of future capacity requirements should be made. This is to ensure that adequate processing power and storage is available. Examples include: monitoring hard disk space, RAM, and CPU on critical servers.

■ *System acceptance.* System acceptance criteria should be established for new information systems, upgrades, and new versions.

■ *Controls against malicious software.* Controls against malicious software usage should be in place including the following:
  – Security policies addressing software licensing issues such as prohibiting usage of unauthorized software.
  – Procedures to verify that all warning bulletins are accurate and informative with regards to malicious software usages.
  – Anti-virus software is installed on computers to check and isolate or remove any viruses from computers and media.
  – Anti-virus software signatures are updated on a regular basis to check for the latest viruses.
  – All traffic originating from an untrusted network into the organization is checked for viruses. Example: Checking for viruses on e-mail, attachments, and on the Web, FTP traffic, and so on.

■ *Information backups.* The backup of essential business information such as production servers, critical network components, configuration, and the like, should be done regularly. The backup media along with procedures to restore the backup should be stored securely and well away from the actual site. Backup media should be regularly tested to ensure they can be restored within the timeframe allotted in operational procedures for recovery.

■ *Operator logs.* Create a policy and procedures addressing operation staff logging their activities and for checking these activity logs on a regular basis to ensure the personnel are following standard operating procedures.

■ *Fault logging.* Develop procedures for logging and maintaining all faults. These procedures should include a review of all relevant fault logs, recording the date, time, system, and relevant user information, as well as the conditions of the fault. These procedures should also include the recording of all actions taken to correct the fault. Where possible, all fault logs and corrective actions should be placed in a repository or database that can then provide fault metrics, as well as act as a knowledge base to resolve future faults.

- *Network controls.* Effective operational controls such as separate network and system administration facilities should be established where necessary. Responsibilities and procedures for management of remote equipment including equipment in user areas should be established. Special controls should exist to safeguard the confidentiality and integrity of data processing over the public network and to protect the connected systems. Example: Virtual Private Networks, other encryption and hashing mechanisms, and so on.

- *Management of removable computer media.* Develop policies and procedures for the management of all removable computer media including backup tapes, optical media (i.e., CDs, DVDs, etc.), disks, cassettes, memory cards, and removable USB storage media. These policies and procedures should specify when such removable computer media can be used, as well as proper procedures for the handling, labeling, and destruction of such media.

- *Disposal of media.* Media that are no longer required should be disposed of in a secure manner. For example: CDs or DVDs, and backup tapes containing sensitive or business-critical information should be properly shredded when no longer required.

- *Information handling procedures.* Develop procedures that address the handling of information which is stored. These procedures should specify how information will be protected from unauthorized disclosure and misuse. They should also include sanctions for employees who violate these procedures.

- *Security of system documentation.* Develop procedures outlining the protections of all system documentation. These procedures should call for the creation of access control lists that specify who should have access to the documentation. In addition, only those personnel who have a need to know the information to perform their duties should be placed on the access control lists. Where possible, the system documentation should be maintained in a central, yet secure, location.

- *Security of media in transit.* Develop procedures detailing how media, such as backup tapes are to be protected from unauthorized access, misuse, or corruption during transport. If third-party vendors are used to transport backup tapes off site, appropriate contract clauses requiring the safeguarding of the tapes should be put in place.

- *Electronic commerce security.* Electronic commerce must be well protected with controls implemented to protect against fraudulent activity, contract dispute, and disclosure or modification of information. Security controls such as authentication and authorization should be considered in the electronic commerce environment. An electronic commerce arrangement between trading partners should include a documented agreement that commits both parties to the agreed terms of trading including details of security issues.

■ *Security of electronic mail.* Policies for the acceptable use of electronic mail should be in place. Controls such as anti-virus checking, isolating potentially unsafe attachments, spam control, anti-relaying, and so on, should be in place to reduce the risks created by electronic e-mail.

■ *Security of electronic office systems.* An acceptable use policy to address the use of electronic office systems should be in place including guidelines to effectively control the business and security risks associated with electronic office systems.

■ *Publicly available systems.* Develop change control procedures that involve business and application owners. Include procedures for requesting and changing the hardening of current systems such as adding firewalls, checks of administrative rights abuses, and the placement of intrusion detection devices.

■ *Other forms of information exchange.* Develop policies and procedures to protect the exchange of information when using voice, facsimile, and video communication facilities. Ensure that these policies and procedures are included in annual security awareness and training programs and that they are communicated to all employees.

■ *Access control policy.* Develop an access control policy that defines business requirements for access control, the rules and rights for each user or group, and helps users and clients gain a clear understanding of how business requirements will be met by access controls.

■ *User registration.* Develop procedures that outline how access is granted and revoked for users of information systems and services. These procedures should include step-by-step instructions for requesting or revoking access, including appropriate approval processes by business or application owners. These procedures should be clearly communicated to all employees as well as all customers and all affected business and application owners.

■ *Privilege Management.* Develop policies and procedures covering the allocation and use of any privileges in a multi-user information systems environment. Such privileges should be restricted and controlled: that is, privileges are allocated on a need-to-use basis; privileges are allocated only after a formal authorization process.

■ *User password management.* Allocation and reallocation of passwords must be controlled through a formal management process. Users should be asked to sign a statement to keep passwords confidential.

■ *Reviews of user access rights.* Develop policies and procedures calling for regular reviews of all systems' access. Normal privileges and access groups should be reviewed at least annually, and special privileges should be reviewed at least semi-annually. Communicate these policies and procedures to customers and employees, and involve them in the review process.

- *Password use.* Develop guidelines to aid users in creating, selecting, and maintaining secure passwords. These guidelines should include such items as password length requirements, character use (i.e., the use of lower case, upper case, numeric, and special characters), and how often passwords should be changed. The guidelines should admonish users not to use dictionary words, names, and dates, as well as advising users not to write down their passwords or leave them in obvious locations. These guidelines should be communicated to all employees.
- *Unattended user equipment.* Establish requirements for automatically locking personal computers or terminating mainframe sessions after no more than 15 minutes. Implement these requirements on all systems.
- *Policy on use of network services.* Develop policies that outline the purposes for which each part or segment of the network may be used. Include procedures that outline how network connections and network services will be protected.
- *User authentication for external connections.* Develop guidelines for all authentication mechanisms, such as hardware tokens and challenge/response protocols, among others, allowed. Communicate these guidelines to all customers and employees.
- *Node authentication.* Develop guidelines that specify how all remote computer connections such as Virtual Private Networks (VPNs) are to be authenticated. Communicate these guidelines to all customers and employees.
- *Remote diagnostic port protection.* Develop policies and procedures identifying all protections that will be placed on diagnostic ports. Ensure that all diagnostic ports are protected by policy, and that they are only open when necessary for diagnostic processes.
- *Segregation in networks.* Develop guidelines for segregating customer data where required. These guidelines should provide alternative methods for segregating data belonging to customers, such as using different servers or regions, adding firewalls, and the like. Communicate these guidelines to all customers and employees.
- *Network connection protocol.* Develop specific procedures for controls to secure shared networks that extend beyond organizational boundaries, for example, procedures covering the use of file transfers using File Transfer Protocol (FTP).
- *Network routing controls.* Develop guidelines that ensure customer applications and their connections and information flows do not breach the access control policies of other customers. For example, make sure that all customer applications utilize proper data validation code. Otherwise buffer overflows, allowing attacks to affect system availability for all customers, could occur. Communicate these guidelines to all customers and employees.

- *Security of network services.* The organization, using public or private network services, ensures that a clear description of security attributes of all services used shall be provided.
- *Terminal log-on procedures.* Access to information systems should be attainable only via a secure log-on process.
- *User identification and authorization.* Develop procedures that specify user identification, authentication, and authorization controls. These procedures should include how log-ins take place, how unique identifiers are provided to all users, and all authentication methods used to substantiate identification. In addition, develop a policy that describes the circumstances under which generic user accounts can be created. This policy should call for a review of all such accounts on a monthly basis.
- *Password management system.* Password management systems enforcing various password controls such as individual password for accountability, password changes, passwords stored in encrypted form, masked passwords onscreen, and so on, must be in place.
- *Use of system utilities.* Develop procedures for the control of system utilities included with computer hardware and software as it is installed. These procedures should include a list of which utilities should be used, and under what circumstances. Access control lists should also be developed to restrict use to these utilities.
- *Information access restrictions.* Create a policy that addresses information access restrictions, put it through the normal review and approval process, and then communicate it to the end users.
- *Event logging.* Create a policy that addresses audit log exceptions, security events, and the retention period, put it through the normal review and approval process, and then communicate it to the end users.
- *Monitoring system use.* Procedures are set up to monitor the use of information processing. The procedures should ensure that the users are performing only the activities that are explicitly authorized.
- *Clock synchronization.* Where possible all system clocks should be synchronized to a real-time clock. This assists in handling security incidents, having accurate system logs, and the gathering of evidence in criminal cases. This is especially important in applications that may cover the trading of stocks or other securities in which the value of a stock may be determined based upon the time of the transaction.
- *Mobile computing.* A formal policy taking into account the risks of working with computing facilities such as notebooks, palmtops, and so on, especially in unprotected environments, is in place. Training is arranged for staff using mobile computing facilities to raise their awareness on the additional risks resulting from this way of working and the controls that need to be implemented to mitigate the risks.

- *Telecommuting.* A policy, procedure, or standard to control telecommuting activities is in place and is consistent with organization's security policy. Suitable protection of telecommuting sites is in place against threats such as theft of equipment, unauthorized disclosure of information, and so on.

- *Security requirements analysis and specification.* Security requirements are incorporated as part of business requirement statements for new systems or for enhancement to existing systems. Security requirements and controls identified reflect the business value of information assets involved and the consequences of failure of security. Risk assessments are completed prior to commencement of system development.

- *Input data validation.* Develop guidelines and procedures for validating all data input fields in applications. These guidelines and procedures should include preventing buffer overflows, structured query language injection attacks, and the types of error messages that should be displayed. Furthermore, these guidelines should specify the role of developers, testers, and end users in the data input process.

- *Control of internal processing.* Develop guidelines outlining minimum requirements for all validation checks, for example, the use of checksums to ensure that data has not been corrupted during processing cycles.

- *Message authentication.* Develop guidelines outlining all acceptable techniques used to detect unauthorized changes to, or corruption of, the contents of a transmitted electronic message. Include such methods as public key infrastructure, digital signatures, encryption, hashing techniques, and so on.

- *Output data validation.* Data output of application systems is validated to ensure that the processing of stored information is correct and appropriate for the circumstances.

- *Policy on the use of cryptographic controls.* Develop a set of guidelines governing the use of cryptographic controls.

- *Digital signatures.* Digital signatures are used to protect the authenticity and integrity of electronic documents.

- *Nonrepudiation services.* Nonrepudiation services are used where it might be necessary to resolve disputes about occurrence or nonoccurrence of an event or action. An example would be a dispute involving use of a digital signature on an electronic payment or contract.

- *Key management.* Management systems to support the organization's use of cryptographic techniques such as secret key technique and public key technique are in place. Key management systems are based on an agreed-upon set of standards, procedures, and secure methods.

- *Control of operational software.* Controls are in place for the implementation of software on operational systems. This is to minimize the risk of corruption of operational systems.

- *Protection of system test data.* System test data is protected and controlled. The use of operational databases containing personal information is avoided for test purposes. If such information is used, the data is depersonalized before use.

- *Access control to program source library.* Develop procedures that outline all controls in place to protect program source libraries. These procedures should outline who has access to program source libraries and the circumstances under which program source libraries should be maintained. In addition, access control lists outlining who has access to the program source libraries should be developed and reviewed on a periodic basis.
- *Change control procedures.* Strict access controls to program source libraries are in place. This is to reduce the potential for corruption of computer programs.
- *Technical review of operating system changes.* Process or procedures are in place to ensure application systems are reviewed and tested after changes in operating system. Controls are in place for periodic upgrades to the operating system (installation of service packs, patches, hot fixes, etc.) in order to limit changes to software packages. Whenever possible the vendor-supplied software packages are used without modification. When changes are deemed essential the original software is retained and the changes applied only to a clearly identified copy. All changes should be clearly tested and documented, so they can be reapplied if necessary to future software upgrades.
- *Covert channels and Trojan code.* Develop strict change control procedures for all code moving from test to production environments. The change control procedure should call for code reviews to ensure that covert channels and Trojan code are not inadvertently moved into production.
- *Outsourced software development.* Develop strict change control procedures for outsource development. The change control procedures should call for code reviews, quality assurance reviews, licensing arrangements, and escrow arrangements.
- *Business continuity management process.* There is a managed process in place for developing and maintaining business continuity throughout the organization. This might include organizationwide business continuity plans, regular testing and updating of the plans, formulating and documenting a business continuity strategy, and so on.
- *Business continuity and impact management.* Events that could cause interruptions to business processes are identified, for example, equipment failure or flood and fire. A risk assessment should be conducted to determine the impact of such interruptions. A strategy plan should be developed based on the risk assessment results to determine an overall approach to business continuity.
- *Writing and implementing continuity plans.* Plans should be developed to restore business operations within the required timeframe following an interruption or failure to the business process. The plans must be regularly tested and updated.

■ *Business continuity planning framework.* There must be a single framework for business continuity planning. This framework shall be maintained to ensure that all plans are consistent and identify priorities for testing and maintenance. Conditions for activation and individuals responsible for executing each component of the plan must be identified.

■ *Testing, maintaining, and reassessing business continuity plans.* Business continuity plans shall be tested regularly to ensure that they are up to date and effective. Business continuity plans shall be maintained by regular reviews and updates to ensure their continuing effectiveness. Procedures shall be included within the organization's change management program to ensure that business continuity matters are appropriately addressed.

■ *Identification of applicable legislation.* All relevant statutory, regulatory, and contractual requirements should be explicitly defined and documented for each information system. Specific controls and individual responsibilities to meet these requirements should be defined and documented.

■ *Intellectual property rights.* Develop procedures outlining the strict control over the installation, registration, and removal of software products purchased under a license agreement. These procedures should include tracking all license agreements and all license keys.

■ *Prevention of misuse of information processing facilities.* Implement a log-on warning message in both client/server and mainframe environments warning users that the system being entered is private and that unauthorized access is not permitted. This should be a standard feature of any log-on process.

■ *Collection of evidence.* When evidence of a crime is discovered, when possible, law enforcement should be called in to assist with the collection of evidence.

■ *Compliance with security policy.* Develop self-assessment policies and procedures that call for periodic review of all areas to ensure compliance with security policies, standards and procedures. Self-assessment and evaluation is an essential part of any information security program.

■ *Technical compliance checking.* Develop self-assessment policies and procedures that call for periodic review of all areas within the organization to ensure that systems, software, and hardware comply with security implementation standards.

■ *System audit controls.* Develop guidelines for conducting all intrusive checks on operational systems. These guidelines should include an approval and notification process for all intrusive tests and scans. The guidelines should also include scheduling such tests to minimize the disruptions to business processes and all business partners.

■ *Protection of system audit tools.* Access to system audit tools such as software and data files should be protected to prevent any possible misuse or compromise.

This is not a complete list of all of the standards found within ISO 27002. However, it is important to understand how the controls represented by these standards represent controls that organizations should consider to protect the information in their systems. Whenever these controls are absent, there is the potential for a weakness or vulnerability to exist.

Code reviews, testing, and the use of scanning tools all require that at least some code has been developed. This means that the earliest these methods can be used within the SDLC is the unit testing stage, and some of these methods such as vulnerability scanning can't be utilized until the implementation phase. Does this mean that risk analysis activities can't be conducted until the design phase? Of course not! Vulnerability analysis can still be conducted during the requirements phase of the SDLC if the development team understands what the common vulnerabilities associated with software development are. In addition a review of current controls, especially when compared to the controls represented by industry standards such as ISO 27002, can reveal potential vulnerabilities as shown when discussing vulnerabilities with the test case below.

5.6 Secure Coding Techniques to Avoid Vulnerabilities

There are a number of coding techniques that, when practiced religiously, can dramatically reduce the number of vulnerabilities associated with an application. These coding techniques are provided here to assist you in developing more secure applications.

5.6.1 Validate Input

Many of the vulnerabilities that plague software development projects today rely upon the ability of users to place script in the input fields of applications. Injection flaws, buffer overflows, and cross-site scripting attacks all rely upon the ability to input malicious code or scripts into an application. Inputs should be validated against a white-list (i.e., a list of acceptable responses) instead of against a black-list (a list of prohibited responses) because the black-list will constantly change as new exploit codes are discovered. Validating all user input against a well-developed white-list will eliminate many different vulnerabilities.

5.6.2 Validate Output to Be Displayed on Browsers

A number of vulnerabilities including injection flaws and cross-site scripting errors rely upon applications to "trust" data that is stored in databases. When this data contains script that was input by a malicious user in the form of a forum comment, or product rating, applications will "trust" that the data should be displayed in the browser. The result is often that malicious script will then be run instead of the display of a forum comment or product rating supplied by a consumer. Validating all output against a good white-list of expected values will eliminate vulnerabilities such as injection errors and cross-site scripting that are associated with Web applications.

5.6.3   Keep It Simple

Common sense in programming means keeping software designs as simple and small as possible. The more complex the design and the more complex the code, the more likely that errors will be made in their coding, implementation, configuration, and use.

5.6.4   Follow the Principle of Least Privilege

The principle of least privilege requires that every procedure should be conducted with the minimum set of privileges necessary to finish the job. Any process that requires elevated permissions should only be held for the time required to complete the elevated job. The benefits of following the principle of least privilege include:

- Better system stability by limiting the scope of changes code can make to a system.
- Better system security: vulnerabilities in one application cannot be used to exploit the rest of the machine.
- Ease of deployment: in general, the fewer privileges an application requires the easier it is to deploy within a larger environment.

5.6.5   Practice Defense in Depth

Risk should be managed by providing multiple layers of defensive strategies so that if one layer of defense turns out to be inadequate, another layer of defense will, it is hoped, prevent vulnerabilities from being exploited. For example, combining input validation routines and output validation routines on a Web application will decrease the likelihood of an injection flaw attack. If the input validation failed to catch the script injected into a forum comment field, then the output validation used when the comment is displayed may stop the injection script from triggering.

5.6.6   Practice Quality Assurance

Quality assurance is essential in identifying and eliminating vulnerabilities. Quality assurance techniques include: code reviews, penetration testing, and source code audits. Independent security auditors and assessors can often catch items that the development team missed and provide an extra set of eyes which view systems and their implementation with an objective eye.

5.6.7   Adopt Coding Standards

Developing and adopting coding standards that require a uniform format and review process can reduce the number of flaws built into a system. These coding standards should be a living document that changes as new flaws are uncovered which affect software development efforts. For example, if information leakage due to improper error-handling routines becomes a vulnerability, then the coding standard should be updated to require that all error-handling routines are developed around a standard that will prevent the information leakage vulnerability. Likewise input and output validation rules can be enforced through such a standard.

5.6.8   Define Security Requirements

Security requirements should be identified and documented early in any software development life cycle. Subsequent development artifacts must be evaluated for compliance with those requirements. When security requirements are not defined, the security of the resulting system cannot be effectively evaluated, and the risks with the resulting system will be difficult to correctly identify and measure.

5.6.9   Practice Threat Modeling

Threat modeling, as defined in the previous chapter is a good mechanism for understanding the attack vectors threats will utilize to conduct an attack. These attack vectors can then be scrutinized for vulnerabilities that may exist. For example, one of the threat categories in the STRIDE model is spoofing identities. Spoofing requires that an attacker assume someone else's identity. If spoofing is a threat, then a search for methods that an attacker could use to assume another identity may reveal possible vulnerabilities in the system.

5.7 Vulnerabilities Associated with the Test Case

Over the course of the previous chapters, we have learned a lot about our test case application that will calculate retirement benefits for retirement plans at the end of a given fiscal year. In the previous chapter, we learned a lot about the proposed architecture of the application. In this chapter, we use the knowledge gained in the previous chapter about the architecture of the test case, and couple it with the knowledge we gained in this chapter about common vulnerabilities, to come up with a list of potential vulnerabilities for our application.

To begin our vulnerability analysis of the test case, we look at the three types of vulnerabilities examined in this chapter and see if they could potentially apply to the test case. We start by looking at buffer overflows.

Buffer overflows in custom applications are generally caused by arbitrarily large user inputs. Our test case allows a number of user inputs including:

- User ID and password
- Plan ID number
- Fiscal year end date
- Contribution amount
- Plan type
- Plan formula
- Notes about the calculation (made by the retirement plan administrator when the administrator saves the calculation results)
- Edits to PII
- Account number (containing the funds that must be distributed to the retirement plan members when posting the results of a calculation)

A number of these input values have the potential for a user to enter an arbitrarily large input including the following:

- Contribution amount
- Fiscal year end date (a date that doesn't exist)
- Notes about the calculation
- Plan formulas (what if we expect that the plan formula (i.e., the company match in a 401k plan) to be 100 percent or less and a user enters 1,000,000 percent?
- Edits to PII (salaries, contribution amounts)

Therefore because the potential exists for a user to enter an arbitrarily large input value, we assume that buffer overflows are potential vulnerabilities within our test case application.

Next, we look at injection flaws. Injection flaws occur when user-supplied data is sent to a subsystem or interpreter as a part of a command or query. In the case of our test case application, there are several instances when user-supplied data is sent to a SQL server interpreter including:

- Retrieving PII data gathered by the mainframe service and placed in the mainframe DB2 database
- Saving (and retrieving) the inputs made to create a specific retirement benefit calculation
- Saving (and retrieving) corrections made to PII when creating a specific retirement benefit calculation
- Saving (and retrieving) the results of a specific benefit calculation so that those results may be posted to the individual retirement plan participants' accounts
- Saving (and retrieving) the notes made by the retirement plan administrator when saving the results of a calculation

Because the potential exists for a user to inject flaws into the SQL interpreter, particularly when saving and retrieving the notes made by the retirement plan administrator, injection flaws are a potential vulnerability that exists for our application.

Finally, let's examine information leakage and error-handling vulnerabilities as they are associated with our application. Of course, as with any application, we want to include a robust error handler so that routine errors will not result in an application crash. Because the calculations and business rules are complex, it is possible for any number of calculation errors including dividing by zero, floating-point decimal errors, and the like to exist within our application. In addition, there are possible exception-handling errors that may be associated with the application resulting from the authentication service. Recall that the authentication service will attempt to do the following:

- Determine if the user ID supplied is a valid user ID.
- Determine if the password supplied is a valid password for the user ID supplied.
- Determine if the plan ID supplied is a valid plan ID.
- Determine if an authenticated user is authorized to view information for the specified Plan ID.

Therefore, because we have a number of exception-handling issues, as well as error-handling issues, information leakage and error-handling vulnerabilities are potential vulnerabilities for our application.

Other potential vulnerabilities for the test case include:

- Broken authentication and session management
- Lack of a policy requiring code and peer reviews
- Lack of a policy that requires the classification of data

5.8   Conclusion

At the scene of the crime right after the crime is reported to the police, the forensic experts from the crime lab swing into action and soon they are busy collecting, categorizing, testing, and logging evidence. A review of the evidence will reveal the means that the criminal used to commit the crime. Much like the forensic experts from a crime lab, software development teams must have the education to spot potential vulnerabilities in software. And like the forensic experts, software developers have a host of vulnerability scanning tools and methods that can be used to aid them in discovering the vulnerabilities or potential vulnerabilities in their code.

Vulnerabilities are the means that threats use to attack assets. In order to provide the proper protection for those assets, software development teams need to understand how these vulnerabilities can affect the software they build. This chapter dealt with ways of determining ways of discovering potential or actual vulnerabilities within software including:

- Understanding what vulnerabilities are and sources to turn to for further information and education
- Code reviews, peer reviews, and buddy reviews
- Testing
- Static code scanning tools
- Dynamic code scanning tools
- Web application scanning tools
- Network vulnerability scanning tools

Now that we have identified the means or vulnerabilities that threats may use to attack our assets, we are ready to "solve the crime" or at least determine the probability or risk that a thief (threat) has the means (vulnerability) to destroy, alter, or steal our valuables (assets). This is the process of determining risk, and that is the subject of our next chapter.

5.9   Checklists

5.9.1   *Sources of Education about Software Vulnerabilities*

☐ OWASP Top 10 (http://www.owasp.org/index.php/OWASP_Top_Ten_Project)
☐ National Vulnerability Database (NIST) (http://nvd.nist.gov/nvd.cfm)
☐ Common vulnerabilities and exposures (http://cve.mitre.org/index.html)
☐ SANS Top 20 (http://www.sans.org/top20/)
☐ U.S. Computer Emergency Readiness Team (US CERT) (http://www.us-cert.gov/cas/alldocs.html)

5.9.2   OWASP Top 10 (2007)

☐ Cross-Site Scripting (XSS)
☐ Injection flaws
☐ Malicious file execution
☐ Insecure direct object reference
☐ Cross-Site Request Forgery (CSRF)
☐ Information leakage and improper error handling
☐ Broken authentication and session management
☐ Insecure cryptographic storage
☐ Insecure communications
☐ Failure to restrict URL access

5.9.3   SANS Top 20 for 2007

☐ Server-side vulnerabilities in:
    ☐ Web applications
    ☐ Windows services
    ☐ Unix and Mac OS services
    ☐ Backup software
    ☐ Anti-virus software
    ☐ Management servers
    ☐ Database software
☐ Client-side vulnerabilities in:
    ☐ Web browsers
    ☐ Office software
    ☐ E-mail clients
    ☐ Media players
☐ Security policy and personnel vulnerabilities including:
    ☐ Excessive user rights and unauthorized devices
    ☐ Phishing
    ☐ Unencrypted laptops and removable media
☐ Application vulnerabilities including:
    ☐ Instant messaging applications
    ☐ Peer-to-peer sharing applications
☐ Network device vulnerabilities including:
    ☐ VoIP servers and phones
☐ Zero day attacks

5.9.4 Methods for Finding Vulnerabilities

- ☐ Review of Current Controls
- ☐ Review of "Best Practice" standards
- ☐ Code/peer/buddy reviews
- ☐ Testing
- ☐ Open Source Static Code scanning tools
    - ☐ Lint (C)
    - ☐ Bandera (Java)
    - ☐ Checkstyle (Java)
    - ☐ ClassCycle (Java)
    - ☐ FindBugs (Java)
    - ☐ Jlint (Java)
    - ☐ PMD (Java)
    - ☐ Soot (Java)
    - ☐ CQual (C)
    - ☐ Sparse (Linux)
    - ☐ Splint (C language)
    - ☐ Flawfinder (C++)
    - ☐ Oink (C++)
    - ☐ ftnchek (Fortran)
    - ☐ JsLint (JavaScript)
    - ☐ Perl::Critic (Perl)
    - ☐ Pixy (PHP 4)
    - ☐ PyChecker (Python)
    - ☐ pylint (Python)
    - ☐ Rough Auditing Tool for Security (RATS) (C, C++, Perl, PHP, and Python)
- ☐ Open Source Web Application Scanning Tools
    - ☐ WebScarab
    - ☐ Paros Proxy
- ☐ Open Source Network Scanning Tools
    - ☐ Nessus
    - ☐ Nmap
    - ☐ Microsoft Baseline Security Analyzer
    - ☐ HFNetChk
    - ☐ NeWT
    - ☐ Tripwire
    - ☐ Nikto
    - ☐ Whisker

5.9.5 *Secure Coding Practices to Avoid Vulnerabilities*

☐ Validate Input
☐ Validate Output in Web Applications
☐ Keep It Simple
☐ Follow the Principle of Least Privilege
☐ Practice Defense in Depth
☐ Practice Quality Assurance
☐ Adopt Coding Standards
☐ Define Security Requirements
☐ Practice Threat Modeling

Chapter 6

Analyzing Security Risks

There comes a point in every detective story where someone, usually the lead detective in the case, has got it all figured out. He knows who committed the crime, why the crime was committed, how the crime was committed, and what the criminal was really out to accomplish. At this point in the story, the detective begins a narrative, describing all of the little twists and turns in the case. The narrative tale the detective spins is for everyone else involved in the case who may not have figured it out yet. Step by step, the detective tells how it all came down: how each piece of evidence, or false lead found fits together to reveal the answers to who the criminal (threat) is, what the criminal's motive, means, and opportunity (vulnerabilities) were, and what he was trying to steal (the asset).

Analyzing security risks is similar to putting all of the clues together in a detective story. The chief difference is that instead of trying to solve a crime, the risk analysis team is trying to prevent an adverse affect from occurring. By identifying the probability that such an adverse event can occur and its relative impact, the risk assessment team can make recommendations to change the possible motive, means, or opportunity for the event, making it less likely that the event will occur. This is the process of risk analysis and risk management.

This chapter covers several steps associated with the risk management process including: threat–vulnerability pairing, likelihood determination, impact determination, and risk determination. These steps and their inputs and outputs are shown in Figure 6.1.

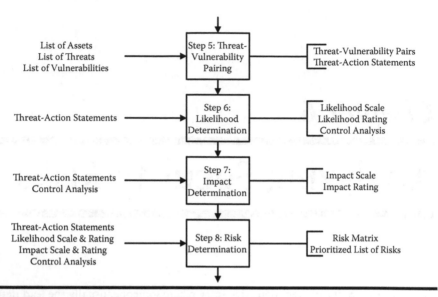

FIGURE 6.1   Steps 5 through 8 of the risk management process

6.1   Threat–Vulnerability Pairs

The potential for a crime exists when someone has the motive, means, and opportunity to commit a crime. Likewise an information security risk (which is the potential for an adverse event to affect an asset), exists when a threat can utilize a vulnerability to steal, alter, disclose, or destroy an asset. Just as the criminal has to have the motive, means, and opportunity to commit the crime for there to be a crime, there must be a vulnerability that a threat can exploit in order for a risk to exist.

In this step of the risk analysis process, the threats for a project that were uncovered utilizing threat modeling or other threat determination methods are paired with a specific vulnerability to produce a threat–vulnerability pair. From this threat–vulnerability pair comes a descriptive statement of how the threat will use the vulnerability to alter, destroy, or disclose an asset. This descriptive statement is called a threat action. To see how this works, consider the following example.

- *Threat*: Hacker or cracker
- *Vulnerability*: Injection flaws
- *Threat Action*: A malicious individual (hacker or cracker) takes advantage of injection flaws to input code into the "Product Review" feature of a commercial e-commerce site, allowing him to steal authentication credentials from other users of the e-commerce site.

Not all threat actions will be this long or this detailed. Some may be very simple, such as the following.

- *Threat*: Errors and Omissions: An employee mistakenly enters 400 hours into a timesheet application.
- *Vulnerability*: Improper Input Validation: The application doesn't check to see if the value input (400 hours) is a valid amount for one week worth of work.
- *Threat Action*: The employee is overpaid.

Other threat-action statements can be found in Table 6.1.

By now you begin to get the picture as to what a threat-action statement is. But why is a threat-action statement necessary? The answer to that question is that threat-action statements help in determining risk likelihood or probability, which is the next step in our risk assessment process.

6.2 Risk Likelihood or Probability

You may recall from Chapter 2 that likelihood of occurrence represents the likelihood that a threat will exploit a vulnerability to affect an asset. In a qualitative risk analysis methodology, likelihood is typically represented by a subjective term such as high, medium, or low instead of an actual value, as is the case in a quantitative risk analysis. At this point a scale based upon how often an event may occur, the

TABLE 6.1   Threat–Vulnerability Pairs

Threat	Vulnerability	Threat Action
Curiosity – An employee browses salary information for celebrity clients	Authorization for client data does not follow the principle of least privilege	An employee brags to other people about how much money a celebrity makes
Improper Disposal of Sensitive Information – Documents are not properly shredded	Policy does not classify data by sensitivity level – therefore not all documents are shredded	Sensitive data is thrown out in the trash where it can be retrieved by anyone
Policy or Procedure Violation – User account management is not informed of an employee termination	Employee accounts are not terminated in a timely manner	A terminated employee logs on from home and alters, destroys, or discloses sensitive data
Shoulder Surfing – Visitors are allowed to freely wander the first floor of a building	Terminal locks are not required when an employee leaves a workstation	A visitor gains access to confidential information when an employee leaves their desk to take a break

motivation of the threat, or what controls or safeguards are already in place to prevent the threat–vulnerability pair can be determined.

In Chapter 2 a number of such scales were provided as examples of simple likelihood tables. One scale was based upon the frequency of occurrence or the probability of a threat–vulnerability pair attacking an asset. Yet another scale was based upon the motivation of the threat and the skill required by the threat to produce the potential outcome. Finally, a scale based upon how effective current (or planned) safeguards and controls are in preventing the threat–vulnerability pair from the ability to attack an asset was presented. Which type is the most effective? In order to help determine the answer to that question, each of the three types of likelihood scale is provided side by side in Table 6.2.

Each one of these scales is subjective in nature and each varies fairly widely in scope. The scales can be a simple three-step scale as was used here, or they can be any number of steps in length. Both descriptive scales (i.e., high, medium, and low) and numeric scales (i.e. 1–5, 0–10, etc.) can be used to describe the relative likelihood of a threat–vulnerability pair attacking an asset. However, the choice of one style of scale over another can often be difficult to make. That is where the threat-action statements come in. Examination of the threat-action statements can often reveal which type of likelihood scale will best suit the current assessment.

Take, for example, the first example from the threat-action statements from Table 6.1: "An employee brags to other people about how much money a celebrity makes." Does this threat-action statement reveal anything about how frequently this threat action may occur? On its own, it does not. Perhaps HR records could be examined to determine how often an employee was reprimanded for accessing

TABLE 6.2 Likelihood Scales

Likelihood of Threat-Action	Scale Type		
	Frequency of Occurrence	Motivation and Skill of Threat	Controls and Safeguards
Low	Threat action occurs less that once/year	Threat lacks motivation and skill to harm asset	Current (or planned) controls prevent the threat action
Medium	Threat action occurs more than once/year and less than once/month	Threat has motivation, but lacks skill or has skill but lacks motivation	Current (or planned) controls impede the threat action
High	Threat action occurs more than once/month	Threat has both motivation and skill to harm asset	Current (or planned) controls ineffective against the threat action

sensitive information he should not have been viewing. However, it may be difficult to gain access to those HR records in order to make this sort of determination. In addition, it would only tell us how often an employee was *reprimanded* for this type of action, not how often the employee actually *committed* this type of infraction!

How about the motivation and skill of the threat: what does our threat-action statement say about motivation and skill? Obviously, the threat had motivation (he was bragging about his knowledge of sensitive information) and also the skill because he obviously knew what the sensitive information was. What about the effectiveness of the controls? At least in this case, the controls were ineffective in preventing the employee from obtaining the sensitive information. If at some point, the employee were to be reprimanded because an audit revealed the employee viewed records that the employee did not need to know, then we might say that the controls impeded, or will impede the threat action.

A similar analysis of the other threat-action statements can be conducted to come to a conclusion about which type of likelihood scale is most appropriate for the threat-action statements collected. First, a review of the remaining example threat-action statements from Table 6.1 is in order.

- Example 2: Sensitive data is thrown out in the trash where it can be retrieved by anyone.
- Example 3: A terminated employee logs on from home and alters, destroys, or discloses sensitive data.
- Example 4: A visitor gains access to confidential information when an employee leaves her desk to take a break.

None of these statements gives any indication of how often the threat action will occur. What about motivation and skill? In Example 2, "sensitive data is thrown out" doesn't appear to say anything about motivation, but it does give an indication that the threat has the skill or capacity to actually throw out the data. Example 3 indicates that the threat is highly motivated and also has the skill required to conduct an attack on an asset. Example 4 doesn't indicate too much about the motivation of the subject, but does indicate that the threat has the skill required to access the asset.

What about the effectiveness of controls and safeguards? Example 2 would seem to indicate that there are no effective controls at all. However, a recall of the threat–vulnerability pair from Table 6.1 indicates that there may be a shredding policy in place, but there is no policy on the sensitivity of data. This would indicate that sensitive information should be shredded, but the policy doesn't indicate in all situations exactly what types of information are sensitive, therefore some sensitive information is not shredded. From this we can conclude that the safeguards and controls are probably a partial deterrent.

If we apply this reasoning to Example 3 we come to the conclusion that although there is a policy in place to prevent this event from occurring, the policy was not enforced. Because there are no additional safeguards to ensure that all of the proper notifications go out when an employee is terminated, then the safeguard by itself is not sufficient to prevent the threat action from occurring. And finally, there is no safeguard for Example 4, because terminal locks are not required or enforced.

What does this analysis reveal about the likelihood scale that should be utilized for a risk analysis effort in which these types of threat-action statements are developed? First, none of the threat-action statements gave any indication at all of how often the threat action would occur, nor was it possible to infer such information from other sources. Therefore, a likelihood scale based upon frequency of occurrence can be eliminated. As you may recall from our discussions in Chapter 2 on determining which type of risk assessment methodology to use, it is often difficult if not impossible to accurately predict the frequency of a threat action occurring.

What about motivation and skill? For each of the example threat actions we were able to determine if the threat had the skill required in order to exercise the vulnerability. However, it was not possible to determine the motivation of the threat source for two of the four examples. What about a likelihood scale based upon controls (or the lack thereof) and how effective those controls are in preventing the threat action? In each of the four examples, it was easy to determine if controls were effective in preventing the threat action. However, it wasn't necessarily clear on the relative level of effectiveness of the control.

In this instance, either a motivation or skill or an effectiveness of controls and safeguard likelihood scale would be appropriate for use in assessing risks. The subjective nature of the scale doesn't require a detailed analysis in order to make a choice. And a compromise might be to utilize a combined scale based both on the motivation and skill required by the threat source as well as the effectiveness of current or planned controls to prevent a threat action from occurring. Such a combined likelihood scale is shown in Table 6.3.

An analysis of our example threat actions from Table 6.1 against this combined likelihood scale reveals the following.

■ Example 1 would be an example of a high likelihood. The threat source had both motivation and skill, and the audit policy that would result in an employee reprimand would count as a deterrent but not prevention.
■ Example 2 would be an example of a moderate likelihood. The threat source had the skill required, and motivation was unknown, but motivation probably was not a factor because we can assume that nobody wants to throw out sensitive information in the trash. The shredding policy is an effective control, but the lack of a data classification policy to go along with the shredding policy makes that control only partially effective.
■ Example 3 would be an example of a critical likelihood. The threat source had the motivation and skill required and there was a policy to prevent the threat action from occurring, but it wasn't effective at all!

TABLE 6.3   Combined Likelihood Scale

Likelihood of Threat Action Occurring	Criteria
Negligible	Threat source does not have the motivation to accomplish the threat action Threat source does not have the skill required to accomplish the threat action Controls are in place that prevent the threat source from accomplishing the threat action
Low	Threat source motivation is unknown or unclear Threat source does not have the skill required to accomplish the threat action Controls are in place that deter the threat source, but will not absolutely prevent the threat action from occurring
Moderate	Threat source has either the motivation or the skill required to accomplish the threat action but not both Controls are in place that deter the threat source, but will not absolutely prevent the threat action from occurring OR Threat source has the motivation and the skill required to accomplish the threat action Controls are in place that prevent the threat source from accomplishing the threat action
High	Threat source has both the motivation and skill required to accomplish the threat action Controls are in place that deter the threat source, but will not absolutely prevent the threat action from occurring OR Threat source has the motivation or the skill required to accomplish the threat action but not both No controls are in place to deter or prevent the threat source from accomplishing the threat action
Critical	Threat source has both the motivation and skill required to accomplish the threat action No controls are in place to deter or prevent the threat source from accomplishing the threat action

■ Example 4 would be an example of a high likelihood. There are no controls in place at all. Although the threat source has the skill necessary to conduct the threat action, the motivation of the threat source is in question. It is highly unlikely that a visitor who is highly motivated will linger in an area until an employee leaves her desk and does not lock her PC without being challenged. Therefore it is unlikely that the threat source is motivated.

6.3   Control Analysis

In the analysis of each of the threat actions conducted in this chapter, assumptions were made as to the effectiveness of controls when performing our analysis. For example, in our analysis of Example 2, we assumed that although there was a no-shredding policy it wasn't a fully effective deterrent because there was no data classification policy to define sensitive and nonsensitive data. However, the opposite might have been true. Perhaps due to the shredding policy, employees shred everything, whether or not there is sensitive data involved. In this case, the absence of a data classification policy would not affect whether sensitive information was shredded or not. Therefore in this instance, Example 2 would be a low likelihood of occurrence because the motivation of the threat is unknown, the skill is available, but there are controls in place (shredding policy) that deter the threat action from occurring.

The same type of analysis could be conducted for Example 3. Previously, an assumption was made that the policy of notifying all required departments when an employee was terminated so that access rights for the terminated employee could be revoked, was not effective. However, it could be that it is almost always effective, but in this particular instance, it was not effective. Therefore the likelihood of this threat may be reduced to high, or perhaps even moderate, depending upon how effective the notification of termination policy truly is.

What about Example 1? An assumption was made that there was an audit policy that would eventually find which employees accessed the data and determine that one or more employees should not have accessed the data and those employees would be reprimanded. But if there were no audit policy in place, then Example 1 would become a critical likelihood, because there are no controls to prevent the employee from repeating this action over again.

Sometimes it may be truly difficult to decide how effective controls and safeguards are, especially when those safeguards are policies and procedures. Will audit checks always catch employees who access information to which they should not have access? Do all employees shred confidential or sensitive information all of the time? Are the proper departments within an organization always notified of employee terminations in a timely manner? Does the fact that there is no policy requiring personnel to lock their workstations when they leave their desk mean that no employee ever locks his workstation when leaving his desk? The answers to all of these questions are very subjective in nature and there are no right and no wrong answers.

When conducting an analysis on the potential effectiveness of safeguards and controls there are a number of methods that can be used to determine if controls might be effective or not. First, simple observation methods can be used. Consider the shredding policy. Observe the office staff. Are they diligent in shredding materials or do they throw most of their material in the trash? Look at the trash. Is sensitive material being discarded? The same type of analysis can be conducted for the workstation process. Do most employees lock their workstations when leaving their desks? How often are visitors or strangers seen wandering about unchallenged? Simple observation can often provide a strong sense of how effective some types of controls may be at preventing a threat action.

A second method of determining the effectiveness of controls and safeguards is to look at organizational records or interview organizational staff such as human resources and internal audit teams. If there is an audit policy in place, then how often are audit checks made? Have employees been investigated or reprimanded for attempting to access information to which they are not supposed to have access? Have employees been caught attempting to access information more than one time? How timely are termination notifications supplied to access control? Are they always timely? Looking at a list of current user IDs and comparing it to a listing of current employees might also reveal how effective a policy requiring the termination of access rights for terminated employees actually is. The answers to these types of questions can reveal how successful a control might be as a deterrent.

Finally a consideration of the effectiveness of controls can look to the future. Are there potential controls or enhancements to controls that are coming on line or will soon come on line which might increase the effectiveness of current controls? For example, perhaps most but not all employees currently lock their workstations when leaving their desk for any period of time. What if a security awareness newsletter were to be issued to employees reminding them that they should lock their workstations when leaving their desks? Would this increase the likelihood that the control would be effective? Or perhaps there are plans in place to roll out an automatic lockout program that would lock workstations after 10 or 15 minutes of inactivity in the next quarter. Likewise, perhaps a data classification policy is currently in draft form but has not yet been implemented. When such a policy is implemented, will it increase the effectiveness of a shredding policy?

When considering the impact of future enhancements on current controls, care should be taken to consider the impact of other decisions that may weaken the effect of current controls. What if a new state governor declares a policy of open government that is open to visitors at all times? Before this announcement, visitors to work areas were rare. After this announcement, visitors will be much more common. If there is no policy on locking workstations or no automatic enforcement of a lockout, then the likelihood of a visitor threat action increases. And what about the announcement of a work from home policy? Previous to this announcement, only a handful of employees could access work applications and data from home. After the work from home program has been implemented, everyone in the company will be able to access work applications and data from home. In this instance, if access control is not revoked from terminated employees in a timely manner, it is much more likely that the control will be ineffective.

6.4 Impact or Severity of Threat Actions

Now that a likelihood scale has been selected or developed, the impact of a threat action upon an asset must be considered. In order to consider the impact a threat action may have on a given organization it is necessary to understand the mission of the business area affected by the threat action, the criticality of the system or data affected by the threat action, and the sensitivity of the system or data affected by the threat action. The criticality of a system and its data represent the relative importance of the value of the system to an organization. The sensitivity of a system represents the relative need to protect data from unauthorized disclosure.

How then are mission, criticality, and sensitivity determined for a given system? One method of determining these factors is to look at the organization's Business Impact Analysis (BIA). A BIA is a document created as the first step in an organization's Disaster Recovery (DR) and Business Continuity Planning (BCP). A BIA will identify the organization's mission, along with the processes or business functions performed by the organization, the resources required to support those business functions, the interdependencies between processes or departments within the organization, and the impact of failing to perform a process. Processes can then be ranked in terms of how critical they are to the organization's ability to meet its mission in a disaster scenario.

For example, if an organization were to be hit by a tornado, or fire, or other disaster that affected the systems of the organization, then it would be necessary for the organization to set up in some other backup location, either pre-selected or not. Which systems should be restored and in what order? Typically, it will be less critical that human resource systems in an organization be restored before systems supporting the organization's external customers. However, it is not enough to simply restore the external customer systems, if the security for those systems is not restored at the same time.

Of course new software development efforts will more than likely not be a part of the BIA, DR, and BCP documentation until some time after they have been implemented. However, similar systems most likely are already a part of the BIA or at least the business unit affected will be a part of the BIA. If, however, the business unit is new, or the organization has never completed a BIA, there are still methods of determining the criticality and sensitivity of systems. Typically, the more protections or safeguards required for a system, the more critical and sensitive those systems are. Also systems that serve external customers are typically more critical (but not necessarily more sensitive) than systems that provide service to the internal departments of an organization.

Typically, any information security effort has three goals in mind: the confidentiality, integrity, and availability of the systems protected. This is known as the CIA triangle. When determining the impact of a threat action upon an asset, we consider the impact in terms of how the confidentiality, integrity, or availability of a system or its data are affected.

6.4.1 Impact on Confidentiality

Determining the impact of a threat action on confidentiality refers to how well the asset is protected from unauthorized disclosure. The impact that disclosure may have on confidential or sensitive information can range from national security issues to data privacy issues. In addition to the criminal and civil penalties associated with potential disclosure issues, an analysis should also consider the loss of public confidence or embarrassment that may be caused if the disclosure should become public knowledge.

6.4.2 Impact on Integrity

An impact on the integrity of an asset means that the asset was improperly modified in some manner. If the improper modification goes unnoticed, then continued use of the contaminated system or data could lead to increasing acts of inaccuracy or fraud. Take for an example an online retail store. The store decides to have an annual 10 percent off sale for a given timeframe. At the beginning of the timeframe, all the prices of goods listed in the database are reduced. But because they are improperly modified, the prices are increased by 10 percent rather than decreased by 10 percent. As a result of the price hike, instead of increased sales, the organization sees a reduction in sales. They may decide to reduce the price even further to increase sales, or they may conclude (inaccurately) that there is no longer a demand for the goods they are selling, so that they change their inventory.

Another example might be the improper modification of account numbers in a system that handles medical insurance claims. As a result, claims may be paid twice to two different account numbers associated with one given provider. This could lead to multiple payments for the same procedure over time. Because a loss of system integrity can also lead to the loss of confidentiality (i.e., if one has the ability to modify data, perhaps one can also see the data being modified), and loss of availability (i.e., if you can modify the data, you can probably also destroy the data) of a system or its data, then a loss of integrity usually implies a greater impact upon a system than a loss of confidentiality or availability.

6.4.3 Impact on Availability

The availability of an asset is affected whenever the asset is not available to its end users. If an organization's e-mail asset is not available, then nobody within the organization will be able to send or receive e-mail. Understanding how important the e-mail function is to an organization is important in understanding the impact of availability upon the e-mail system. If e-mail is vital to the organization or its mission, then a spam attack that fills the e-mail mailboxes of the organization to capacity with unwanted advertisements will have a critical impact on the e-mail asset.

It is possible to quantify the impact of a threat action to the confidentiality, integrity, and availability of a specific asset. For example, if a virus were to infect the e-mail system of an organization, the impact could be calculated in terms of the number of hours spent quarantining and cleaning up from the attack and the labor rates of the individuals who cleaned up. Or it could be the cost associated in paying for credit monitoring services for the customers of an organization who had their personal information disclosed when a laptop containing names, account numbers, and credit card numbers of customers is lost or stolen.

But what about the impact to public confidence or credibility of an organization when the confidentiality of an asset is breached? This figure is much more difficult to ascertain. In some instances, such as the case of Arthur Andersen LLC with the Enron scandal, once the problem became public knowledge, the loss in public confidence was so massive that most of the customers and staff of the organization walked away. Yet with other companies, such as TJX and the loss of more than 50 million credit card records, the loss in public confidence hasn't nearly been as great.

Because a qualitative risk analysis is based upon subjective criteria, it is enough to be able to determine the relative impact upon public confidence and credibility and not the actual impact. Therefore, we now have enough information to begin building a scale that will measure the relative impact of a threat action upon an asset. Consider Table 6.4.

Continuing the analysis of the examples from earlier in this chapter, a relative magnitude of impact can be determined for each example. Let's begin with Example 1: the employee who accessed confidential information for a celebrity and who passed along that information to others. Little or no impact has been made to the mission of the organization. Is there a financial impact? Only if the celebrity finds out about the threat action and sues the organization or threatens to take her business from the organization. What about loss in confidence or credibility? Again, this depends upon whether the threat action becomes public knowledge and what action the celebrity chooses to take. Because the threat action was an employee bragging about the news within the company, we will assume that nobody outside the company found out about the threat action, and therefore there is no financial impact, nor is there a loss in confidence. In this instance, the magnitude of impact will be low.

TABLE 6.4   **Magnitude of Impact Scale**

Magnitude of Impact	*Criteria*
Low	Minor impact upon business mission Minor financial loss No loss in confidence or credibility
Moderate	Minor impact upon business mission Financial loss caused Some loss in confidence or credibility No legal liability
High	Major impact or interruption of business mission Major financial loss Loss of customer confidence and credibility Legal liability

Example 2 is also a threat action that affects the confidentiality of an asset. Again, there is no impact upon the business mission if the confidential information is thrown in the trash. As to whether there is a financial loss or a loss in confidence it depends again on if any of the confidential information is retrieved from the trash. If not, then the magnitude of impact will be low. However, it is just as possible that a financial loss could occur if the confidential information were to fall into the wrong hands. And it would also be an embarrassment if it became public knowledge that confidential information was thrown out in the trash. In this instance, the threat action would have a moderate impact.

Example 3 is a threat action that can affect the confidentiality, integrity, and availability of systems and data. Depending upon the action that the terminated employee takes, data could be copied out to a public Web site, or destroyed, or altered to perpetuate fraudulent acts. In this case, the impact of the threat action would be high, because a major impact of a business function could occur, along with a major financial loss, loss of credibility to customers, as well as potential legal liabilities associated with revealing confidential information.

Example 4 is a threat action that most likely affects the confidentiality of information, but which could also affect the integrity of information, and to a lesser extent the availability of information. It all depends upon what the visitor does with the time allotted when the employee is away from her desk. Typically this won't be for an extended period of time, so the amount of data that could be destroyed, or altered, or disclosed will be limited to a degree. In this instance, the magnitude of the threat action would be moderate.

Of course, just as with likelihood scales, it is possible to build many different types of impact scales. Numeric scales with values of 1–5 or 0–10 are possible, as are various types of subjective scales such as low-medium-high, or insignificant-minor-significant-damaging-severe-critical. The wider the scale, the easier it becomes to determine the relative risk associated with the threat action. However, the wider the scale, the more difficult it becomes to truly determine if the impact should be a 6 or a 7 on the scale.

It is also possible to determine the magnitude of impact using a slightly less subjective approach. Consider the following magnitude of impact scale shown in Table 6.5.

Table 6.5 simply provides a number of criteria for which a yes or no answer is required. Then, based upon how many yes answers are provided, the magnitude of impact rises. Of course significant financial impact may be a bit subjective still, but this is a much more subjective table than Table 6.4.

6.5 Determining Risk Levels

Once both magnitude of impact and likelihood of occurrence scales have been developed, it is possible to create a risk matrix. The risk matrix represents the relative amount of risk associated with a threat action based upon the likelihood of occurrence and the magnitude of impact that threat action has upon the asset. This then is how risk is measured as defined back in Chapter 1 as the net negative impact of the exercise of a vulnerability or weakness, considering both the probability and the impact of occurrence. Consider the risk matrix in Table 6.6.

Table 6.6 represents a typical risk matrix. The results of such a risk table often depend upon how the scales for likelihood of occurrence and magnitude of impact were developed. In the case in Table 6.6, it may be that a low magnitude of impact will never result in a high risk, regardless of how often that threat action may occur. As an example, consider the second example from this chapter, where confidential information is thrown out in the trash. If the trash is never searched for confidential information, then it doesn't matter how often the confidential information is thrown out. Of course we can't be certain that somehow, a piece of garbage won't blow off a garbage truck and into the hands of someone who is interested in the

Table 6.5 Alternative Magnitude of Impact

Magnitude of Impact	Criteria	No. of Criteria That Apply
Insignificant	Impact upon business mission	No more than 1
Minor	Significant financial impact	2
Moderate	Loss of reputation or confidence	3
Significant	Legal liability	4
Critical	Personal safety affected	5

Table 6.6   Risk Matrix

	Magnitude of Impact		
Likelihood of Occurrence	*Low*	*Moderate*	*High*
Negligible	Low	Low	Low
Low	Low	Low	Moderate
Moderate	Low	Moderate	High
High	Moderate	High	High
Critical	Moderate	High	High

confidential information, and therefore the more confidential information that is thrown out, the greater the chance becomes that someone who will do something with the information will get their hands on it.

Of course it is possible to combine subjectively worded scales with numeric values to come up with a more subjective scale. Consider Table 6.7 which uses the following scale: 1–25 = Low, 26–50 = Moderate, 51–100 = High.

An examination of the relative risks associated with the examples used in this chapter reveals the following.

- Example 1 is a low risk because although it has a high likelihood of occurrence it has a low magnitude of impact.
- Example 2 is a moderate risk because it has both a moderate likelihood of occurrence and a moderate magnitude of impact.
- Example 3 is a high risk because it has a critical likelihood of occurrence and a high magnitude of impact.
- Example 4 is a moderate risk because although it has a high likelihood of occurrence, it only has a moderate magnitude of impact.

Once threat actions have been given a rating, they can be ordered in descending order of the level of risk associated with the threat. Ranking of risks is important,

Table 6.7   Numerical Risk Matrix

	Magnitude of Impact		
Likelihood of Occurrence	*Low (1)*	*Moderate (5)*	*High (10)*
Negligible (1)	Low (1)	Low (5)	Low (10)
Low (3)	Low (3)	Low (15)	Moderate (30)
Moderate (5)	Low (5)	Moderate (30)	Moderate (50)
High (8)	Low (8)	Moderate (40)	High (80)
Critical (10)	Low (10)	Moderate (50)	High (100)

because eliminating the biggest risks first will have the greater impact upon the organization. Because resources associated with eliminating or reducing risks may be scarce, it is important to utilize those resources where they will have the greatest impact upon the organization. Going back to the examples used in this chapter we find the following.

- Example 3 is the biggest risk uncovered.
- Examples 2 and 4 represent the next most likely risks.
- Example 1 represents the lowest risk uncovered.

Additional controls and safeguards can now be considered to *mitigate* (i.e., reduce or eliminate) the risk involved with each threat action either by preventing its occurrence, or by reducing the likelihood of occurrence, the magnitude of impact, or both. This is the process of risk mitigation and risk management and is covered in the next chapter.

6.6 Sources of Scales and Tables

There are a number of good sources of likelihood of occurrence scales, magnitude of impact scales, and risk matrix tables if you are having difficulty in developing your own. Some of these sources include the following:

- The National Institute of Science and Technology (NIST) (http://csrc.nist.gov/)
- The Centers for Medicare and Medicaid Services (CMS) (http://www.cms. hhs.gov/)
- The SysAdmin, Audit, Security, Network (SANS) Institute (http://www. sans.org/)
- The Software Engineering Institute (SEI) at Carnegie-Mellon University (http://www.sei.cmu.edu/)

6.7 Determining Security Risks for the Test Case

It is now possible to begin to determine the risks for the test case. The first step is to begin pairing threats with possible vulnerabilities to come up with a list of threat actions. A recap of the threats discovered in Chapter 4 and the vulnerabilities discovered in Chapter 5 can be found in Sections 6.7.1, 6.7.2, and 6.7.3 of this chapter.

6.7.1 Human Threats

Human threats for the test case include the following:

- Shoulder surfing could allow nonauthorized personnel to observe the authentication process.
- Impersonation could allow users with stolen identity credentials (i.e., a stolen user ID and password) to view information they are not authorized to see.
- Errors and omissions in updating the IRS limitation file could result in the application applying incorrect business rules to the calculation. Likewise errors and omissions in the entries made by the retirement plan administrator, such as the plan formula, fiscal year end date, or amount to be contributed could all result in an incorrect calculation.
- Inadvertent acts or carelessness could result in programming errors that do not apply the complex business rules properly, resulting in incorrect calculations or incorrect error handling or other potential vulnerabilities that could allow an attacker to gain access.

6.7.2 Technical Threats

Technical threats for the test case include the following:

- *Data contamination.* The error log designed for this application placed all of the details associated with the error into an error log including sensitive information that the log administrator was not authorized to see.
- *Corruption by system failures.* If the mainframe service that gathers the PII required for the calculation is interrupted due to a mainframe system failure, the data placed in the DB2 tables could be garbled or corrupted. Or likewise the call to the DB2 table to pull the PII into the application could be corrupted by system failures such as the gateway to the mainframe, resulting in data that is garbled or corrupted.
- *Failures and intrusions not properly logged.* It is possible for the authentication service to determine that the user has not properly supplied log-in credentials, or is not authorized to view a specific pension plan. If these types of intrusions are not properly logged (i.e., the user is simply denied access to the information and no log entry is made) then no audit trail will exist that a user was attempting to view unauthorized information.
- *Environmental and natural threats.* The application will run on Web server located in the main data center for the company. This data center is also the home of the mainframe computer where all of the data files are stored. Therefore natural and environmental threats such as fire, flood, power fluctuations,

tornadoes, and the like all could affect the operation of the application or its associated information.

■ *Malicious code.* Viruses, worms, or other malicious programs could attempt to alter or destroy the IRS limitations data file, or interrupt calls through the gateway between the Web-based application and the mainframe service or the mainframe DB2 database.

■ *Eavesdropping.* Keystroke loggers could capture user IDs and passwords supplied to the authentication service. Network sniffers could detect, intercept, and corrupt or replace packets sent between the application and the gateway to the mainframe.

■ *Intrusion.* Backdoors to the application could be programmed by the development staff.

■ *Takeover of authorized sessions.* If an authorized retirement plan administrator left a workstation unattended and unlocked then it would be possible for an unauthorized individual to gain access to the information in the application.

6.7.3 Vulnerabilities

Vulnerabilities for the test case include the following:

■ Buffer overflows
■ Injection flaws
■ Information leakage
■ Broken authentication and session management
■ Lack of a policy requiring code and peer reviews
■ Lack of a policy that requires the classification of data

The threat–vulnerability pairs and their associated threat-action statements for the test case might be represented by the data in Table 6.8.

6.7.4 Threat-Action Statements

These do not represent all of the threat-action statements possible for the test case, but provide a representative sampling of possible outcomes. However, it is relatively easy to perform an analysis for including or excluding some of the remaining threats. Take, for example, the shoulder-surfing threat. Although it would be very possible for an unauthorized individual to view the authentication process, there is not an associated vulnerability that might allow that threat to get to the test case system. Policy requires that all visitors to the facility must be escorted by an employee at all times, and the floor plans of the data processing areas are open, making it nearly

Table 6.8 Test Case Threat—Vulnerability Pairs

Threat	Vulnerability	Threat Action
Errors and omissions by the retirement plan administrator when entering data into the application	Buffer overflow	1. The retirement plan administrator could erroneously enter a buffer overflow causing the application to crash
Data contamination	No controls on who can see the error and user log files	2. Sensitive information can be disclosed to unauthorized individuals by reading the error log files
Impersonation	No controls available on detecting if impersonation is occurring	3. An inside employee who had obtained the authentication credentials of another employee could view sensitive information in the application
Inadvertent acts of carelessness in programming	Injection flaws, information leakage	4. A programmer could inadvertently allow injection flaws or information leakage which would reveal information to an unauthorized user
Corruption by system failures	No error messages passed between services used by the application when an error occurs	5. An incorrect calculation could result from data contamination caused by a failure of the mainframe service
Failures and intrusions not properly logged	Broken authentication and session management	6. Unauthorized attempts to gain access to certain plans are not detected.
Intrusion	Lack of a policy requiring code and peer reviews	7. A developer programs a backdoor into an application allowing access to the application and its data.

impossible for an intruder to observe a log-in process and then be able to sit down at an empty workstation and use the credentials observed. In addition, screen-savers with passwords and automatic lockouts are required on all workstations, which when coupled with the requirement that visitors must be escorted would also make it practically impossible for takeover of unauthorized sessions to occur.

6.7.5 Likelihood of Occurrence

Now that the threat-action statements have been developed, a likelihood of occurrence scale can be developed. Looking at our threat-action statements reveals nothing at all of how often these threat actions will occur. Therefore, we can rule out a scale based upon frequency of occurrence. Looking at the threat-action statements we can see that in most cases, the motivation and skill of the threat source can be determined, as can the effectiveness, or lack of effectiveness, of controls. Therefore, we utilize the simple scale outlined in Table 6.9.

6.7.8 Control Analysis

Now that the likelihood scale has been created, we can conduct a control analysis to make sure that we understand how the controls or lack thereof might affect the likelihood of occurrence for each of the threat actions and rate our threat actions on the likelihood of occurrence scale. The likelihood of occurrence for each of our threat action statements might be as follows:

- Example 1 represents a high likelihood. We assume that the threat source is completely lacking in motivation, because the retirement plan administrator does not want to enter an erroneous value that may cause the system to crash. Of course the retirement plan administrator does have the skill required to make such an error. If there are no controls at all that validate the input of the retirement plan administrator, then there is nothing that will prevent a buffer overflow from occurring if the retirement plan administrator enters a very high value.
- Example 2 represents a medium likelihood. In this instance, we assume that the threat source has the motivation to want to read the confidential information contained within the error log file. However, simply because the threat source wants to read the confidential information does not necessarily mean that the threat source has the capability to understand the error log contents. And even if the error log is unprotected, the threat source may not know where the error log is located. Therefore we assume that the threat source does not have the skill, and that the controls are at least partially effective.

Table 6.9   Test Case Likelihood Scale

Likelihood of Occurrence	Criteria
Very Low	Threat source lacks motivation and skill Controls fully effective
Low	Threat source lacks motivation and skill Controls partially effective OR Threat source lacks motivation or skill but not both Controls fully effective
Medium	Threat source lacks motivation or skill but not both Controls partially effective OR Threat source has motivation and skill Controls fully effective OR Threat source lacks motivation and skill Controls completely ineffective
High	Threat source has motivation and skill Controls partially effective OR Threat source has motivation or skill but not both Controls completely ineffective
Very High	Threat source has motivation and skill Controls completely ineffective

■ Example 3 represents a medium likelihood. If an employee were to imperson-ate another employee, we must assume that the employee has the motivation to do so. Does the employee have the skill required? Are the controls that pre-vent impersonation effective? It would depend upon how the authentication credentials were stolen. Because we are unlikely to know for sure, then we are forced to make an assumption based upon a control analysis. We already know that shoulder surfing is difficult to accomplish due to the physical con-trols in place within our organization. If there are controls that search for keystroke loggers, and policies in place that prevent recording passwords and user IDs and leaving them in plain sight, then it is possible that the user would either not have the skill required or the controls are effective. In this instance, from the author's personal knowledge of the organization in ques-tion, we assume that the user does not have the skill required, but that the controls in place are only partially effective.

■ Example 4 represents another high likelihood. The threat source is assumed to lack the motivation required; most programmers do not want to introduce vulnerabilities into their code. Of course, being human, it is possible for a programmer to make a mistake, therefore the threat source does have the skill required. Because there are no code or peer reviews required within the organization, it is highly unlikely that these vulnerabilities will all be caught during testing; therefore we judge the controls to be completely ineffective.

■ Example 5 represents a medium likelihood. There is no motivation behind most system failures, but the fact that they do happen means that the threat source possesses the skill required. The fact that the mainframe service does not always return an error code when it has been interrupted by a system failure means that the controls are only partially effective.

■ Example 6 represents a very high likelihood. The fact that someone is attempting to access unauthorized information is an indication of motivation. The fact that someone can attempt to do so also implies that the source has the skill to do so. And finally, because there is no log that records access attempts and their failures, the controls are completely ineffective.

■ Example 7 also represents a very high likelihood. The fact that someone could put in a backdoor within the application implies both motivation and skill. And because there are no controls to detect such a backdoor, the controls are completely ineffective.

6.7.9   Magnitude of Impact

Now that we have determined the likelihood for each of the threat actions in the test case, we can build a scale to represent the magnitude of impact the threat actions could have on the assets of our test case. Such a scale might look something like the scale shown in Table 6.10.

An analysis of each of the threat-action statements against this scale reveals the following.

■ Example 1 would represent an insignificant impact. If the retirement plan administrator did cause a buffer overflow, the worst that would happen would be that the business mission is affected while the application is brought back on line,

Table 6.10   Test Case Magnitude of Impact Scale

Magnitude of Impact	Criteria	No. of Criteria That Apply
Insignificant	Impact upon business mission	0
Minor	Significant financial impact	1
Moderate	Loss of reputation or confidence	2
Significant	Legal liability	3
Critical	Personal safety affected	4 or more

and it would be more likely that the employee simply had to restart the application which would not be a significant impact upon any business mission.

- Example 2 would represent a moderate impact. If someone were to gather sensitive information from the error log file and make use of it, it is possible that a loss of reputation or confidence on the part of the customer could be affected as well as some sort of legal liability to pay for credit monitoring services. It is highly unlikely that a significant financial impact could occur, although it is possible if enough confidential information were in the error log file.
- Example 3 represents a significant impact. If an employee were to gain the credentials of another user and use the application over time to view unauthorized sensitive information, and then used the information to commit fraud, then it is highly likely that significant financial impact would result, along with a loss of reputation or confidence as well as legal liabilities.
- Example 4 represents an insignificant impact. Because the users of this application are all internal employees then injection errors and information leakage errors would only reveal information to authorized users of the application to begin with. This doesn't affect any of the criteria within our impact scale. However, if at some future point, the application were to be made available on the Internet to external customers so that they could do their own retirement plan calculations, then these types of vulnerabilities could mean that this threat action could represent a significant impact.
- Example 5 represents a moderate impact. A miscalculated retirement plan benefit could easily result in a loss of confidence or reputation, as well as potentially representing a significant financial loss depending upon when the error was discovered. Again, depending upon the nature of the error, it could also represent a legal liability, although in this instance, the organization had a policy of making right all financial errors it made without the need for legal proceedings.
- Example 6 represents an insignificant impact. As you might recall from the discussion on the application architecture from Chapter 5, we discussed the potential outcomes of the authentication service. They were:
  - The user ID does not exist.
  - The password for a given user ID is incorrect.
  - The plan ID does not exist.
  - The user ID is not authorized to view the information for the given plan ID.
  - If an incorrect password is provided for a user ID three times, then that user ID is locked out and a new password must be established by the user. However, if the user ID is not authorized to view the information for a given plan ID, nothing happens other than the user is told that she does not have the proper authorization for that particular plan ID. However,

because the user did not gain access to any unauthorized information there is no impact on any of the criteria in our magnitude of impact scale.

■ Example 7 represents a critical impact. A backdoor into the application can allow a disgruntled employee to plant a logic bomb, to alter the data used by the application, to commit fraud by writing confidential information to a file that could then be used for identity theft, or to shut down the application itself. Therefore although personal safety is probably not affected, all of the other criteria could be.

6.7.10   Risk Levels

Now we can begin to determine the levels of risk associated with the test case. First a risk matrix must be created. Table 6.11 represents the risk matrix for our test case.

Now that we have a risk matrix, we can rank order all of our threat actions according to risk level.

■ High risk: Example 7
■ Medium risk: Example 2, Example 3, Example 5, Example 6
■ Low risk: Example 1, Example 4

Now that we have determined the level of risk associated with our application development effort, we can begin to determine what additional controls or safeguards we can build into the application in order to reduce or eliminate these threats. That is the process of risk mitigation and risk management and is the subject of the next chapter.

Table 6.11   Test Case Risk Matrix

Likelihood of Occurrence	Magnitude of impact				
	Insignificant	Minor	Moderate	Significant	Critical
Very low	Low	Low	Low	Low	Medium
Low	Low	Low	Low	Medium	Medium
Medium	Low	Low	Medium	Medium	High
High	Low	Medium	Medium	High	High
Very high	Medium	Medium	High	High	High

6.8   Conclusion

The detective story is now over. The detective has revealed the criminal (threat source) along with his motive, means (vulnerabilities), and opportunities, along with the true item of value (asset) the criminal was after. The detective can go to bed that night, knowing that he's solved his problem, and now he can go on to another case. But that isn't the case with the software development team. Although the risks associated with the case have been identified, it is the job of the software development team to prevent those risks from being realized.

In this chapter we have seen how to develop threat–vulnerability pairs resulting from our threat identification processes (Chapter 4) and vulnerability identification process (Chapter 5). We have turned these threat–vulnerability pairs into a threat action that describes how the threat will affect an asset. From there, we learned how to create likelihood of occurrence scales that indicate the relative occurrence of our threat actions. We then rated our threat actions against this scale using a control analysis.

Next, we turned to developing a scale that would represent the relative impact that a threat action might have upon our assets. This scale took into account the impact the threat actions had against the confidentiality, integrity, and availability of the test case system and its data. We then rated our threat actions against this scale.

Finally, we developed a risk matrix based upon our likelihood of occurrence and magnitude of impact scales. This allowed us to rank the threat actions based upon the amount of risk they represented to the assets in our test case. Now, all that remains is to eliminate or reduce the risks associated with the test case and that is the subject of our next chapter.

6.9   Common Risk Scales and Tables

In this section a number of different scales and tables are presented in order to provide you with a true representation of some of the relative levels of simplicity or complexity that can be utilized when creating scales and tables.

6.9.1   Likelihood of Occurrence Scales

This section displays some common likelihood of occurrence scales that you may wish to use in your risk assessment efforts. Tables 6.12 and 6.13 represent both a simple and a more complex likelihood of occurrence scale.

Table 6.12   Example 1 Likelihood Scale

Likelihood of Occurrence	Criteria
Low	The threat source lacks motivation or capability, or controls are in place to prevent, or at least significantly impede, the vulnerability from being exercised.
Medium	The threat source is motivated and capable, but controls are in place that may impede successful exercise of the vulnerability.
High	The threat source is highly motivated and sufficiently capable, and controls to prevent the vulnerability from being exercised are ineffective.

Table 6.13   Example 2 Likelihood Scale

Likelihood of Occurrence	Criteria
Negligible	Unlikely to occur
Very low	Likely to occur two/three times every five years
Low	Likely to occur once every year or less
Medium	Likely to occur once every six months or less
High	Likely to occur once per month or less
Very high	Likely to occur multiple times per month
Extreme	Likely to occur multiple times per day

6.9.2   Magnitude of Impact Scales

This section displays some common magnitude of impact scales that you may wish to use in your risk assessment efforts. Tables 6.14 and 6.15 represent both a simple and a more complex magnitude of impact scale.

6.9.3   Risk Matrixes

This section displays some common risk matrixes that you may wish to use in your risk assessment efforts. Tables 6.16 and 6.17 represent different complexities in risk matrixes.

Table 6.14   Example 1 Magnitude of Impact Scale

Magnitude of Impact	Criteria
Low	Exercise of the vulnerability (1) may result in the loss of some tangible assets or resources or (2) may noticeably affect an organization's mission, reputation, or interest.
Medium	Exercise of the vulnerability (1) may result in the costly loss of tangible assets or resources; (2) may violate, harm, or impede an organization's mission, reputation, or interest; or (3) may result in human injury.
High	Exercise of the vulnerability (1) may result in the highly costly loss of major tangible assets or resources; (2) may significantly violate, harm, or impede an organization's mission, reputation, or interest; or (3) may result in human death or serious injury.

Table 6.15   Example 2 Magnitude of Impact Scale

Magnitude of Impact	Criteria
Insignificant	Will have almost no impact if the threat occurs. Will result in minimal loss of functional integrity. Requires little or no recovery cost.
Minor	Will have some minor effect on the business function. Will not result in negative publicity or loss in confidence, but may cause minor financial loss. Will require only minimal effort to complete corrective actions and continue or resume operations.
Significant	Will result in some tangible harm, albeit negligible, and perhaps only realized by a few individuals or clients. May cause loss of confidence, negative publicity, and moderate financial loss. Will require a moderate expenditure of resources to repair.
Damaging	May cause damage to the reputation of the organization, or notable loss of confidence in the ability for the organization to complete its stated business mission. May result in legal liability, and will require significant expenditure of resources to complete corrective actions and restore operations.
Serious	May cause considerable disruption in the business function or loss of customer or business partner confidence. May result in compromise of large amount of confidential information or services, a substantial financial loss, and the failure to deliver organizational programs and services.
Critical	May cause an extended disruption in the business function, and may require recovery in an alternate site environment. May result in full compromise of the organization's ability to provide programs and services, and complete the stated business mission.

Table 6.16   Example 1 Risk Matrix

Likelihood of Occurrence	Magnitude of Impact		
	Low	Medium	High
Low	Low	Low	Low
Medium	Low	Low	Medium
High	Low	Medium	High

Table 6.17   Example 2 Risk Matrix

Likelihood of Occurrence	Magnitude of Impact					
	Insignificant	Minor	Significant	Damaging	Serious	Critical
Insignificant	Low	Low	Low	Low	Low	Low
Very low	Low	Low	Low	Low	Moderate	Moderate
Low	Low	Low	Moderate	Moderate	High	High
Medium	Low	Low	Moderate	High	High	High
High	Low	Moderate	High	High	High	High
Very high	Low	Moderate	High	High	High	High
Extreme	Low	Moderate	High	High	High	High

6.9.4   *Risk Assessment Reporting Template*

All risk assessment activities need to be documented. The following is a template that can be used to document risk assessment activities.

System Documentation

[This section is used to identify the name of the system and to provide the names and contact information of those individuals who are responsible for developing, testing, maintaining, and securing the system, as well as identifying the business owner of the system under development.]

System Purpose and Description

[Identify the assets utilized by the system and provide a complete and concise description of the function and purpose of the system and the organizational business processes supported, including functions and processing of data. Include all supported services, data flows, and databases, as well as functions and information processed.]

System Environment
[Provide a complete and concise technical description of the system. Discuss any environmental factors that raise special concerns and document the physical location of the system. Provide a network diagram or schematic to help identify, define, and clarify the system boundaries for the system, and a general description of the system.]

System Interconnections and Information Sharing
[Show how the various components and services of the application connected or interconnected to any other services or application(s) or other software interdependencies.]

System Sensitivity and Criticality
[Document the level of sensitivity of the data handled by the application, and the level of criticality associated with how the application supports the business mission of the organization.]

Risk Determination
[This portion of the risk assessment documentation will support the calculation of the level of risk for each threat–vulnerability pair based on: (1) the likelihood of a threat exploiting a vulnerability; and (2) the severity of impact that the exploited vulnerability would have on the system, its data, and its business function in terms of loss of confidentiality, loss of integrity, and loss of availability. Business impact to threat and vulnerability pairs should be mapped and listed in a table in order of highest risk to lowest risk. For each risk identified the following information should be supplied.]

Threat description

- Vulnerability description
- Threat action
- A list of existing controls that may partially or completely protect the risk
- Likelihood of occurrence
- Severity of impact
- Resulting risk level

A risk determination table might look something like the following in Table 6.18.

Table 6.18   Risk Determination Table

Threat Action	Existing Controls	Likelihood of Occurrence	Severity of Impact	Resulting Risk
Threat action statement one	List of controls that affect likelihood or impact	High	High	High
Threat action statement two	List of controls	Moderate	High	High
Threat action statement three	List of controls	Moderate	Moderate	Moderate
Threat action statement four	List of controls	Low	Moderate	Moderate
Threat action statement five	List of controls	Moderate	Low	Low
Threat action statement six	List of controls	Low	Low	Low

Safeguards Determination

[The safeguard determination portion of the document involves identification of additional safeguards to minimize the threat exposure and vulnerability exploitation for each threat–vulnerability pair identified in the risk determination portion. For each risk identified the following information should be supplied.]

- Threat action
- Recommended safeguard description
- Residual likelihood of occurrence if the additional safeguard would be implemented
- Residual severity of impact if the additional safeguard would be implemented
- Residual risk level if the additional safeguard would be implemented

Table 6.19 represents a typical safeguards determination table.

Implementation Analysis

[The implementation analysis is used to provide an implementation priority and rationale for any additional safeguards that are selected for implementation as a result of the safeguards determination. For each safeguard identified that will be implemented, the following information should be supplied.]

Table 6.19   Safeguards Determination Table

Threat Action	Recommended Safeguard	Residual Likelihood of Occurrence	Residual Severity of Impact	Residual Risk Level
Threat action statement one	Recommended safeguard one	Moderate	Moderate	Moderate
Threat action statement two	Recommended safeguard two	Low	Moderate	Moderate
Threat action statement three	Recommended safeguard three	Moderate	Low	Low
Threat action statement four	Recommended safeguard four	Low	Low	Low
Threat action statement five	Recommended safeguard five	Low	Low	Low
Threat action statement six	Recommended safeguard six	Low	Low	Low

- Threat description
- Vulnerability description
- Threat action
- List of existing controls
- Current level of risk
- Description of recommended safeguard
- Priority for implementing the safeguard
- Rationale for why the safeguard should be implemented and why it was given the priority it received

Table 6.20 represents a typical implementation analysis.

6.9.5 Alternate Risk Assessment Reporting Template

The previous section represented a simple and straightforward risk assessment template. This section provides a more detailed reporting template that may suit the needs of your organization more clearly. This template also includes more detailed examples of the types of information that might be found in a risk assessment report. It is also based upon a different methodology to provide you with a further example of how risk assessments may be approached and conducted.

Table 6.20   Implementation Table

Threat Action	Existing Controls	Current Level of Risk	Recommended Safeguard	Safeguard Priority	Safeguard Rationale
Threat action statement one	List of controls that affect likelihood or impact	High	Recommended safeguard one	High	Reasons why safeguard needs to be implemented right now
Threat action statement two	List of controls	High	Recommended safeguard two	High	Reasons why safeguard needs to be implemented right now
Threat action statement three	List of controls	Moderate	Recommended safeguard three	Medium	Reasons why safeguard needs to be implemented
Threat action statement four	List of controls	Moderate	Recommended safeguard four	Low	Reasons why safeguard can wait
Threat action statement five	List of controls	Low	Recommended safeguard five	Low	Reasons why safeguard can wait
Threat action statement six	List of controls	Low	Recommended safeguard six	Low	Reasons why safeguard can wait

6.10   Risk Assessment Summary

6.10.1   Overview

A risk assessment was conducted for [ORGANIZATION] using the [METHOD NAME] risk assessment methodology. The risk assessment was completed in [DATE].

The purpose of the risk assessment was to identify [ORGANIZATION] critical assets and create risk mitigation plans to protect the critical assets identified.

6.10.2 OCTAVE Risk Assessment Methodology

OCTAVE is a self-directed information security evaluation developed by Carnegie-Mellon University. OCTAVE is a risk management approach that focuses on understanding which information assets are important to meeting the mission of the organization and using that knowledge to prioritize risk mitigation actions.

OCTAVE uses a workshop-based analysis. A small group of people (an analysis team) leads the process and gathers information using workshops. The analysis team reviews and analyzes the information that has been gathered and creates mitigation plans.

The assessment is divided into three phases. Phase 1 workshops elicit knowledge from participants at various levels within the organization about critical assets, areas of concern, security requirements, and current protection strategy practices. This information is used to create threat profiles for each identified critical asset. Phase 2 is a technical vulnerability assessment. The critical assets identified in Phase 1 are examined for vulnerabilities using various scanning and vulnerability assessment tools. In Phase 3, the analysis team identifies and prioritizes risks to the organization. This prioritized list is then used to create a protection strategy for the organization.

Four workshops are held in Phase 1. Participants in the first workshop were members of the [ORGANIZATION] Leadership Team. The second workshop involved key operational area managers representing various programs throughout [ORGANIZATION]. The third workshop was for information technology staff and the fourth workshop in this phase involved staff members from various areas within [ORGANIZATION]. Attachment 1 contains a list of workshop participants and the names of the analysis team members.

6.10.3 Identified Assets

An asset is something of value to [ORGANIZATION]. Assets can fall into five categories. An information asset is documented (paper or electronic) information or intellectual assets. System assets are information systems that process and store information. Systems are a combination of information, software, and hardware assets. Software assets include software applications, operating systems, database applications, networking software, office applications, and custom applications. Hardware assets are IT physical devices such as workstations and servers. People assets include [ORGANIZATION] staff, including their skills, training, knowledge, and experience.

6.10.4 Critical Assets

The critical assets determined by the Leadership Team are listed below.

6.10.4.1 Critical Asset #1

[A description of the critical asset and the rationale behind why it was selected as a critical asset is described in this section.]

6.10.4.2 Critical Asset #2

[A description of the critical asset and the rationale behind why it was selected as a critical asset is described in this section.]

6.10.4.3 Critical Asset #3

[A description of the critical asset and the rationale behind why it was selected as a critical asset is described in this section.]

6.10.4.4 Critical Asset #4

[A description of the critical asset and the rationale behind why it was selected as a critical asset is described in this section.]

6.10.5 Vulnerability Assessment

The technical vulnerability assessment addresses the need within the risk assessment for an analysis of all workstations, servers, and other network mediums. The analysis of these devices focuses on actual vulnerabilities that have been identified as misconfigurations, operating system software defects, network holes, or other application vulnerabilities that compromise individual layers of security within a network environment.

Although it is necessary for a successful business to leave certain identified vulnerabilities unaddressed, the technical vulnerability assessment assists in identifying which issues are considered acceptable risk and which issues are not.

A technical report has been generated and provided to authorized personnel for their review. The report will be reviewed by IT personnel. Recommended mitigation actions for the identified vulnerabilities have been included in the risk mitigation plans for the critical assets.

6.10.6 Security Requirements

Security requirements outline the qualities of an asset that are important to protect. The following security requirements were examined.

- Confidentiality: the need to keep proprietary, sensitive, or personal information private and inaccessible to anyone who is not authorized to see it
- Integrity: the authenticity, accuracy, and completeness of an asset
- Availability: when or how often an asset must be present or ready for use

Security requirements were identified and prioritized for each critical asset. The security requirements types were refined by the Analysis Team from the original security requirements prioritized by the workshop participants. Security requirements for each critical asset are listed below in priority order.

6.10.6.1 Asset #1

- Integrity: [Describe the impact to the asset caused by system integrity problems. Example: Errors associated with data integrity for this asset could lead to potential cases of fraud.]
- Availability: [Describe the impact to the asset caused by system availability problems. Example: The system must be available 24/7, or the system must be operational 90% of the time.]
- Confidentiality: [Describe the impact to the asset caused by system confidentiality problems. Example: The system contains unique identifying information that must be protected from unauthorized access.]

6.10.6.2 Asset #2

- Integrity: [Example: The information stored on the system must be accurate or improper financial transactions will result.]
- Availability: [Example: The system must be available during regular business hours.]
- Confidentiality: [Example: The requirement for confidentiality of the information stored on the system is minimal because the information is available upon request.]

6.10.6.3 Asset #3

- Integrity: [Example: The system contains payroll information that must be protected from unauthorized modification.]
- Confidentiality: [Example: The system contains payroll information that must be kept confidential.]
- Availability: [Example: Normal business operations hours.]

6.10.6.4 Asset #4

- Availability: [Example: System should be available during normal business hours.]
- Integrity: [Example: System information must be accurate to ensure that payments are made correctly.]
- Confidentiality: [Example: System information must be protected from unauthorized access.]

6.10.7 Sources and Potential Impacts of Threats

A threat is any circumstance or event with the potential to harm an information system through unauthorized access, destruction, disclosure, modification of data, or denial of service. Threats to critical assets can come from both inside and outside sources. Motivation can be accidental or deliberate.

6.10.7.1 Sources of Threat

The sources of threats explored during the risk assessment were as follows:

- *Deliberate actions by people.* This group includes people both inside and outside the organization who might take deliberate action against critical assets.
- *Accidental actions by people.* This group includes people inside and outside the organization who might accidentally harm critical assets.
- *System problems.* These are problems with information technology systems. Examples include hardware defects, software defects, unavailability of related systems, viruses, malicious code, and other system-related problems.
- *Other problems.* These are problems that are outside the control of the organization. Other problems can include natural disasters (e.g., floods and earthquakes) that can affect IT systems, unavailability of systems maintained by other organizations, and interdependency issues. Interdependency issues include problems with infrastructure services, such as power outages, broken water pipes, and telecommunication outages.

6.10.7.2 Outcomes

The outcomes of threats typically fall into four categories:

- Disclosure or viewing of sensitive information
- Modification of important or sensitive information
- Destruction or loss of important information, hardware, or software
- Interruption of access to important information, software, applications, or services

Table 6.21 outlines the critical assets, the potential threats to those assets, and the impact of those threats.

Table 6.21   Sources of Threat and Potential Outcomes

Threat	Asset #1	Asset #2	Asset #3	Asset #4
Deliberate, inside, using network access	Disclosure Modification Destruction Interruption	Disclosure Modification Destruction Interruption	Disclosure Modification Destruction Interruption	Disclosure Modification
Deliberate, outside, using network access	Disclosure Modification Destruction Interruption	Disclosure Modification Destruction Interruption	Disclosure Modification Destruction Interruption	Disclosure Modification
Accidental, inside, using network access	Disclosure Modification Destruction Interruption	Modification Destruction Interruption	Disclosure Modification Destruction Interruption	Disclosure Modification
Accidental, outside, using network access	Disclosure Modification Destruction Interruption	Disclosure Modification Destruction	Disclosure Modification Destruction Interruption	
Deliberate, inside, using physical access	Disclosure Modification Destruction Interruption	Disclosure Modification Destruction Interruption	Disclosure Modification Destruction Interruption	Disclosure Modification
Deliberate, outside, using physical access	Disclosure Modification Destruction Interruption	Disclosure Modification Destruction Interruption	Disclosure Modification Destruction Interruption	Disclosure Modification Destruction Interruption
Accidental, inside, using physical access	Destruction Interruption	Disclosure Modification Destruction Interruption	Destruction Interruption	Disclosure Modification
Accidental, outside, using physical access		Disclosure Modification Destruction Interruption		
Software defects	Disclosure Modification Destruction Interruption	Disclosure Modification Destruction Interruption	Disclosure Modification Destruction Interruption	Interruption

—continued

Table 6.21   Sources of Threat and Potential Outcomes (continued)

Threat	Asset #1	Asset #2	Asset #3	Asset #4
Malicious software	Destruction Interruption	Destruction Interruption	Destruction Interruption	
System crashes	Destruction Interruption	Destruction Interruption	Destruction Interruption	
Hardware defects	Interruption	Destruction Interruption	Interruption	Interruption
Power supply problems	Interruption	Destruction Interruption	Destruction Interruption	Interruption
Telecom problems	Interruption			
Third-party problems	Modification Destruction Interruption	Modification Destruction Interruption	Modification Destruction Interruption	Interruption
Natural disasters	Interruption	Destruction Interruption	Interruption	Interruption

6.10.8 Impact Descriptions

The Analysis Team next looked at the possible outcomes of each threat, described what the potential impact of each threat would be to a particular critical asset and assigned it an impact value of high, medium, or low. Evaluation criteria were created by defining what constitutes a high, medium, or low impact for [ORGANIZATION] in five categories: reputation/client confidence, customer well-being, productivity, financial, loss of facilities, and loss of network functionality. The evaluation criteria were developed by the Analysis Team and reviewed by members of the [ORGANIZATION] Leadership Team. Evaluation criteria for each category are shown in Table 6.22.

6.10.8.1 High Impacts

Three outcomes of potential threats were considered to have a "high" impact on [ORGANIZATION] ability to continue critical business functions. The outcome of disclosure would have a high impact on both Asset #1 and Asset #4. Destruction or loss of information would have a high impact on the Asset #1 system.

6.10.8.2 Medium Impacts

Disclosure of information was considered to be medium impact threat to Asset #1 and Asset #2. Unauthorized modification of information creates a medium-to-

Table 6.22 Evaluation Criteria Examples

Impact Area	High	Medium	Low
Reputation/customer confidence	Calls received from compliance organizations regarding interruption of service.	Escalating calls to IT regarding interruption of service.	Minimal calls made to customer service repts regarding interruption of service.
	Failure to meet financial commitments (lease payments, vendor payments, payroll, etc.).	Delay of one week in meeting financial commitments.	Delay of less than one week in meeting financial commitments.
Customer well-being	Inability to report Asset #4 eligibility information for one week.	Inability to report Asset #4 eligibility information for 3–4 days.	Inability to report Asset #4 eligibility information for less than 3 days.
	Inability to pay benefits for one week.	Inability to pay benefits for less than 3 days.	Inability to pay benefits for less than 3 days.
Productivity	Unable to meet contractual or statutory obligations for 3 days.	Unable to meet contractual or statutory obligations for 2 days.	Unable to meet contractual or statutory obligations for 1 day.
	Mandatory overtime for employees.	Voluntary overtime for employees.	No overtime for employees.
Financial	Inability to draw down funds for more than 3 days.	Inability to draw down funds from the Federal government for 2 days.	Inability to draw down funds from the Federal government for 1 day.
	Loss of use of administrative office facilities.	Loss of use of major regional office facilities.	Loss of use of small remote facilities.
Other: Facilities	Damage to facilities requires relocation.	Damage to facilities requires partial shutdown.	Damage to facilities requires repair but no relocation or shutdown.
	Access to facility by unauthorized person with malicious intent.	Unauthorized person removed from facility without incident.	No unauthorized access.

high impact on the Asset #2 system and the Asset #3 system and creates a medium impact on Asset #1 and Asset #4.

Destruction or loss of information would create a medium impact on the Asset #2 system and a medium-to-high impact on the Asset #3 system. Interruption was considered to be a medium-to-high impact for Asset #3 and a medium threat to Asset #1 and Asset #4.

6.10.8.3 Low Impacts

The only impact considered to be low was the impact of interruption on the Asset #2 system.

6.10.9 Current Protection Strategies

The objective of a protection strategy is to provide a direction for future information security efforts rather than trying to find an immediate solution to every security vulnerability. Protection strategies include risk management plans, security policies and procedures, security awareness training, and business continuity planning.

Workshop participants were given a survey to fill out before the workshop. The survey included questions about current security practices within [ORGANIZA-TION]. Workshop participants were asked to circle "yes" if they knew the practice was in use by [ORGANIZATION], "no" if they knew the practice was not used by [ORGANIZATION], and "don't know" if they did not know if the practice was in use by [ORGANIZATION].

Each section of the survey was discussed by workshop participants and a determination was made as to whether there were security strategy practices in place or whether there were organizational vulnerabilities. This information was then used by the Analysis Team to formulate specific security protection strategies for [ORGANIZATION]. The protection strategies were divided into two categories, strategic practices and operational practices. Strategic practices address areas such as security awareness and training, security management, and security policy development. Operational practices address physical security, information technology security, and staff security.

Proposed protection strategies for strategic practices are outlined in Table 6.23. Proposed protection strategies for operational practices are in Table 6.24.

6.10.9.1 Impact Assessment and Risk Table

The risk table (Table 6.25) includes information about the risks determined for each system assessed. The risk level was determined by examining the impacts described above and reviewing the protection strategies that are already in place as well as

Table 6.23   Example Protection Strategies for Strategic Practices

Protection Strategies for Strategic Practices	
Security awareness and training	Comply with security policy training requirement.
	Make signing of the security statement part of initial training and refresher training. Consider using an electronic signature method.
	Incorporate completion of physical and information security training into the annual review process.
	Implement plan for regularly scheduled e-mails about security best practices from IT.
Security strategy	Continue to incorporate security considerations into business strategies.
Security management	Establish security team to make recommendations and provide input to management regarding security planning.
Security policies and regulations	Create a separate security manual online to make security policies more accessible to all staff and increase awareness.
Collaborative security management	Continue to review and update policies and procedures for protecting information when working with external organizations.
Contingency planning/ disaster recovery	Create and test disaster recovery plans.

Table 6.24   Example Protection Strategies for Operational Practices

Protection Strategies for Operational Practices	
Physical security	Review physical access to buildings and make recommendations for improvements including security cameras, key card system, new locks, etc.
	Develop a plan for enforcement of physical security.
Information technology security	Train management on IT security risks.
	Add enforcement of IT security policies to all management job descriptions.
Staff security	Document best practice security procedures in a separate online security manual.

organizational vulnerabilities to assist in determining the likelihood of occurrence. The following formula was used to determine the risk level.

$$\text{Risk Level} = \text{Likelihood of Occurrence} \times \text{Severity of Impact}$$

Threats types were derived from the threat trees created for each critical asset.

6.10.10 Risk Analysis

When examining the risk table, the level of risk to the physical security of systems and information is noticeable. One risk created by the threat of unauthorized physical access to systems or information was rated as high, six risks were rated as medium, and ten were ranked as low. Of the ten ranked as low risk, two would have high impacts to the organization if the threat were realized, two would have medium-high impacts, and six would have medium impacts. This would indicate that although the risk is low when occurrence likelihood is considered, there is potential for noticeable impact to the organization if one or more of these threats were realized. Therefore, every effort should be made to mitigate the risk of occurrence.

System problems created by the accidental or deliberate downloading of malicious software were ranked as medium risks. The outcome of these system problems is interruption, which has an impact level of medium-high for Asset #3 and medium for both Asset #1 and Asset #4.

Power outages were considered to have a medium risk level for Asset #3 and a low risk level for Asset #1 and Asset #4. Again, the impact to these systems of interruption of service needs to be considered along with the level of risk.

Disclosure and interruption were the two outcomes with the most critical impacts. These two outcomes were primarily associated with physical threats and system problems.

6.10.11 Risk Mitigation Plans

Risk mitigation plans are intended to reduce the risks to critical assets. The focus of mitigation plans is assets. Because all four of the critical assets are accessed from the same physical locations and have the same network connections, the plans to mitigate risk are very similar.

Additional recommended actions for mitigation of risks to technical systems are outlined in the Technical Vulnerability Assessment Report. This report is available to appropriate [ORGANIZATION] personnel upon request from the IT department.

6.10.12 Summary

The [METHOD NAME] risk assessment of [ORGANIZATION] critical information assets revealed that physical security and the prevention of system problems are the most crucial to the ongoing functions of the organization's business operations. Mitigation plans for reducing the level of impact and the likelihood of occurrence for these threats have been submitted as part of this report.

The protection strategies for strategic and operational practices stress the importance of ongoing training on security best practices and incorporating security factors in overall organizational planning. The re-establishment of a security team with representatives from each level in the organization would be instrumental in defining security responsibilities, reviewing policy and information security audits and assessments, as well as recommending appropriate actions for managing information security risk. Overall, management's support of security policy and procedure development and enforcement is critical to the management of information security risk.

Table 6.25   Risk Level Examples

Item No.	Critical Asset	Threat Type	Outcome	Risk Description	Existing Controls	Occurrence Likelihood	Impact Severity	Risk Level
1	#1 #4	Human actors using network access, accidental	Modification	Staff data entry errors such as incorrect values or misspellings can result in a compromise of data integrity.	Training Direct supervision	Low	Medium	Low
2	#2 #3	Human actors using network access, accidental	Modification	Staff data entry errors such as incorrect values or misspellings can result in a compromise of data integrity.	Training Direct supervision	Low	Medium-High	Low
3	#3	Human actors using network access, accidental	Interruption	Insertion of malicious code or software is the malicious intent to change a system's configuration without authorization by the addition or modification of software or information. Users who access unsafe Web sites or open e-mails with attachments from unknown sources may inadvertently download malicious software.	Signed security statement Training Anti-virus software	Medium	Medium-High	Medium

4	#1 #4	Signed security statement	Interruption	Insertion of malicious code or software is the malicious intent to change a system's configuration without authorization by the addition or modification of software or information. Users who access unsafe Web sites or open e-mails with attachments from unknown sources may inadvertently download malicious software.	Signed security statement Training Anti-virus software	Medium	Medium	Medium
5	#1 #4	Human actors using network access, deliberate	Modification	Impersonations are threats that often become enablers for other threats. Impersonation for electronic or system access could include use of others' identification and authentication. Could significantly affect data integrity.	Access control procedures Password policy Multiple passwords Basic security training Signed security statement ID badge system	Very Low	Medium	Low

(continued)

Table 6.25   Risk Level Examples (continued)

Item No.	Critical Asset	Threat Type	Outcome	Risk Description	Existing Controls	Occurrence Likelihood	Impact Severity	Risk Level
6	#2 #3	Human actors using network access, deliberate	Modification	Impersonations are threats that often become enablers for other threats. Impersonation for electronic or system access could include use of others' identification and authentication. Could significantly affect data integrity.	Access control procedures Password policy Multiple passwords Basic security training Signed security statement ID badge system	Very Low	Medium-High	Low
7	#2 #3	Human actors using network access, deliberate	Modification	Lack of sufficient tools for filtering and monitoring network traffic can result in intrusions into internal networks and systems.	Firewall Perimeter router Firewall and router logs	Low	Medium-High	Medium
8	#1 #4	Human actors using network access, deliberate	Modification	Lack of sufficient tools for filtering and monitoring network traffic can result in intrusions into internal networks and systems.	Firewall Perimeter router Firewall and router logs	Low	Medium	Low

9	#3 #4	Human actors using network access, deliberate	Disclosure	Unauthorized individuals may gain access to system resources. The intent could be malicious or nonmalicious (e.g., curiosity seeker) in nature. Could significantly affect data confidentiality.	Access control procedures Firewalls Multi-layer security	Very low	High	Low
10	#1 #2	Human actors using network access, deliberate	Disclosure	Unauthorized individuals may gain access to system resources. The intent could be malicious or nonmalicious (e.g., curiosity seeker) in nature. Could significantly affect data confidentiality, integrity, and availability.	Access control procedures	Very low	Medium-High	Low
11	#3	Human actors using network access, deliberate	Interruption	Unauthorized individuals may gain access to system resources. The intent could be malicious or nonmalicious (e.g., curiosity seeker) in nature. Could significantly affect data confidentiality.	Access control procedures Firewalls Multi-layer security	Very low	Medium-High	Low

(continued)

Table 6.25 Risk Level Examples (continued)

Item No.	Critical Asset	Threat Type	Outcome	Risk Description	Existing Controls	Occurrence Likelihood	Impact Severity	Risk Level
12	#1 #4	Human actors using network access, deliberate	Interruption	Unauthorized individuals may gain access to system resources. The intent could be malicious or nonmalicious (e.g., curiosity seeker) in nature. Could significantly affect data confidentiality, integrity, and availability.	Access control procedures	Very low	Medium	Low
13	#3 #4	Human actors using physical access, deliberate	Disclosure	Improper disposal or discarding of media including hard copies of documentation can result in compromise of sensitive information.	Shred bins Shredders	Medium	High	High
14	#1 #2	Human actors using physical access, deliberate	Disclosure	Improper disposal or discarding of media including hard copies of documentation can result in compromise of sensitive information.	Shred bins Shredders	Medium	Medium	Medium

| 15 | #3 | Interruption | Environmental conditions are controlled and noncontrolled factors that exist where systems are physically located. This includes climate control, safe and efficient placement of wiring and cabling, fire control equipment, etc. | Locked data center | Low | Medium-High | Medium |
| 16 | #1 #4 | Interruption | Environmental conditions are controlled and noncontrolled factors that exist where systems are physically located. This includes climate control, safe and efficient placement of wiring and cabling, fire control equipment, etc. | Locked data center | Low | Medium | Low |

(continued)

Table 6.25   Risk Level Examples   (continued)

Item No.	Critical Asset	Threat Type	Outcome	Risk Description	Existing Controls	Occurrence Likelihood	Impact Severity	Risk Level
17	#1 #2	Human actors using physical access, deliberate	Disclosure	Shoulder surfing is the deliberate attempt to gain knowledge of protected information from observation. Primarily affects data confidentiality, but in combination with other threats could affect integrity and availability.	Physical security procedures ID badge system Workstation locking procedures Training Password policy Multiple passwords Signed security statement	Low	Medium	Low
18	#3 #4	Human actors using physical access, deliberate	Disclosure	Shoulder surfing is the deliberate attempt to gain knowledge of protected information from observation. Primarily affects data confidentiality, but in combination with other threats could affect integrity and availability.	Physical security procedures ID badge system Workstation locking procedures Training Password policy Multiple passwords Signed security statement	Low	High	Medium

19	#1	Human actors using physical access, deliberate	Destruction or loss	Theft of equipment, destruction of resources, or intrusions that include penetrating system security could result in data loss. Could significantly affect data integrity and availability, and to a lesser extent data confidentiality.	Physical security procedures Document destruction service ID badge system	Very Low	High	Low
20	#2	Human actors using physical access, deliberate	Destruction or loss	Theft of equipment, destruction of resources, or intrusions that include penetrating system security could result in data loss. Could significantly affect data integrity and availability, and to a lesser extent data confidentiality.	Physical security procedures Document destruction service ID badge system	Very Low	Medium	Low

(continued)

Table 6.25   Risk Level Examples (continued)

Item No.	Critical Asset	Threat Type	Outcome	Risk Description	Existing Controls	Occurrence Likelihood	Impact Severity	Risk Level
21	#3	Human actors using physical access, deliberate	Destruction or loss	Theft of equipment, destruction of resources, or intrusions that include penetrating system security could result in data loss. Could significantly affect data integrity and availability, and to a lesser extent data confidentiality. Theft of equipment or destruction of data could disrupt operations.	Physical security procedures Document destruction service ID badge system	Very Low	Medium-High	Low
22	#3	Human actors using physical access, deliberate	Interruption	Theft of equipment or destruction of data could disrupt operations.	Physical security procedures Document destruction service ID badge system	Very Low	Medium-High	Low
23	#1 #4	Human actors using physical access, deliberate	Interruption	Theft of equipment or destruction of data could disrupt operations.	Physical security procedures Document destruction service ID badge system	Very Low	Medium	Low

24	#3 #4	Human actors using physical access, deliberate	Disclosure	Physical security and environmental security are the measures taken to protect systems, buildings, and related supporting infrastructures against threats associated with their physical environment. Primarily affects the confidentiality of the data in the system. Also affects business operations.	ID badge system Physical security procedures Visitor sign-in procedures	Low	High	Medium
25	#1 #2	Human actors using physical access, deliberate	Disclosure	Physical security and environmental security are the measures taken to protect systems, buildings, and related supporting infrastructures against threats associated with their physical environment. Primarily affects the confidentiality of the data in the system. Also affects business operations.	ID badge system Physical security procedures Visitor sign-in procedures	Low	Medium	Low

(continued)

Table 6.25 Risk Level Examples (continued)

Item No.	Critical Asset	Threat Type	Outcome	Risk Description	Existing Controls	Occurrence Likelihood	Impact Severity	Risk Level
26	#3	System problems	Interruption	Insertion of malicious code or software is the malicious intent to change a system's configuration without authorization by the addition or modification of software or information. Users who access unsafe Web sites or open emails with attachments from unknown sources may inadvertently download malicious software.	Signed security statement Training	Medium	Medium-High	Medium

27	#1 #4	System problems	Interruption	Insertion of malicious code or software is the malicious intent to change a system's configuration without authorization by the addition or modification of software or information. Users who access unsafe Web sites or open emails with attachments from unknown sources may inadvertently download malicious software.	Signed security statement Training	Medium	Medium	Low
28	#3	Other problems: power outage	Interruption	Primarily affects the availability of the system	Backup power generation for east wing of 1000 E. Grand building Contingency plan	Low	Medium-High	Medium
29	#1 #4	Other problems: power outage	Interruption	Primarily affects the availability of the system	Backup power generation for east wing of 1000 E. Grand building Contingency plan	Low	Medium	Low

Chapter 7

Managing Security Risks

Over the course of the past four chapters a detective story of sorts has unfolded. This story has focused on a number of distinct elements typically associated with a crime or investigative story. As the story opened, the focus was on the crime itself—or at least in determining what the principal target of the perpetrated was—the object of value (or asset) that the criminal wanted to steal, alter, disclose, or destroy. Next, the focus shifted to the "criminal" (or threat source) that caused the crime. After going through the list of "usual suspects," a number of strategies were considered in how to identify our threat sources, along with their motivation and opportunities.

Next, the means (or vulnerabilities), those weaknesses in the protections that are designed to deter criminals, became the focus of the investigation. We discovered that vulnerabilities provide the avenue of attack that the threat source uses to steal, alter, disclose, or destroy our assets. We also learned that although there are many technical vulnerabilities associated with software development efforts, there are also nontechnical vulnerabilities including weaknesses in physical and administrative safeguards that can affect software development. We also learned that much like a crime lab, discovering vulnerabilities can require tests of numerous types in order to be discovered.

Finally, the detective story came to an end when we put all of the facts together, the object of the criminal (asset), who the criminal is (threat source), and the means (vulnerabilities) the criminal used to carry out his crime. This is where our investigation began to diverge from the true detective story, because we found that we are faced with more than one asset to protect, there are a number of potential threat sources that could affect our assets, and several vulnerabilities that provide the opportunity for the threat sources to attack the assets. We learned how to pair threat sources with vulnerabilities and come up with threat actions which are descriptive statements of how the crime could occur. We then developed subjective scales for both the likelihood that the threat action would occur, and the impact upon our organization if the threat action should occur. Finally, we developed a level of "risk" based upon the likelihood of occurrence and magnitude of impact the threat action might have.

Determining what potential risks exist in a software development effort represents just half of the story. Unlike the detective novel where the story ends when the case is solved, our story continues. Our risk analysis is complete, but risk management is just beginning. Unlike the detective novel where the goal was to solve the crime, our goal is to prevent the crime from occurring in the first place! This is the process of risk mitigation and risk management.

7.1   Definitions

Risk management is the process of managing uncertainty through the assessment of risks and developing strategies to manage and reduce risk. *Risk mitigation* represents the process of developing a strategy to deal with risk. Chapters 2 through 6 of this book were dedicated to the process of risk assessment. In this chapter, the focus is on risk mitigation. The inputs and outputs of the risk mitigation step of the risk management process are shown in Figure 7.1.

7.2   Risk Mitigation Strategies

There are four primary strategies for mitigating risks: assumption, avoidance, limitation, and transference. Not all of these strategies may be available in all situations. These strategies often involve trade-offs that may not be acceptable to management. Other strategies may not be possible due to the resources required in order to pursue the particular mitigation strategy. At times it may not be possible to avoid risks at all, due to political or other situations. However, before a potential strategy can be rejected it must first be considered.

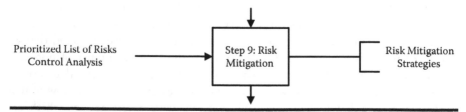

FIGURE 7.1   Inputs and outputs associated with risk mitigation

7.2.1   Risk Assumption

The first risk mitigation strategy is *risk assumption.* True self-insurance is an example of risk assumption. With risk assumption, an organization assumes the responsibility for the risk, and accepts any consequences associated with the threat action. In some instances, such as with projects for government agencies, in particular the Department of Defense, risk assumption may not be a possible strategy, particularly for high and moderate risks. However, for many other organizations, risk assumption is a valid strategy. For example, some state and local government agencies may place the ability to provide services to its constituency above the potential risk associated with allowing visitors open access to facilities, where they could potentially observe sensitive information.

Other organizations may decide to assume risk because the cost of the potential safeguards or controls necessary to reduce a risk may be more costly than the magnitude of impact caused by a threat action. An example of this might be a situation such as the following. Let's assume that an organization maintains all of its data on mainframe hardware. The cost of this hardware has been fully depreciated. All of the organization's applications are Web-based applications that retrieve data from the mainframe hardware through a gateway. The threat action in this instance is data becoming corrupted when passing through the gateway due to the increasing age of the mainframe hardware and gateway. Additional manual checks of data are required when these instances are recorded. However, the cost associated with making these manual checks is less than it would take to replace the aging hardware, and also modifying all of the legacy code from the applications that utilize the gateway to retrieve data.

Finally, some organizations may decide to assume risk simply because they can afford the potential loss associated with the risk. Many organizations choose to assume the potential risk associated with those risks rated low on a scale of high, medium, and low for various reasons including: lack of resources to eliminate or reduce all risk, the cost to eliminate the risk is greater than the magnitude of risk, or the potential drawbacks (e.g., a reduction in customer service) associated with the elimination of risk.

7.2.2   Risk Transference

Risk transference is the strategy of transferring the responsibility for the impact associated with a risk to another organization. Insurance is a prime example of risk transference. Most organizations deal with environmental threats (fire, HVAC failure, power failure, etc.) or natural threats (tornadoes, floods, hurricanes, etc.) by purchasing insurance to cover the physical losses associated with these threats. However, when selecting such a strategy, it is also necessary to consider not only the cost of repairing and replacing physical assets, but also to consider the costs of business continuity and disaster recovery should enough damage be caused to require a relocation, or significant downtime required to repair the damage caused by such a disaster.

Another method of risk transference that is seeing increased use in the IT field is the use of managed services. Managed services are a process whereby organizations turn over the day-to-day management responsibilities for a particular system to another organization. Managed services are popular for numerous different IT services including, but not limited to:

- Intrusion detection and intrusion prevention services
- Data backup and storage
- Network management
- User management
- E-mail services
- Data encryption
- Communications
- Business continuity and disaster recovery services

Organizations utilizing managed services often do so to gain improved efficiencies, reduced costs, or simply to obtain expertise that the current organization doesn't have. Managed services can provide cost-effective and efficient solutions for software development programs. Take, for example, a health insurance Web site that wants to add a feature which allows the members of the health insurance plans the opportunity to ask questions to a registered nurse, doctor, or pharmacist. The nature of these questions may require that certain confidential medical information be shared in the question. The health insurance organization has a secure e-mail system. However, its customers, who will ask the questions, do not. Therefore, the health insurance organization can choose to build a custom application in order to allow clients the ability to communicate with them securely. Or the health insurance organization could hire a managed service to provide the ability for customers to communicate securely, often at a price that is lower than the custom application could be built, and certainly have a solution in place more quickly.

Organizations can also choose to internally transfer the risk to other departments within the organization, or to other agencies within a government. For example, many state government agencies that share physical space in a building may also share a data center together. Although each agency or department may have its own segregated space within the data center, the overall responsibility for the physical security associated with that data center, as well as the environmental security associated with the data center, may be transferred to another organization or agency.

Another example of internal risk transfer is when one department or agency within an organization has developed an expertise that the other departments or agencies within the organization have not had the time or resources necessary to develop on their own. For example, because business continuity and disaster recovery planning and testing is a very specialized field that often requires considerable resources, some of the larger departments within an organization might have business continuity and disaster recovery plans, but the smaller departments may not have the expertise or resources required to develop their own plans. In this instance, the smaller departments may transfer the internal risk of developing such plans to the larger departments who have the expertise required.

7.2.3   Risk Avoidance

Risk avoidance is the strategy of eliminating the risk completely. Although risk avoidance is often the most secure strategy, because risk is completely eliminated, it may only be possible through the deployment of additional controls and safeguards that may cost more than the assets they protect, or by eliminating a product or service.

As an example, let's look at a small government agency that has recently begun taking credit card payments for the permits it issues, via a Web application that allows the public to apply and pay for permits online. This process has allowed the agency to cut back on the personnel hours at some of its regional offices, because the public no longer has to pay for permits in person, but can do so over the Web. Because the agency began taking credit cards for payment, the Payment Card Industry (PCI) Data Security Standard (DSS) version 1.1 applies to that agency. This new standard requires that the agency must protect its Web application by either code reviews, or an application firewall. The risk is that if the agency does nothing, and has a breach of its Web application that accepts credit card applications, then it may have to pay a large fine, and may also no longer be able to accept credit card payments for the permits. However, it may not be able to afford the application firewall or the cost of the code reviews. Therefore in order to eliminate the risk completely, the organization may be faced either with costly controls (application firewall or code reviews) which may cost more than the fine would be, or it may be forced to drop the service of having the public pay for the permits over the Internet altogether.

In some instances, for example, when dealing with risks that may affect national security, or when dealing with risks that may cause significant bodily harm or even death, then there may be no alternative other than to completely eliminate the risk. Take, for example, software that controls or assists in controlling such actions as:

- Air traffic control
- Railroad routing and switching
- Electrical power grids and power routing
- Municipal water supplies and dams
- Autopilots for ships or aircraft
- Petroleum or petrochemical pipelines or refineries
- Guidance systems for missiles

If any of these types of system or software controlling such a system had risks associated with them, risk avoidance may be the best bet in order to avoid the potentially dangerous consequences of not eliminating the risk completely. However, it is not always possible to completely eliminate risk, short of dropping a product or service altogether. In these instances, risk limitation may be the only acceptable choice.

7.2.4   Risk Limitation

Risk limitation is the strategy of applying additional controls and safeguards in order to reduce the amount of risk to an acceptable level. By applying additional controls, one may be able to reduce a risk from high to moderate or even low, by reducing either the frequency of occurrence of the threat action, the magnitude of impact the threat action may have, or both. Let's go back to our detective story analogy. A burglar alarm or a dog may make it less likely that someone would break into the house, or that if someone did break into the house, make it less likely that that individual would have the time to truly search for the assets and still get away. If we add a safe to put the assets in, cameras to record any activity, and outdoor lights with a motion sensor, then we are even less likely to suffer an adverse break-in. The same is true for information technology systems. The more difficult it becomes for someone to hack a system, and the less likely that when the individual does hack the system that anything will be accomplished, then the less likely an attacker is to even try. This is the essence of risk limitation. However, in applying risk limitation the following guidelines should still be applied.

- The cost of a safeguard should never be greater than the amount of damage that can be applied to the asset(s) the safeguard is protecting.
- The earlier in the software development life cycle that the additional safeguards can be applied, the cheaper those safeguards will cost to implement.

As an example of a risk limitation, consider the following situation. An e-commerce site has been found to be vulnerable to SQL injection vulnerabilities, especially when coupled with information leakage vulnerabilities through the site's error-handling routine; that is, an attacker gains knowledge of the system through the SQL injection error, which is displayed to the attacker in the form of an error message. The associated risk with this situation is high because of a high magnitude of impact and a high likelihood of occurrence because similar attacks have been launched on the e-commerce site in the past year. Elimination of the risk would require extensive coding changes to the application. If the resources necessary to make and test the coding changes were not available due to other priorities, risk elimination may not be possible.

However, it may be possible to reduce the impact of the threat by applying an application firewall on the database and monitoring this firewall for suspicious activity at the database level. When the suspicious activity is detected, then the database can be isolated or cut off from the e-commerce application, or at least the activity that is suspect. In this instance, the vulnerability hasn't been changed at all: the SQL injection vulnerability still exists. Nor has the likelihood of occurrence changed. However, the magnitude of impact has changed, because the suspicious activity may be halted before any significant damage is done to the database. This will change the risk level to moderate or even low, depending upon how good the monitoring solution is, and how quickly the attacker can be isolated and cut off from the attack.

However, if the cost of the application firewall and monitoring is greater than the damage an attacker could cause to the database, then another solution for limiting the risk associated with the SQL injection should be considered. For a moment, let's assume that this is the case. Therefore we must consider other risk limitation strategies. Let's also assume that some programming resources are available. These programming assets aren't trained how to prevent SQL injection. However, they do have the knowledge to change the error-handling routine so that it does not reveal any information when an error occurs. In this instance, the SQL injection vulnerability still exists, but we have limited the information an attacker can gather from the SQL injection vulnerability by eliminating the associated information leakage vulnerability.

Risk assumption, risk transference, risk avoidance, and risk limitation are all valid strategies for mitigating risk. All have their strong points and weak points to recommend them. Typically, most risk mitigation plans will utilize more than one of these strategies. It may be possible to avoid some low risks by adopting additional controls and safeguards. It may also be possible to limit high and moderate risks, changing them to low risks by changing the likelihood of occurrence, the magnitude of impact, or both. Some risks may be transferable to others using managed services or the services of other departments within an organization. And it may also be necessary to assume some risks, simply because there is no cost-effective method of eliminating, limiting, or transferring the risk without discontinuing a product or service. Let's look at how some of these risk mitigation strategies can be applied to our test case.

7.3   Protection Strategies

Protection strategies are long-term initiatives that an organization may use to increase its long-term security posture. They are not the same as a risk mitigation plan, yet they are often created or at least updated at the same time because they require the same types of thinking. Both focus on providing increased security protections and mitigating risk. The primary difference is that a risk mitigation plan is tactical in nature: that is, what can be done to reduce the effectiveness of current threats, where a protection strategy is strategic in nature; that is, how can we increase the overall security posture of an organization within the software development life cycle.

In a risk mitigation plan, the focus is on how to eliminate or reduce a specific threat. First, a question is posed that describes what we want to accomplish. Then an action plan is developed to answer that question. Take a look at the following examples.

Question: How can we prevent an attacker from exploiting the SQL injection vulnerability?
Action Plan: Implement strong input validation against a white-list.
Question: How do we prevent an attacker from exploiting the Reflective XSS vulnerability?
Action Plan: Implement strong output validation against a white-list.

The protection strategy works much the same way, except that the questions are strategic in nature. For example:

Question: How can we ensure that the custom applications our organization develops are more secure?
Action Plan: Implement security risk management practices throughout the software development life cycle.
Question: Are security issues incorporated into our organization's business strategy? What can we do to improve the way security issues are integrated into our organization's business strategy?
Action Plan: Make sure that information security becomes part of the requirements analysis for avll new projects. Implement a training and awareness program designed to highlight how information security can integrate with business strategies.

The types of protection strategies adopted will depend upon the specific organization and its business needs. Business needs should drive all protection strategies. Some further examples of protection strategies include the following:

■ Update individual training plans and communicate to all personnel.
■ Periodically update training; conduct refresher courses.
■ Ensure compliance by requiring sign-off after completing training.
■ Provide additional technical training for all personnel.
■ Increase education and awareness of security issues as part of initial planning and decision making.
■ Background checks should be required for specific classes of employees, particularly those with access to sensitive information and those who have financial responsibilities.
■ Establish positions with specific responsibilities and authority for setting security strategy.

- Review and update existing security policies.
- Document procedures for creating, updating, and communicating security policies.
- Implement annual security reviews.
- Create business associate agreement with security requirements and have the agreement signed by appropriate managed service providers.
- Update current disaster recovery and contingency plans.
- Communicate plans to employees.
- Conduct training on disaster recovery and contingency plans.
- Technical staff should receive periodic training in security best practices.
- Position(s) responsible for information security should be clearly defined.

7.4 Mitigating Risks in the Test Case

Recall from the previous chapter that we identified seven distinct risks, one high risk, four moderate risks, and two low risks. The high risk was:

- A developer programs a backdoor into an application allowing access to the application and its data.

The moderate risks included:

- Sensitive information can be disclosed to unauthorized individuals by reading the error log files.
- An inside employee who had obtained the authentication credentials of another employee could view sensitive information in the application.
- An incorrect calculation could result from data contamination caused by a failure of the mainframe service.
- Unauthorized attempts to gain access to certain plans are not detected.

And low risks identified were:

- The retirement plan administrator could erroneously enter a buffer overflow causing the application to crash.
- A programmer could inadvertently allow injection flaws or information leakage that would reveal information to an unauthorized user.

Typically, when considering risk mitigation strategies, high risks are mitigated first, because of their potential for greater impact upon the organization, and also because oftentimes some of the additional safeguards and controls considered for the high risk items will also affect the likelihood of occurrence or magnitude of impact for some of the lower risk items. For example, requiring peer reviews could reduce the likelihood of occurrence and the magnitude of impact for the backdoor programmed into our test case. Code and peer reviews would also make it much more likely that injection flaws and information leakage flaws would be caught before such code was implemented.

The detection of backdoors is not easy, especially in an application that may have hundreds of thousands, or even millions of lines of code. There are some code scanning software packages that can detect some forms of backdoors. But even the best of these software packages will not detect each and every instance of a backdoor. The best methods of detecting backdoors are code and peer reviews conducted as each module of code is written, along with code source control software and configuration management processes designed to compare versions of code.

For the test case, the organization did require the use of code source control software, but it was not monitored closely. As a direct result, a backdoor was programmed into the application in question and remained undetected for some time until it was uncovered during the testing for a bug that affected the calculations within the application. As a direct result of this incident (and others like it), code and peer reviews were instituted for all new code, and the source code control software was monitored. This will change the likelihood of occurrence from high to medium because the controls are now more effective. It will also change the likelihood of impact from critical to moderate because the types of backdoors that can now be programmed will be less devastating than previously. Therefore, the risk level is limited to moderate. As a direct result of these changes, the likelihood of occurrence for the risk associated with injection flaws or information leakage is also reduced from high to low.

The moderate risk associated with the error log files may also be limited. It was not possible to change the settings on the error log file to restrict its access. However, a process was developed that moved the error log files to a secure location at the end of each day. In this manner, the likelihood of occurrence was reduced from medium to low because the controls became more effective in preventing the user from viewing sensitive data that may have been in the log file. The overall risk level was reduced to low because our risk matrix associates a low risk when a threat action has a low likelihood of occurrence and a moderate level of impact.

It was decided to accept the risk associated with an inside employee gaining the log-in credentials of another employee for a number of reasons. First, employees were required to change their passwords every 30 days, so that the risk would only exist for a 30-day window at best. Second, only PCs within the retirement plan administration department would have the access to the application; it wouldn't be available from a PC elsewhere in the company, even with stolen log-in credentials. Finally, the open floor plan of the retirement plan administration department made it unlikely that a strange individual could sit down at a PC in the department without being challenged by someone, at least during regular business hours.

The data contamination that could occur when the mainframe service suffered an error can be eliminated. By passing an error message to the application from the mainframe service whenever anything went wrong with the mainframe service, the application would know when potential data contamination occurred. The application was programmed to attempt to request a fresh set of data from the mainframe service when this occurred. If three or more errors of the mainframe service occurred in a row, the application would inform the user that the mainframe service was unavailable, and to report the situation to the help desk for resolution. In this instance, the likelihood that the data would be corrupt was completely eliminated, thus eliminating the risk altogether.

The risk associated with unauthorized attempts to gain access to certain retirement plans was caused by the authentication service. The authentication service required three pieces of information, user ID, password, and a plan ID. If the user ID and password were valid, but the plan ID was not valid (i.e., the user was not authorized to see the information for the plan ID provided) then the authentication service would not return an error. The user would not be allowed to continue, but no error would be provided to the user, nor would an entry be made in an error or access log. In this case, the risk was transferred to the management of the retirement plan administration area. When the application was informed that the user ID and password were not authorized for the plan ID provided, an e-mail was generated by the application and sent to a management mailbox in the retirement plan administration area. The e-mail provided the details of the user who was attempting to access unauthorized information, which plan that user was attempting to view, and the date and time of the attempt. It then became the responsibility of the retirement plan administration management staff to investigate the unauthorized access attempt and take any appropriate action.

Finally, the risk associated with buffer overflows was eliminated. Although this buffer overflow problem had little impact upon the organization, future plans called for the application to be made available to customer service representatives so that they could initiate their own calculations (rather than require the retirement plan administrator). This would have changed both the likelihood of occurrence and the magnitude of impact for this risk. Therefore, the risk was eliminated by enforcing strict input validation rules on all input fields.

7.5 Conclusion

Our detective story has changed from one of crime detection to that of crime prevention. Risk management is the process of managing the day-to-day uncertainties of any operation by assessing and mitigating risks. Up until this chapter, the focus was on the process of risk assessment, or the detection of those uncertainties that may affect the day-to-day operations of any organization. In this chapter, our focus switched to the second part of risk management, that of risk mitigation: strategies for reducing or eliminating risk. A number of different strategies were discussed for mitigating risk including: risk acceptance, risk transference, risk avoidance, and risk limitation. All of these are valid strategies for reducing or eliminating the risk associated with software development. Any given risk mitigation process will involve the employment of at least one, if not several of these strategies.

7.6 Risk Mitigation Checklists

The following checklist may be helpful in determining a risk mitigation strategy. Each risk should be considered separately when determining a risk mitigation strategy, beginning with the highest level of risk first.

☐ Risk Mitigation Strategies
    ☐ *Risk Acceptance.* No action is taken to mitigate risks. Risk assumption may be considered when:
        ☐ The organization is self-insured.
        ☐ The level of risk is relatively low, particularly the magnitude of impact associated with the risk.
        ☐ The cost of additional safeguards or controls to reduce or eliminate the risk any further is greater than the cost caused by the threat action.
        ☐ The organization is forced to accept the risk due to a political or managerial decision.
        ☐ The organization would be forced to discontinue a product or service in order to eliminate or reduce the risk.
    ☐ *Risk Transference.* The responsibility for the impact associated with the risk is transferred to another organization or entity. The impact associated with the risk is typically transferred through written agreements with:
        ☐ Insurance agencies
        ☐ Managed services
        ☐ Other departments, individuals, or agencies within an organization
    ☐ Risk transference should only be considered when:
        ☐ The cost of the risk transference (i.e., the cost of insurance, managed services, or departmental chargeback) is less than the cost of the impact associated with a threat action.
        ☐ The transference of risk does not create additional risk. (For example: using managed services often may expose data and systems to other organizations. In the case of a shared data center, controls must be in place to ensure that employees from various organizations only have access to their own data and systems stored within the shared data center.)
    ☐ *Risk Avoidance.* Risks are avoided by:
        ☐ Dropping products or services associated with the risk.
        ☐ Eliminating the risk either by completely eliminating the vulnerability, or by implementing additional safeguards which reduce the

likelihood of occurrence of the threat action, reduce the magnitude of impact of the threat action or both to zero.

☐ Risk avoidance should be considered when:

☐ The associated risk could result in the bodily injury or death of an individual or individual(s).

☐ *Risk Limitation.* The likelihood of occurrence for a threat action, or the magnitude of impact for a threat action are reduced through the adoption of additional controls and safeguards. This reduces the level of risk to a point where the residual risk may be accepted. Risk limitation may be considered when:

☐ The cost of the additional safeguards and controls are not greater than the cost of the impact associated with a threat action.

☐ Any remaining residual risk will be acceptable to the organization.

7.7 Risk Mitigation Reporting Template

Whatever risk mitigation strategy is selected, it is important to document the decisions that were associated in selecting the strategy. This will provide evidence that due diligence was performed. Typically a documentation of risk mitigation strategies will include the following.

7.7.1 Risk Mitigation Documentation

[Documenting risk mitigation efforts describe how risk mitigation activities will be carried out and the decisions associated with risk mitigation. Through risk mitigation, the organization will prioritize, evaluate, and implement appropriate risk-reducing controls recommended from the risk assessment process. An example of risk mitigation documentation is found below.]

The elimination of all risk is usually impractical or close to impossible. Therefore, it is the responsibility of the organization's senior management and functional and business managers to use the least-cost approach and implement the most appropriate controls to decrease mission risk to an acceptable level, with minimal adverse impact on the organization's resources and mission.

7.7.2 Risk Mitigation Options

Risk mitigation is a systematic methodology used by the organization's senior management to reduce mission risk. The organization will achieve risk mitigation through any of the following risk mitigation options:

- *Risk Assumption*. Accepting potential risk and continue operating IT system(s) or implementing controls to lower the risk to an acceptable level.
- *Risk Avoidance*. Avoiding the risk by eliminating the risk cause or consequence (e.g., forgo certain functions of a system or shut down the system when risks are identified).
- *Risk Limitation*. Limiting the risk by implementing controls that minimize the adverse impact of a threat's exercising a vulnerability (e.g., use of supporting, preventive, or detective controls).
- *Risk Transference*. Transferring the risk by using other options to compensate for the loss, such as purchasing insurance.

The organization's goals and mission shall be considered in selecting any of these risk mitigation options. Because it may not be practical to address all identified risks, the organization shall give priority to the threat and vulnerability pairs that have the potential to cause significant mission impact or harm. Because the organization has a unique environment and objectives, the option used to mitigate the risk and the methods used to implement controls may vary. The organization will use the "best of breed" approach by selectively using appropriate technologies from among various security products, along with the appropriate risk mitigation option and nontechnical administrative measures.

7.7.3 Risk Mitigation Strategy

As a general guideline, the organization will provide implementation of control actions at appropriate points in the SDLC using the following guidelines:

- When a vulnerability (or flaw/weakness) exists. The organization will implement appropriate assurance techniques to reduce the likelihood of the vulnerability being exercised.
- When a vulnerability can be exercised. The organization will apply layered protections, architectural designs, and administrative controls as appropriate, to minimize the risk of, or prevent, the vulnerability being exercised.
- When the attacker's cost is less than the potential gain. An attacker represents someone or something intentionally attempting to violate the security of an asset. The organization will apply appropriate protections to decrease an attacker's motivation by increasing the attacker's cost. For example, by applying system controls to limit what a system user can access and accomplish, the organization could significantly reduce a potential attacker's gain.
- When a potential loss would be too great. The organization will apply appropriate design principles, architectural designs, and technical and nontechnical protections to limit the extent of the attack, thereby reducing the potential for loss.

7.7.4 Control Implementation Approach

When control actions must be taken, the organization will address the greatest risks and strive for sufficient risk mitigation at the lowest cost, with minimal impact on other mission capabilities. The organization will use the following risk mitigation methodology when implementing controls:

- Step 1: Prioritize actions. Based on the risk levels presented in the risk assessment report, the implementation actions will be prioritized. In allocating resources, top priority will be given to risk items with unacceptably high risk rankings. These vulnerability–threat pairs will require immediate corrective action to protect the organization's interests and mission.
- Step 2: Evaluate recommended control options. The organization will analyze the feasibility (e.g., compatibility, user acceptance) and effectiveness (e.g., degree of protection and level of risk mitigation) of the recommended control options. The organization will then adopt the most appropriate control option for minimizing risk.
- Step 3: Conduct cost-benefit analysis. The organization will conduct a cost-benefit analysis to aid management in decision making and to identify cost-effective controls.
- Step 4: Select controls. On the basis of the results of the cost-benefit analysis, management shall determine the most cost-effective control(s) for reducing risk to the organization's mission. The controls selected should combine technical, operational, and management control elements to ensure adequate security for the system and the organization.
- Step 5: Assign responsibility. Appropriate persons who have the appropriate expertise and skillsets to implement the selected control will be identified, and responsibility will be assigned.
- Step 6: Develop an action plan. At a minimum, the plan shall contain:
  - Risks (vulnerability–threat pairs) and associated risk levels
  - Recommended controls
  - Prioritized action list
  - Selected planned controls based upon the results of the cost-benefit analysis
  - Required resources for implementing the selected controls
  - Lists of responsible teams and staff
  - Start date for implementation
  - Target completion date for implementation
  - Maintenance requirements
- Step 7: Implement selected controls. Depending upon individual situations, the implemented controls may only reduce the risk, instead of eliminating it. These reduced risks shall be documented for auditing purposes.

Chapter 8

Risk Assessment and Risk Mitigation Activities in the SDLC

Software development is a constant balancing act among functional requirements, business drivers, deadlines, limited resources, risk, and flexibility. This balancing act is governed by the Software Development Life Cycle (SDLC) methodology selected for the software development effort. Unfortunately, many of the SDLC methodologies in use today do not recognize security as a functional requirement that must be a part of any development effort. The following major SDLCs do not have a concrete notion of security:

- Waterfall
- Incremental Build
- Spiral
- Rational Unified Process (RUP)
- Extreme Programming (XP)

Within these SDLC methodologies, security is treated as just one more non-functional requirement. And experience has taught that nonfunctional requirements are often the first thing to go in the face of budget cuts, scarce resources, and tighter schedules. Eliminating security controls from a software development effort will increase the risks associated with that software development project.

Regardless of the SDLC methodology an organization selects, there are a number of common steps or phases that can be identified. And within each of these steps, there are risk assessment or risk mitigation activities that can be conducted. The following sections describe risk management activities that are appropriate for the SDLC phases of:

- Requirements gathering and analysis
- Design
- Development
- Test
- Implementation/maintenance

Figure 8.1 is a graphical representation of risk management activities and how they fit into the phases of the SDLC.

There are several general rules that can be applied to any step in the risk management process. First and foremost, make sure that all risk management activities follow the quality assurance principles, rules, and guidelines of the organization. Quality assurance should be the foundation for any process within an organization. Quality does not happen by accident. Rather it comes from following standards and processes which ensure that all documentation and deliverables follow a well-defined process that allows for oversight. This oversight must come from multiple levels within an organization, and at multiple points within a life cycle. Second, all information, activities, requirements, and decisions should be thoroughly documented. The history of why decisions were made, and what information was available when those decisions were made is essential in understanding the risks that may be associated with later phases of a development effort. Finally, all documentation and deliverables should fall under configuration and change management processes. Too often it becomes impossible to understand the circumstances under which a document or piece of code changed without change management and version control. When this happens, risks may occur because information essential to understanding the history of decisions made may be altered or lost.

8.1   Requirements Gathering and Analysis

There are several elements of the risk analysis effort that may be accomplished during the requirements gathering phase of the SDLC. First, this is a good point to begin the identification of assets. During the requirements phase, the information required for the software begins to be identified. As these information elements are identified, they may also be classified to determine if the information is sensitive or critical to the mission of the organization. Assets other than sensitive or critical information such as services, databases, other applications, accounts, business rules, functions, formulas, and people may be identified. Items that are important

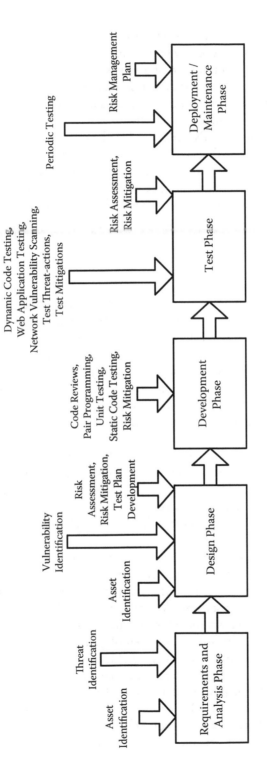

FIGURE 8.1 **Risk management activities within the SDLC**

to business managers will be uncovered during this phase, as will the consequences of failing to protect assets. A review of legislative or other regulatory requirements that might lead to the identification of assets will often occur during this phase. Additionally, a review of organizational standards and policies undertaken to understand requirements may also reveal assets such as passwords, authentication processes, and encryption methods and keys.

In addition, threats may also begin to be identified during this phase. *Abuse cases* are a form of use case that can be used to identify threats. Whereas use cases document expected behavior, normal inputs, and functional requirements, abuse cases can be used to document unexpected behavior by malicious agents, unexpected inputs, and missing security requirements. Abuse cases are a form of threat modeling discussed in Chapter 4 of this book.

8.2   Design

During the design phase, there are a number of additional risk assessment as well as some risk mitigation activities that may take place. First, during the design phase additional asset identification activities may take place as asset libraries from earlier development efforts are reviewed for possible reuse in the current development effort. In addition, as the architecture of the software is designed, additional assets may be identified by looking at data flows, authentication processes, transmission protocols, and other services that may be required by the design.

During the design phase, vulnerabilities are considered for the first time. Although no code has been written at this point and therefore no vulnerability testing will have been completed, common vulnerabilities from OWASP, SANS, NIST, and other sources can and should be considered. When the design of the architecture is complete, then lists of common vulnerabilities can be consulted and considered. A control analysis can be conducted using a list of current and planned controls for the system to end up with a list of vulnerabilities that could affect the software once it enters production.

At the end of the design phase, a risk analysis should be completed utilizing the assets, threats, and vulnerabilities that have been discovered up to this point. This risk analysis should then form the basis for risk mitigation decisions that will affect the remaining phases of the software development life cycle. For example, if vulnerabilities such as injection flaws and buffer overflows are found to represent a significantly high risk, a risk mitigation strategy employed might be to attempt to avoid or limit the risk by ensuring that all input fields in the application require strong input validation code, and furthermore, that each and every input field within the application will be thoroughly tested to ensure that the input validation code is in place and functioning correctly. By identifying such risks at this point in the software development effort, risk mitigation efforts will generally be cheaper than if these risks were discovered after the application had entered production.

Test cases for all risks uncovered by the risk assessment should also be developed. These test cases should be written in order to test each and every threat action, with the goals of:

- Understanding the likelihood of occurrence and magnitude of impact a threat action may have
- Testing to ensure that any risk mitigation strategies selected will be effective

For example, injection flaws represent a risk and the risk mitigation strategy is to limit this risk by application of input validation; then the test plan should call for testing all input for potential risk injection vulnerabilities, and if such a vulnerability is uncovered during the test phase, then conducting further testing in order to see how far the injection vulnerability can be exploited.

This risk assessment and the associated risk mitigation strategies employed must be thoroughly documented and placed under change management.

8.3   Development

During the development phase, coding actually begins. It is at this point that additional vulnerabilities may be uncovered by using processes such as the following:

- *Peer, buddy, and code reviews* that search for code (or the absence of code) which might allow a vulnerability to exist within an application. Code reviews often find and remove common vulnerabilities such as buffer overflows, improper error-handling routines, and lack of improper field validation rules. Code reviews help find and fix defects earlier, which helps eliminate costly repairs later in the development cycle. These reviews do not need to be costly in terms of schedule and often make for one of the best mentoring techniques. Remember: code reviews are not meant to be a competition and that cooperation and communication are keys to success.
- *Pair programming* where two authors develop code together at the same workstation can also reduce the probability that vulnerabilities will be introduced into software.
- *Unit testing* can also be used to detect vulnerabilities. Common vulnerabilities such as buffer overflows, injection flaws, and information leakage can all be easily detected through testing.
- *Static code scanning tools* look for vulnerabilities and inconsistencies within the style of the code. These scanners will point out potential vulnerabilities within an application.

In addition to vulnerability detection, risk mitigation strategies selected during the design phase also begin to take effect. Decisions such as the enforcement of certain coding standards including ensuring that all input fields in the application require strong input validation code, and furthermore, that each and every input field within the application will be thoroughly tested to ensure that the input validation code is in place and functioning correctly will be made. Risks uncovered in the design phase may have resulted in risk mitigation decisions to make changes to the design of the architecture, data flows, or services and functions that will begin to be coded in this phase.

8.4   Test

During the testing phase, a number of different tools can be brought into play in order to further detect vulnerabilities associated with the software development effort. Dynamic code scanning tools can attempt to find vulnerabilities while the code is actually executing. Also Web application scanning tools can be utilized during this phase by "crawling" the Web pages associated with the application, investigating each Web page, input field, and link and finding vulnerabilities while attempting to "break" the application. Finally, vulnerability scanning tools can be utilized to look for vulnerabilities within the organization's network which may be open to known vulnerabilities that may affect the application. All of these tools can and should be used within test environments in an attempt to find as many vulnerabilities associated with the software development as possible. All testing using network vulnerability scanners, even on limited test environments, needs to be coordinated, because many vulnerability scanners are intrusive by nature and may eat up bandwidth, shut down running services, or potentially damage systems.

In addition to testing for vulnerabilities utilizing dynamic code scanning tools, Web application scanning tools, and network vulnerability scanners, application testing in this phase can and should be conducted that focuses on vulnerabilities and threats which were discovered in earlier phases of the SDLC. For example, ensuring that all input fields have data validation routines behind them could be one way of testing that buffer overflow and injection type attacks have been mitigated. Likewise, trying to break an application and view the information supplied to the user by the error-handling routine(s) of an application can also be utilized in order to check for possible information leakage threats.

During the test phase, after all testing for vulnerabilities has been completed, but before the decision on migrating the application to production has taken place, another risk assessment should be conducted. This risk assessment should consider the assets, threats, and vulnerabilities identified since the original risk assessment was conducted, and should also consider the residual risk remaining after any risk mitigation efforts were conducted. In addition, risk mitigation recommendations should be made for any new threat-action statements identified since the original risk analysis. The risk analysis and any mitigation recommendations should be made available to the individual(s) who will make the decision on implementing the application in production. Providing this information to the implementation decision maker(s) will ensure that the decision is made with the full knowledge of any remaining residual risk.

8.5   Production and Maintenance

During the production phase, testing should still continue to uncover potential threats and vulnerabilities associated with the production of the application. If the application is a Web-based application, it should be scanned utilizing Web-based application scanning tools to ensure that there are no unknown vulnerabilities with the production configuration of the application or the environment in which it now functions. Additionally, periodic vulnerability scanning should be conducted on the network environment to ensure that no network-based vulnerabilities that could affect an application creep in. For example, network vulnerability tools can often identify critical patches that should be applied to Web servers, database servers, or operating systems. If these patches are not tested and applied in a timely manner, they could affect the overall level of risk associated with applications that are deployed on those systems.

In addition, periodic risk assessments should be conducted during the production and maintenance phases of any software development effort. They should be conducted at least every other year, or when any significant changes are made to the application, the services upon which it relies, or the environment in which it operates. This process should be defined in a risk management plan that is continually reviewed (at least annually) and updated as necessary. As we learned in the previous chapter, the third element of risk management is continual assessment and improvement. Threats and vulnerabilities continue to become more sophisticated, and therefore organizations must continually improve in the assessment, mitigation, and management of risks in order to provide a more secure computing environment.

8.6   Risk Management Activities within the Test Case

Throughout the course of this book, we utilized a test case to illustrate some of the principles associated with assessing and mitigating risks during a software development life cycle. This test case was based upon the real-life experiences of the author with a project which was very similar to that utilized in the test case. Each chapter looked at a different step in the risk assessment, risk mitigation, or risk management process. The story began with the selection of a risk assessment methodology. From there we looked at identifying assets, threats, and vulnerabilities, and then utilizing these items to assess some of the risks associated with the test case development effort. We then examined strategies to mitigate these risks.

In this chapter, the focus is not on how the risk assessment and risk mitigation efforts should be conducted, but rather when they were conducted in the actual test case. We look at each of the assets, threats, and vulnerabilities associated with the test case and discuss the circumstances under which they were uncovered. We also look closely at the risk mitigation strategies selected, and discuss their relative effectiveness as well as the decision-making process involved.

8.6.1 Test Case Assets

The assets for the test case were as follows:

- PII utilized by the application to calculate retirement benefits
- The proprietary business rules used within the application to calculate retirement benefits
- The Web portal used by external customers to access and view the results of a retirement benefit calculation
- The application of IRS business rules as they apply to the calculation of retirement benefits
- The passwords utilized by internal employees to access the PII used by the application
- Corporate reputation
- The collective knowledge of the only business analysts within the organization who understand the complexity of the calculations involved

From the beginning it was obvious that the PII required for the application was already an asset to the organization, due to the sensitive nature of much of the data that was required in order to calculate the retirement benefits. The PII was identified during the requirements phase as an asset, as was corporate reputation, as the organization had always placed a high value upon its reputation as an industry leader in this field.

However, many of the other assets were not recognized as assets until later phases of development. Until the system architecture was fully designed, it was not easy to recognize that the application of IRS business rules and the proprietary business rules should be an asset. These were uncovered as assets towards the end of the design phase as the architecture of the application became more apparent. It was also at this time when the design of the authentication service came under discussion that passwords were recognized as potential assets for the application. The authentication service that was in use by the organization at the time was able to not only authenticate user IDs but also to authorize specific user IDs to specific plan IDs. This was necessary to ensure that only the retirement plan administrator for a given plan, and her assistants and manager would have access to the information within that plan. This was necessary to ensure that retirement plan administrators and their assistants could not have access to plans they did not administrate, particularly the organization's own retirement plan which held salary information for every employee within the organization who was a participant in the plan.

The Web portal was not a part of the original design of the application. In a later phase of the project, the additional requirement to provide a method for customers to see the results of a retirement calculation more quickly was added. It was only during this phase of the development effort that the Web portal was selected as a solution to this problem and at that point, it became an asset.

Finally, it wasn't until the development phase that the body of knowledge held by the handful of business analysts was really appreciated as the asset it represented. The business rules behind the calculations were incredibly complex, and by this time, there were only three business analysts in the entire organization who truly understood how all of the calculations worked, especially in conjunction with the IRS rules. When one of those business analysts retired during the middle of the development effort, which left two individuals who understood the business rules, then it became very apparent that their knowledge needed to be thoroughly documented in case something happened to them.

8.6.2 Test Case Threats

The threats from the test case included the following:

- Shoulder surfing could allow nonauthorized personnel to observe the authentication process.
- Impersonation could allow users with stolen identity credentials (i.e., a stolen user ID and password) to view information they are not authorized to see.
- Errors and omissions in updating the IRS limitation file could result in the application applying incorrect business rules to the calculation. Likewise, errors and omissions in the entries made by the retirement plan administrator, such as the plan formula, fiscal year end date, or amount to be contributed could all result in an incorrect calculation.
- Inadvertent acts or carelessness could result in programming errors that do not apply the complex business rules properly, resulting in incorrect calculations or incorrect error handling or other potential vulnerabilities that could allow an attacker to gain access.
- Data contamination. The error log designed for this application placed all of the details associated with the error into an error log including sensitive information that the log administrator was not authorized to see.
- Corruption by system failures. If the mainframe service that gathers the PII required for the calculation is interrupted due to a mainframe system failure, the data placed in the DB2 tables could be garbled or corrupted. Or likewise the call to the DB2 table to pull the PII into the application could be cor-

rupted by system failures such as the gateway to the mainframe, resulting in data that is garbled or corrupted.

- Failures and intrusions not properly logged. It is possible for the authentication service to determine that the user has not properly supplied log-in credentials, or is not authorized to view a specific pension plan. If these types of intrusions are not properly logged (i.e., the user is simply denied access to the information and no log entry is made) then no audit trail will exist that a user was attempting to view unauthorized information.
- Environmental and natural threats. The application will run on a Web server located in the main data center for the company. This data center is also the home of the mainframe computer where all of the data files are stored. Therefore natural and environmental threats such as fire, flood, power fluctuations, tornadoes, and the like all could affect the operation of the application or its associated information.
- Malicious code. Viruses, worms, or other malicious programs could attempt to alter or destroy the IRS limitations data file, or interrupt calls through the gateway between the Web-based application and the mainframe service or the mainframe DB2 database.
- Eavesdropping. Keystroke loggers could capture user IDs and passwords supplied to the authentication service. Network sniffers could detect, intercept, and corrupt or replace packets sent between the application and the gateway to the mainframe.
- Intrusion. Backdoors to the application could be programmed by the development staff.
- Takeover of authorized sessions. If an authorized retirement plan administrator left a workstation unattended and unlocked then it would be possible for an unauthorized individual to gain access to the information in the application.

Most of the threats of the test case were uncovered using threat modeling techniques during the design phase of the development effort. However, there were a couple of threats that weren't uncovered until much later in the development effort. The data contamination threat was not uncovered until the acceptance testing phase, when the development team was trying to debug an error in the application and noticed that the error log file contained sensitive information including Social Security numbers and salary information. Neither piece of information was obvious at first, because the Social Security numbers appeared simply as a nine digit number (i.e., 123456789 not 123-45-6789) and the salary information also appeared just as a number 67459.25 or something similar, all jumbled together amidst a jumble of other information. But eventually, the development team realized that some of the information within the log file represented confidential information.

Likewise the corruption by system errors was not recognized as a threat until user testing. Test results during a two-day period were not bringing back consistent results for the PII retrieved by the mainframe service. Tracking back the problem revealed that the test environment from the mainframe during those two days was experiencing some stability problems from a batch testing patch that had just been installed and was in the process of being tested before it was passed on to production.

The failures and intrusions not properly logged threat was not detected as a potential threat until after the first phase of development had been rolled into production. It was only uncovered when a new retirement plan administrator repeatedly attempted to gain access to a specific plan ID and kept getting blocked by the authentication service. Because the administrator was new, this individual did not know who to report the problem to and so kept trying over the course of two weeks. Eventually, it was determined that when this individual was assigned a new caseload, the proper individuals were not notified, so she was not properly authorized for the plan as she should have been. However, this revealed the threat that an individual could make repeated attempts to access information she was not authorized to view, and no log was being kept of the attempts.

Finally, the backdoor to the application was discovered during phase 3 of the development effort. The backdoor had been placed by members of the development staff after the initial test phase when it was discovered that some testers were only partially completing a calculation effort, and then leaving the application running all night long. This prevented some of the cleanup efforts of logging test data, and locked some rows in the test database. The backdoor allowed them to shut off the access of the users who were leaving the application running. A different method was found to handle the situation without requiring a backdoor, and the backdoor was removed.

8.6.3   Test Case Vulnerabilities

Vulnerabilities for the test case included the following:

- Buffer overflows
- Injection flaws
- Information leakage and error handling
- Broken authentication and session management
- Lack of a policy requiring code and peer reviews
- Lack of a policy that requires the classification of data

Of these vulnerabilities, only buffer overflows, lack of a policy requiring code and peer reviews, and lack of a policy requiring the classification of data were considered during the initial risk assessment conducted during the design phase. Both code and peer reviews and data classification policies for the organization were under consideration at the time of the development effort, and the development team had experienced buffer overflows on a recent project. However, the injection flaws and information leakage were not uncovered until the test phase, when they were discovered at the same time by one of the testers who knew about SQL injection. This tester noticed some of the information that was being passed back to him from the error-handling routine of the application was actually revealing information about the database tables, and that by utilizing a SQL query in an input field, he could find out more information including some of the information stored within those tables. The remaining vulnerability was not discovered until the production phase of the application development effort, at the same time the failures and intrusions not properly logged threat was uncovered.

8.6.4 Test Case Risks and Mitigation Efforts

Risks associated with the threat case included the following:

- The retirement plan administrator could erroneously enter a buffer overflow causing the application to crash.
- Sensitive information could be disclosed to unauthorized individuals by reading the error log files.
- An inside employee who had obtained the authentication credentials of another employee could view sensitive information in the application.
- A programmer could inadvertently allow injection flaws or information leakage that would reveal information to an unauthorized user.
- An incorrect calculation could result from data contamination caused by a failure of the mainframe service.
- Unauthorized attempts to gain access to certain plans are not detected.
- A developer programs a backdoor into an application allowing access to the application and its data.

Of the risks listed here, only the first and third ones were uncovered prior to the development phase. The other risks were not discovered until much later in the development effort, near the end of the testing phase. And at least two risks were not uncovered until after the first two phases of the development effort had been put into production. The reason for this is that at the time of the development effort, the author and the development team did not fully understand how to program applications securely, and although program reviews were conducted, application risk assessments were not required by the organization. If they had been, it is probable that many of the risks not uncovered until the production phase would have been detected earlier.

Still, when the risks were discovered, or at least the vulnerabilities and threats, risk mitigation efforts were conducted. Because code and peer reviews were already under consideration, when the backdoor was discovered in this application (and in others at the time) the code and peer reviews were established and helped discover a great many flaws in a great many applications. A static code analysis tool was purchased to assist in this effort, and proved to be very effective. It was not too expensive, and use of the tool did not increase development timelines by a significant amount. It also resulted in some of the fixes for injection flaws and buffer overflows.

It is difficult to say if the mitigation efforts associated with moving the log files were effective or not. It is unlikely that anyone knew where the error log files were kept. However, it was also impossible at that time to tell if anyone had copied or otherwise had accessed the error log files. Likewise, it is impossible to detect how often credentials of employees were stolen or discovered through other means (some individuals did write down passwords and hide them somewhere within their desks), and many individuals did work during the weekends and at night when they could have logged in at any workstation in the company and would not have been noticed. However, because passwords were reset every 30 days, the risk associated with this possibility was acceptable to the organization.

Once the possible data contamination error was discovered during testing, the fix of returning an error code solved the problem, and no further data contamination errors were uncovered. The same can be said of the information leakage problem and some of the SQL injection flaws that were uncovered in testing. The code put in place as a result eliminated these errors from the application.

The final risk dealt with the authentication service. The risk, as you may recall, resulted when the authentication service was provided with a valid user ID and password, but an invalid plan ID. In this particular instance, the employee was attempting to access information to a plan that she was not authorized to see. The risk was the result of a clerical error made on a new employee. The employee was authorized to access information for the plan ID in question, but had never been granted the proper access rights. Therefore, the application simply stopped at the authentication point, and would go no further. The true underlying risk was the fact that an employee could attempt to access information for a plan that they were not authorized to see, and could make multiple attempts at such access, without anyone realizing that the employee was attempting to make an unauthorized attempt. However, as a direct result, the authentication service itself was changed to log all unauthorized requests. Further automation would provide the details of who attempted to access unauthorized information, when the attempt occurred, and an e-mail containing the information was sent to that employee's supervisor as well as human resources for appropriate action.

In short, the mitigation efforts proved successful in transferring, eliminating, or limiting the risk associated with the threat actions. However, because the organization did not at that time practice application risk assessments, many of the risks associated with the development effort were not detected before they rolled out in production. Luckily, none of the risks uncovered after production ended up affecting the organization in any significant manner. However, if the application had been placed on the Internet to allow customers to calculate their own retirement plan benefits as had originally been planned, then going to production with these types of vulnerabilities could have resulted in a significant risk to the organization. In addition, some of the vulnerabilities and threats were only discovered due to anomalies or problems with other systems (the mainframe patch) or administrative services (the clerical error). It is lucky that they were uncovered before any real impact occurred. Had a thorough risk analysis been conducted, it is more likely that they would have been discovered much earlier in the development process.

8.7   Conclusion

Risk assessment and risk mitigation efforts are conducted throughout the various phases of the software development life cycle. When these activities are conducted in earnest, in their proper order within the SDLC, risks may be discovered much earlier in the life cycle, allowing risk mitigation efforts to be applied much earlier, and at much less cost to an organization.

8.8   Risk Assessment and Risk Mitigation Activity Checklist

☐ Requirements Gathering and Analysis Activities
  ☐ Identification of Assets
      ☐ Information elements and classification of information
      ☐ Identification of additional requirements such as:
          ☐ Services
          ☐ Databases
          ☐ Software
          ☐ Accounts
          ☐ Business rules
          ☐ Functions
          ☐ Formulas
          ☐ People
      ☐ Interviews of business managers to understand what is important to business managers about the software development effort and the potential consequences of not protecting those assets
          ☐ Review of regulatory or legislative requirements
          ☐ Review of organizational standards and policies
      ☐ Identification of threats through:
          ☐ Development of abuse cases
          ☐ Threat modeling

☐ Design Phase Activities
    ☐ Further identification of assets through:
        ☐ A review of asset libraries used in earlier design efforts
        ☐ A review of the application architecture including:
            ☐ Data flows
            ☐ Authentication processes
            ☐ Transmission protocols
            ☐ Other services identified
        ☐ An identification of vulnerabilities through a review of typical vulnerabilities which plague similar software projects found at:
            ☐ OWASP Top 10 (http://www.owasp.org/index.php/OWASP_Top_Ten_Project)
            ☐ National Vulnerability Database (NIST) (http://nvd.nist.gov/nvd.cfm)
            ☐ Common Vulnerabilities and Exposures (http://cve.mitre.org/index.html)
            ☐ SANS Top 20 (http://www.sans.org/top20/)
            ☐ U.S. Computer Emergency Readiness Team (US CERT) (http://www.us-cert.gov/cas/alldocs.html)
    ☐ Conducting a risk assessment utilizing:
        ☐ Assets determined at this point
        ☐ Threats determined at this point
        ☐ Common lists of vulnerabilities
    ☐ Conducting risk mitigation efforts that will affect the remaining SDLC life cycles
    ☐ Developing test plans that:
        ☐ Test all threat-action statements
        ☐ Test all risk mitigation strategies
        ☐ Document risk assessment and risk mitigation efforts
☐ Development Phase Activities
    ☐ Identification of further vulnerabilities through:
        ☐ Peer, buddy, and code reviews
        ☐ Pair programming techniques
        ☐ Unit testing
        ☐ Static code analysis tools
    ☐ Enforcing risk mitigation strategies which were decided during the design phase. Such mitigation strategies could call for:
        ☐ Enforcement of coding standards
        ☐ Additional unit testing
        ☐ Design changes including:
            ☐ System architecture
            ☐ Data flows
            ☐ Services and functions

☐ Test Phase Activities
    ☐ Conduct dynamic source code scanning for vulnerabilities
    ☐ Conduct Web application scanning for vulnerabilities
    ☐ Conduct network vulnerability scanning
    ☐ Test threat-action statements discovered during the initial risk assessment
    ☐ Test risk mitigation strategies implemented as a result of the initial risk assessment
    ☐ Conduct a risk assessment utilizing assets, threats, and vulnerabilities discovered since original risk assessment
        ☐ Consider residual risk of items that have been mitigated
    ☐ Recommend additional risk mitigation strategies for new risks
    ☐ Provide risk assessment report and risk mitigation recommendations to decision makers for application implementation decisions
☐ Production and Maintenance Phase Activities
    ☐ Periodic testing
        ☐ Web application scanning
        ☐ Network vulnerability scanning
    ☐ Development of a risk management plan identifying:
        ☐ Periodic assessment of risk
        ☐ Risk mitigation strategies
        ☐ Continuous evaluation and improvement

Chapter 9

Maintaining a Security Risk Assessment and Risk Management Process

---

Picture the following scene. A set of faint footsteps lead up to a darkened door. There is a sense of tension in the air, a sense that something is about to happen. A gloved hand reaches out to the door and tries to turn the knob and discovers that it is securely locked. A hooded figure swivels his head, this way and that, and there is a pause to listen. A gloved hand with a crowbar reaches for the door and swiftly jams one end into the crack between the door and the door jamb. Hesitantly, the hand with the crowbar waits and pauses for breath, then with a mighty shove, wrenches hard on the lever. There is the sound of cracking as the wood around the jamb gives way, and the door swings inward. Another pause for breath, listening for some sign that whoever might be in the area might have heard the sound of the door being opened. However, there is no noise above the heartbeat of the individual at the door. With great hesitancy the door is pushed open and a step inside is taken. Another pause is taken to listen. There is no noise. A hand switches on a flashlight and dimly illuminates the room.

The sight that is revealed brings a slight sigh from the person at the door as the crowbar finds its way silently into a backpack. The camera backs out to reveal a room loaded with choice goodies: TVs and stereos, expensive artwork, and collectable items. Furniture of exquisite taste fills the room. Lamps and other ceramic items speak of the great wealth of the owner. Opulence fills the room. The thief quickly makes his way into the bedroom. A jewelry box sits in plain sight on the vanity. The thief opens the lid and shines his flashlight down on the jewels inside only to discover: costume jewelry? Where's the good stuff? The thief pauses. He notices that one picture in the room is slightly ajar. He moves quickly to the picture and pulls it off the wall to reveal a hardened safe! The thief takes one look at the safe and knows his crowbar will be of little use against it. The house has been thoroughly protected and by the looks of it, by some very professional people. That fact is instantly brought to the attention of the thief, as the flashing lights of police cars can be seen outside the house.

The scene switches to a later time period. The house is swarming with police, and cameras flash, taking photographs of the damaged door. The detectives are talking with the homeowner. "Can you please confirm for us that nothing has been taken? How long have you had that alarm system installed?" The homeowner, pleased to find only minor damage to his home and the thief in custody, answers that he doesn't know if anything is missing but would be glad to check and make sure, and that they installed the alarm system some time ago.

We seldom see such scenes as the one just described in our favorite television crime shows or read them in mystery novels. They spoil the story. The crime is prevented with minimal intrusion. There is no story to impart to an eager viewer or reader. However, this is what the homeowner really wants: his valuables have been protected, and the intrusion has been relegated to a rather minor event in his life. This is what the process of risk management is all about.

9.1   Definitions

The process of *risk management* is managing the day-to-day uncertainties that arise during the operations of any organization. Risk management is comprised of three distinct pieces as shown in Figure 9.1. The first is risk assessment, which is the process of identifying and classifying the risks associated with the operations of an organization. Risk assessment methodologies and the steps required to conduct a risk assessment for a software development project were covered in Chapters 2 through 6 of this book. The second part of a risk management process is that of risk mitigation. Risk mitigation is the process of selecting a strategy for dealing with the risks uncovered during the risk assessment process. Finally, the last part of any risk management process is the continual evaluation and improvement of risk management activities and strategies. There is some degree of uncertainty associated with any project, therefore it is necessary to practice a continual evaluation and improvement practice to ensure that risk does not creep back in, and so that the process of finding and mitigating risks becomes easier over time, taking less time and fewer resources.

This chapter is all about the entire risk management process which includes risk assessment and risk mitigation as well as continual evaluation and improvement. The inputs and outputs associated with risk management are shown in Figure 9.2.

FIGURE 9.1 Risk management process

FIGURE 9.2 Risk management inputs and outputs

9.2 Risk Management Plans

Risk management plans provide the means for organizations to accomplish their missions by:

- Securing IT systems that store, process, or transmit data that are critical to mission success
- Enabling management to make well-informed risk management decisions to justify the expenditures on safeguards or controls that are part of the organization's budget
- Assisting management in self-regulating the organization's IT systems on the basis of the results of annual risk assessments

In short, a risk management plan will spell out the conditions under which risk assessment, risk mitigation, and continual evaluation and improvement efforts will be carried out.

Some common elements of a risk management plan include:

■ *A purpose statement:* A purpose statement summarizes the purpose of the plan and the overall goals to be accomplished by the plan. As with an executive summary, it should briefly describe the goals of the plan and how those goals will be accomplished.

■ *A list of objectives:* A list of objectives ties the scope of the risk management plan to specific business goals, objectives, or purposes. A risk management plan should always be tied to a business need.

■ *A list of references:* The list of references includes other documents that may be pertinent to the risk management plan or a phase of the risk management process. Such documents could include, but are not limited to:

  − Specific risk management methodologies.
  − Policies, procedures, standards, and guidelines of the organization. These documents may:

    ■ Specify the requirements of performing risk management activities.
    ■ Provide requirements that must be met when mitigating risks.
      − Form the basis of a control analysis in helping to determine the likelihood of occurrence for a threat action or the magnitude of impact for a threat action.
      − Provide the specifications required for any additional safeguards or controls that are selected as part of a risk mitigation effort.
      − Agreements with managed services organizations or other internal departments that spell out the responsibilities of each party.
    − Insurance documents.

■ *Legal basis:* The legal basis section of a risk management plan often spells out the legal or regulatory requirements of developing, conducting, or maintaining risk management activities. For example, HIPAA, GLB, SOX, and the PCI DSS all require risk management activities of some kind. Other regulatory organizations, particularly federal government organizations such as the General Accounting Office (GAO), Centers for Medicare and Medicaid Services (CMS), the Department of Defense (DoD), and others may require that organizations which do business with them meet the requirements spelled out in various regulatory procedure documents.

■ *Definitions:* The terms found in a risk management plan may not always be understood by those required to read such a plan. Terms such as *asset, risk, vulnerability,* and *threat* should be defined, as should any terms that may be specific to the organization conducting the risk management activities. Most organizations have their own acronyms which are often used, and they should be described in this section.

■ *Risk management overview:* The risk management methodology used by the organization, how the methodology fits into each phase of the System Development Life Cycle (SDLC), and how the risk management process is tied to the process of system authorization must be described. In addition the results of the most recent risk assessment along with the risk mitigation actions and

TABLE 9.1   Risk Mitigation Status

Risk Assessment				Risk Management	
Vulnerability	*Risk Level*	*Recommended Safeguard*	*Residual Risk*	*Status of Safeguard*	*Updated Risk*

their status should be listed. Often the risks and their mitigation actions are described in a table much like that shown in Table 9.1.

■ *Risk management strategy:* This section of the risk management plan encompasses the processes of risk assessment, risk mitigation, and continuing evaluation and assessment. It is an overview of the risk assessment process, which includes the identification and evaluation of risks and risk impacts, and recommendation of risk-reducing measures. It is also an overview of risk mitigation, including how risks are prioritized, as well as how appropriate risk-reducing measures are to be prioritized and implemented. Finally, it is an overview of the continual evaluation process and keys for implementing a successful risk management program.

■ *Risk management in the SDLC:* This section describes how risk management activities are introduced into the SDLC from investigation of initial requirements through analysis, design, implementation, and maintenance.

■ *Key roles:* There are many individuals and roles that are involved in a risk management process. This section of the risk management plan identifies each of those roles and outlines the responsibilities of those roles in regard to the risk management process.

■ *Risk assessment:* Risk assessment is the first process in risk management. This section of the risk management plan describes the risk assessment methodology selected along with a justification for why that methodology was selected. In addition, this section of the document spells out the following:

– The scope of the assessment effort
– Key success factors required for a successful assessment
– Who will be involved in the assessment effort
– The processes used to identify assets
– The processes used to identify threats
– The processes used to identify vulnerabilities
– The processes used to identify threat–vulnerability pairs and to develop threat-action statements
– The process used in performing control analyses
– The processes used to develop risk evaluation criteria:

> > ■ Likelihood of occurrence scale
> > ■ Magnitude of impact scale
> - Top-down support

■ *Risk mitigation:* This part of the risk management plan describes how risk mitigation activities will be carried out. Through risk mitigation, the organization will prioritize, evaluate, and implement appropriate risk-reducing controls recommended from the risk assessment process.

■ *Continual evaluation and assessment:* This section of the risk management plan describes the ongoing activities that the organization will undertake to ensure that risks are managed. It may spell out such activities as when risk assessment and risk mitigation activities will be undertaken on a timeline, or within phases of the SDLC. It also describes plans for continuous improvement in all of the processes associated with risk management activities.

9.3   Supporting Risk Management Practices

Sometimes it is difficult within an organization to get the support required to practice and sustain risk management activities. There are a number of different approaches to take in obtaining this support including: top-down support from senior management; support from the organization's policies and procedures; support from legislative, regulatory, and compliance requirements; support from certification and accreditation requirements; and support from change management requirements. Each of these methods is detailed below.

9.3.1   Top-Down Support

Senior management, under the standard of due care and ultimate responsibility for the organization's mission accomplishment, must ensure that the necessary resources are effectively applied to develop the capabilities needed to accomplish the mission. They must also assess and incorporate results of risk assessment activities into the decision-making process. An effective risk management program that assesses and mitigates IT-related mission risks requires the support and involvement of senior management. Without that support, any risk management effort is bound to fail. But how do you get the support of senior management, especially when many individuals within an organization view information security as an additional cost? Many articles have been written on that subject, and books could be written on that subject alone. However, the basic principles involved are the same as the rationale for conducting risk management activities in the first place!

Firstly, risk management provides insight into how limited resources may best be applied. Let's return to an example from Chapter 7 to illustrate this process. Imagine a small government organization responsible for collecting fees from the public for various permits that are required. Currently, the organization must have offices open throughout a regional area in order to allow the public to come in, request a permit, and pay for that permit. This requires that the organization keep open multiple offices throughout their geographical area in order to make it convenient for the public to pay for their permits. Many of these offices must be open a reasonable number of hours per week and staffed appropriately. To save money, the organization decides to develop a custom Web application so that the public can request a permit, pay for it, then print the permit online without the need to have so many offices opened and staffed.

However, the organization does not realize the risks associated with collecting credit card payments electronically, because it has never conducted e-commerce before. A malicious individual breaches the application and steals credit card numbers. As a result of this breach, the PCI requires that the organization apply specific and very expensive controls to the system if it wishes to have the ability to continue to take credit card payments for its permits. The organization may or may not have the funds to install these controls. And it may be just as expensive, or even more so, for the organization to reopen the regional offices that were closed when the Web application was implemented. Had a risk analysis been conducted during the development of the Web application, perhaps the vulnerabilities that allowed the threat action to occur could have been discovered and eliminated, or limited at a fraction of the cost that is now facing the organization. At least the organization could have been made aware of the possibility that a malicious individual could steal credit card information, and the relative impact such an event would have produced upon the organization.

Secondly, although risk mitigation efforts may represent a cost to an organization, that cost should be looked at as very similar to the cost of insurance. Most organizations do not hesitate to spend money on property and casualty insurance for their physical assets. They don't even hesitate to spend money insuring their human assets through life and health insurance programs. But they often hesitate to spend money to protect information assets by spending money on additional controls and safeguards. It must be made clear to management that the additional funds spent for code reviews, code analysis, intrusion detection and prevention software and hardware, firewalls, and other similar controls and safeguards represent a form of insurance for information systems and the data within those systems. The case for this can best be made through a risk assessment that provides evidence of the level of risk associated with a particular system, and a cost-benefit analysis that can provide a level of assurance that the cost associated with the additional controls is less than the cost associated with a threat action damaging an asset.

Finally, it is important to involve other stakeholders in the risk management process. System and information owners are responsible for ensuring that proper controls are in place to protect the systems they own. They have a stake in what may happen should the confidentiality, integrity, and availability of their systems or information should be jeopardized. Risks associated with their systems can affect the ability of their departments to function, and could definitely affect the bottom line of their departments, as well as department morale. The organization's managers responsible for business operations and IT procurement process must also take an active role in the risk management process. These managers are the individuals with the authority and responsibility for making the trade-off decisions essential to mission accomplishment. Their involvement in the risk management process enables the achievement of proper security for the IT systems, which, if managed properly, will provide mission effectiveness with a minimal expenditure of resources.

9.3.2   Support from Policies and Procedures

Oftentimes, support for a risk management program can come from within an organization's standards, guidelines, policies, and procedures. These documents may require management to make sound decisions based upon due diligence and make trade-off decisions that are essential to mission accomplishment. If the risks associated with these types of decisions have not been identified or understood, then the soundness of the decision may come into question. In our example of the government organization discussed earlier in this chapter, it is apparent that not all of the risks were fully identified or understood when the organization decided to close down regional offices and provide the services those offices provided through means of a Web-based application.

In addition, an organization's policies and procedures may often spell out the requirement to assess risks on a periodic basis, either explicitly or implicitly. For example, an organization may have a standard or guideline that spells out how project management activities are to be applied to any project undertaken by the organization. Project management activities often require the assessment of risks associated with a project. Although the sorts of risks assessed as a part of project management activities are often those associated with accomplishing the requirements of the project within the time, scope, and resources assigned to the project, they could also be extended to include application security risk assessment activities as well.

To illustrate this premise, consider the following. A project is currently underway for a government organization to develop a new application governing the payment of medical claims made for a healthcare program such as Medicare or Medicaid. The project management team must consider all of the risks associated with the management of this project, including risks to the implementation schedule of the payment system, risks to the budget set aside to pay for the project, risks associated with the resources assigned to the project, and risks associated with the implementation of the project. However, if there are information security risks associated with implementation of the project, they must also be considered by the project management team. In this example, because the application is a healthcare application, application security risks associated with HIPAA must be considered.

Policies and procedures within an organization may also spell out other types of risk management and risk assessment activities that must take place on a periodic basis. For example, policy may require that organizational information security risks be assessed on an annual basis. Additionally, organizational policies and procedures may specifically spell out the requirements for the following:

- Software development life cycles
- Data classification guidelines
- Destruction of equipment containing sensitive or confidential information
- Data backup
- Disaster recovery
- Business continuity
- Personnel security
- Identification and authentication processes
- Proper use of computing resources
- Workstation security
- Application security
- Firewalls
- Intrusion detection and prevention
- Configuration of servers

The requirements entailed in any of these types of policies, procedures, standards, and guidelines may either implicitly or explicitly require that the risks associated with these topics are understood and that some measure of risk prevention be applied in order to be in compliance with a policy or procedure. Take, for example, a policy which requires that notifications be made to a number of different departments within an organization whenever an employee is to be terminated. The purpose of this policy is so that the employee may be physically escorted out of the building, and that the employee's access to company assets is terminated so that the employee is not able to damage those assets. Such a policy may imply that there is a risk associated with not notifying the proper individuals in a timely manner to remove access.

9.3.3 *Legislative, Regulatory, or Compliance Support*

Finally, many risk management activities may be implicitly or explicitly implied by legislative or regulatory organizations, regardless of whether the organization actually has a policy or procedure that requires such a process. For example, HIPAA requires that organizations conduct periodic assessments of risk and have risk management programs in place. If an organization is subject to the requirements of the

HIPAA legislation, then it is required to do these things regardless of whether the organization actually develops a policy or procedure to do so.

9.3.4   Certification and Accreditation Support

Information is an asset requiring security commensurate with its value, criticality, and sensitivity. An organization is entrusted with information and is accountable for its protection. Measures must be taken to protect information from unauthorized modification, destruction, or disclosure, whether accidental or intentional, and to ensure its confidentiality, integrity, and availability. To accomplish this, it is necessary for organizations to understand the risks and other factors that could adversely affect their mission. Moreover, an organization must understand the current status of their security programs and the security controls planned or in place to protect their information and information systems so they can make informed judgments and investments that appropriately mitigate risk to an acceptable level. The ultimate objective is to conduct the day-to-day operations of the organization and to accomplish the organization's stated missions with security that is commensurate with risk, including the magnitude of harm resulting from the unauthorized access, use, disclosure, disruption, modification, or destruction of information.

Security *accreditation* is the official management decision given by an organization to authorize operation of an information system and to explicitly accept the risk to organization operations, organization assets, or individuals based on the implementation of an agreed-upon set of security controls. By accrediting an information system, an organization accepts responsibility for the security of the system and is fully accountable for any adverse impacts to the organization if a breach of security occurs. Thus, responsibility and accountability are core principles that characterize security accreditation.

The information and supporting evidence needed for security accreditation is developed during a detailed security review of an information system, typically referred to as security certification. Security *certification* is a comprehensive assessment of the management, operational, and technical security controls in an information system, made in support of security accreditation, to determine the extent to which the controls are implemented correctly, operating as intended, and producing the desired outcome with respect to meeting the security requirements for the system. The results of a security certification are used to reassess the risks and update the system security documentation, thus providing the factual basis for rendering a security accreditation decision. Completing a security accreditation ensures that an information system will be operated with appropriate management review, that there is ongoing monitoring of security controls, and that reaccreditation occurs periodically in accordance with state or organization policy and whenever there is a significant change to the system or its operational environment.

Typical requirements of a security certification and accreditation process include the following:

Purpose: The purpose of a certification and accreditation program is to provide guidelines governing the security certification and accreditation of information systems supporting an organization. The guidelines are developed to help achieve more secure information systems within an organization by:

■ Enabling more consistent, comparable, and repeatable assessments of security controls in the organization's information systems
■ Promoting a better understanding of business-related mission risks resulting from the operation of information systems
■ Creating complete, reliable, and trustworthy information for authorizing officials to facilitate more informed security accreditation decisions

Scope: For the purpose of meeting certification and accreditation requirements, security is defined as the ability to protect the integrity, confidentiality, and availability of information processed, stored, and transmitted by an organization. Security also involves the ability to protect information technology assets from unauthorized use or modification and from accidental or intentional damage or destruction. In general, information technology assets covered by certification and accreditation processes include those that process, store, transmit, or monitor digital information. Information technology assets also include the security of information technology facilities and off-site data storage; computing, telecommunications, and applications-related services purchased from other entities; and Internet-related applications and connectivity. Minimum guidelines must be established and be met by organizations in certification and accreditation of their information systems.

Compliance: Certification and accreditation affect system owners, data owners, program managers, security officers, system architects, system administrators, and network administrators who are responsible for planning, approving, developing, establishing, maintaining, or terminating information systems. All employees, interns, volunteers, and customers that use, develop, implement, or maintain information technology systems are responsible for understanding and complying with certification and accreditation guidelines. This includes using, building, configuring, and maintaining systems in accordance with these guidelines. There is an element of risk in operating any Information Technology (IT) system. However, by planning for security, ensuring that proper individuals are assigned security responsibility for those systems, reviewing the security controls in place in all IT systems, and authorizing systems prior to operations and periodically thereafter, we can mitigate those risks to an acceptable level. Therefore it is important that all organizations understand the risks and other factors that could adversely affect their missions. Moreover, organizations must understand the current status of their security programs and the security controls planned or in place to protect their information and information systems so they can make informed judgments and investments that appropriately mitigate risk to an acceptable level. Outsourced processing and storage facilities, such as service bureaus, vendors, partnerships, and alliances, must be monitored and reviewed to ensure compliance with certification and accreditation guidelines.

Responsibilities: The following describes the roles and responsibilities of key participants involved in an organization's security certification and accreditation process. The security certification and accreditation process is flexible, allowing organizations to effectively accomplish the intent of the specific tasks within their respective organizational structures to best manage the risks to organization operations, organization assets, or individuals.

Chief Information Officer (CIO): The CIO should work closely with authorizing officials and their designated representatives to ensure that an organizationwide security program is effectively implemented, that the certifications and accreditations required across the organization are accomplished in a timely and cost-effective manner, and that there is centralized reporting of all security-related activities. To achieve a high degree of cost effectiveness with regard to security, the CIO should encourage the maximum reuse and sharing of security-related information including: threat and vulnerability assessments, risk assessments, results from common security control assessments, and any other general information that may be of assistance to information system owners and their supporting security staffs. In addition to the above duties, the CIO and authorizing officials should determine the appropriate allocation of resources dedicated to the protection of the organization's information systems based on organizational priorities.

Authorizing Official: The authorizing official is a senior management official with the authority to formally assume responsibility for operating an information system at an acceptable level of risk to organization operations, organization assets, or individuals. Through security accreditation, the authorizing official assumes responsibility and is accountable for the risks associated with operating an information system. The authorizing official should have the authority to oversee the budget and business operations of the information system within the organization and is often called upon to approve system security requirements, security plans, and memoranda of agreement or memoranda of understanding. In addition to authorizing operation of an information system, the authorizing official can also issue an interim authorization to operate the information system under specific terms and conditions, or deny authorization to operate the information system (or if the system is already operational, halt operations) if unacceptable security risks exist.

Chief Information Security Officer (CISO): The CISO is the individual responsible for ensuring the appropriate operational security posture is maintained for an information system or program. The CISO also serves as the principal advisor to the authorizing official or information system owner on all matters (technical and otherwise) involving the security of the information system. The CISO typically has the detailed knowledge and expertise required to manage the security aspects of the information system. This responsibility may also include, but is not limited to, physical security, personnel security, incident handling, and security training and awareness. The CISO may be called upon to assist in the development of the system security policy and to ensure compliance with that policy on a routine basis. In close coordination with the information system owner, the CISO often plays an active role in developing and updating the system security plan as well as in managing and controlling changes to the system and assessing the security impact of those changes.

Information System Owner: The information system owner is that individual responsible for the overall procurement, development, integration, modification, or operation and maintenance of an information system. The information system owner is responsible for the development and maintenance of the security plan and ensures the system is deployed and operated according to the agreed-upon security requirements. The information system owner is also responsible for deciding who has access to the information system (and with what types of privileges or access rights) and ensures that system users and support personnel receive the requisite security training (e.g., instruction in rules of behavior). The information system owner informs the organization of the need to conduct a security certification and accreditation of the information system, ensures that appropriate resources are available for the effort, and provides the necessary system-related documentation to the certification agent. The information system owner receives the security assessment results from the certification agent. After taking appropriate steps to reduce or eliminate vulnerabilities, the information system owner assembles the security accreditation package and submits the package to the authorizing official for adjudication.

Information Custodian: The information custodian is the individual operational authority for specified information and responsibility for establishing the controls for its generation, collection, processing, dissemination, and disposal. The information custodian is responsible for establishing the rules for appropriate use and protection of the subject information (e.g., rules of behavior) and retains that responsibility even when the information is shared with other organizations. The custodian of the information stored within, processed by, or transmitted by an information system may or may not be the same as the information system owner. Also, a single information system may utilize information from multiple information custodians. Information custodians should provide input to information system owners regarding the security requirements and security controls for the information systems where the information resides.

Certification Agent: The certification agent is an individual, group, or organization responsible for conducting a security certification, or comprehensive assessment of the management, operational, and technical security controls in an information system to determine the extent to which the controls are implemented correctly, operating as intended, and producing the desired outcome with respect to meeting the security requirements for the system. The certification agent also provides recommended corrective actions to reduce or eliminate vulnerabilities in the information system. Prior to initiating the security assessment activities that are a part of the certification process, the certification agent provides an independent assessment of the system security plan to ensure the plan provides a set of security controls for the information system that is adequate to meet all applicable security requirements. To preserve the impartial and unbiased nature of the security certification, the certification agent should be in a position that is independent from the persons directly responsible for the development of the information system and the day-to-day operation of the system. The certification agent should also be independent of those individuals responsible for correcting security deficiencies identified during the security certification. The independence of the certification agent is an important factor in assessing the credibility of the security assessment results and ensuring the authorizing official receives the most objective information possible in order to make an informed, risk-based, accreditation decision. When the potential impact on organization operations, organization assets, or individuals is low, a self-assessment activity may be reasonable and appropriate and not require an independent certification agent. When the potential organization-level impact is moderate or high, certification agent independence is needed and justified.

User Representatives: Users are found at all levels of an organization. Users are responsible for the identification of mission/operational requirements and for complying with the security requirements and security controls described in the system security plan. User representatives are individuals that represent the operational interests of the user community and serve as liaisons for that community throughout the system development life cycle of the information system. The user representatives assist in the security certification and accreditation process, when needed, to ensure mission requirements are satisfied while meeting the security requirements and employing the security controls defined in the security plan.

9.3.4.1 Certification and Accreditation Definitions

Selected terms used in certification and accreditation efforts are defined below:

- *Accreditation:* The official management decision given by an organization to authorize operation of an information system and to explicitly accept the risk to organization operations (including mission, functions, image, or reputation), organization assets, or individuals, based on the implementation of an agreed-upon set of security controls.
- *Accreditation Package:* The evidence provided to the authorizing official to be used in the security accreditation decision process. Evidence includes, but is not limited to: the system security plan, the assessment results from the security certification, and the plan of action and milestones.
- *Authorization Official:* Official with the authority to formally assume responsibility for operating an information system at an acceptable level of risk to organization operations (including mission, functions, image, or reputation), organization assets, or individuals.
- *Availability:* Ensuring timely and reliable access to and use of information.
- *Certification:* A comprehensive assessment of the management, operational, and technical security controls in an information system, made in support of security accreditation, to determine the extent to which the controls are implemented correctly, operating as intended, and producing the desired outcome with respect to meeting the security requirements for the system.
- *Certification Agent:* The individual, group, or organization responsible for conducting a security certification. This agent should be independent of the information system owner's chain of management in order to provide an unbiased opinion. Organizations may act as certification agents for other organizations, provided that they have the required level of expertise necessary to review the security controls in place.
- *Confidentiality:* Preserving authorized restrictions on information access and disclosure, including means for protecting personal privacy and proprietary information.
- *Countermeasures:* Actions, devices, procedures, techniques, or other measures that reduce the vulnerability of an information system. Synonymous with security controls and safeguards.
- *Integrity:* Guarding against improper information modification or destruction, including ensuring information nonrepudiation and authenticity.
- *Management Controls:* The security controls (i.e., safeguards or countermeasures) for an information system that focus on the management of risk and the management of information system security.
- *Operational Controls:* The security controls (i.e., safeguards or countermeasures) for an information system that primarily are implemented and executed by people (as opposed to systems).

- *Risk:* The level of impact on organization operations (including mission, functions, image, or reputation), organization assets, or individuals resulting from the operation of an information system given the potential impact of a threat and the likelihood of that threat occurring.
- *Safeguards:* Protective measures prescribed to meet the security requirements (i.e., confidentiality, integrity, and availability) specified for an information system. Safeguards may include security features, management constraints, personnel security, and security of physical structures, areas, and devices.
- *Security Controls:* Protective measures used to meet the security requirements specified for IT resources.
- *Security Incidents:* Adverse events that possess a threat to the shared state IT infrastructure in respect to confidentiality, integrity, or availability.
- *Security Plan:* Formal document that provides an overview of the security requirements for the information system and describes the security controls in place or planned for meeting those requirements.
- *System Owner:* The individual responsible for establishing the rules for appropriate use and protection of the data/information within a system. The system owner retains that responsibility even when the data or information is shared with other organizations.
- *Technical Controls:* The security controls (i.e., safeguards or countermeasures) for an information system that are primarily implemented and executed by the information system through mechanisms contained in the hardware, software, or firmware components of the system.
- *Threat:* Any circumstance or event with the potential to adversely affect organization operations (including mission, functions, image, or reputation), organization assets, or individuals through an information system via unauthorized access, destruction, disclosure, modification of information, or denial of service.
- *Vulnerability:* Weakness in an information system, system security procedures, internal controls, or implementation that could be exploited or triggered by a threat source.

9.3.4.2 Certification and Accreditation Guidelines

The security certification and accreditation process consists of a number of distinct tasks. The security certification and accreditation activities can be applied to an information system at appropriate phases in the system development life cycle. Additionally, the activities can be tailored to apply a level of effort and rigor that is most suitable for the information system undergoing security certification and accreditation. The following guidelines may be used by organizations in their certification and accreditation efforts.

Information System Description: Organizations shall confirm that the information system has been fully described and documented in a system security plan or equivalent document.
Typical system descriptions include the following:

- The name of the information system
- The status of the information system with respect to the system development life cycle
- The name and location of the organization or organization responsible for the information system, contact information for the information system owner or other individuals knowledgeable about the information system
- Contact information for the individual(s) responsible for the security of the information system
- The purpose, functions, and capabilities of the information system
- The types of information processed, stored, and transmitted by the information system
- The functional requirements of the information system
- The applicable laws, directives, policies, regulations, or standards affecting the security of the information and the information system
- The individuals who use and support the information system (including their organizational affiliations, access rights, and privileges, if applicable)
- The architecture of the information system
- Hardware and firmware devices (including wireless)
- System and applications software (including mobile code)
- Hardware, software, and system interfaces (internal and external)
- Information flows (i.e., inputs and outputs)
- The network topology
- Network connection rules for communicating with external information systems
- Interconnected information systems
- Encryption techniques used for information processing, transmission, and storage
- Public key infrastructures, certificate authorities, and certificate practice statements
- The physical environment in which the information system operates
- Web protocols and distributed, collaborative computing environments (processes, and applications)

Threat Identification: Organizations shall confirm that potential threats that could exploit information system flaws or weaknesses have been identified and documented in a system security plan, risk assessment, or equivalent document.
A number of potential threats can cause harm to information systems. It is important to consider all potential threats that may affect the confidentiality,

integrity, or availability of the system or the data processed, stored, or transmitted by the system. Threats of nature (i.e., flood, tornado, blizzard, fire, etc.), human (events enabled by or caused by humans), or environmental (power failures, pollution, chemical spills, water leaks, etc.) should be considered. However, only those threats that are relevant to the security of the system need to be listed.

Initial Risk Determination: Organizations shall confirm that the risk to organization operations, organization assets, or individuals has been determined and documented in a system security plan, risk assessment, or equivalent document.

Many different risk assessment methodologies have been developed and are available for use by organizations. The methodology selected is not important provided that the following major factors of risk management are considered:

■ Threats to, and vulnerabilities within, the information system
■ The potential impact and magnitude of harm to operations, assets or individuals resulting from the unauthorized access, use, disclosure, disruption, modification, or destruction of the information system or the data stored, transmitted, or processed by the system
■ An assessment of the effectiveness of current or proposed security controls
■ Vulnerabilities resulting from the absence of security controls, or the ineffectiveness of such controls (i.e., controls not configured correctly, not operating correctly, or achieving desired results)

Notification, Planning, and Resources: Organizations shall inform the CISO, authorizing official, certification agent, user representatives, and other interested organization officials that the information system requires security certification and accreditation support. Furthermore, organizations shall determine the level of effort and resources required and prepare a plan of execution.

This is one of the key steps in the certification and accreditation process. The notification can serve as an early warning to help potential participants prepare for the upcoming tasks necessary to plan, organize, and conduct the certification and accreditation effort. The level of effort required for certification and accreditation depends upon: the size and complexity of the system, the controls employed to protect the system, and the methods that will be used to measure the effectiveness of those controls.

System Security Documentation Analysis: Organizations shall analyze the system security plan, risk management plan, risk assessment, or similar documentation to determine if vulnerabilities in the information system and the resulting risk to operations, assets, or individuals are actually what the plan would produce, if implemented. If not previously documented formally, organizations shall formally document this analysis in a system security plan, risk management plan, or similar document.

A system security plan provides an overview of the information system security requirements and describes the security controls in place or planned for meeting those requirements. An independent review of system security documentation by the certification agent, authorizing official, and CISO, determines if security planning is complete and consistent with the requirements documentation for the information system. If the independent review reveals flaws with the planned system security controls, then the plans should be revised to bring them into compliance before it is approved.

Security Assessment and Recommendations: Organizations shall assess the management, operational, and technical security controls in the information system.

This security assessment shall determine the extent to which the security controls are implemented correctly, operating as intended, and producing the desired outcome with respect to meeting the security requirements for the system. The results of the security assessment, including recommendations for correcting any deficiencies in security controls, shall be documented in an assessment report.

The assessment report shall provide the information system owner with an assessment of the security controls in the system, and shall also provide specific recommendations on how to correct deficiencies in those controls. This provides an opportunity for the system owner to act on those recommendations and correct deficiencies before the accreditation package is finalized.

Plan of Action and Milestones: Organizations shall prepare a plan of action and milestones based on the results of the security assessment.

This document shall describe actions taken or planned by the information system owner to correct deficiencies found in the security controls and address any remaining vulnerabilities in the information system; in doing so, it shall identify the following:

■ All tasks requiring completion along with a priority for those tasks
■ The resources required to accomplish the tasks
■ Scheduled completion dates for all milestones

Accreditation Package: Organizations shall assemble an accreditation package and submit it to the authorizing official.
The accreditation package shall contain the following:

■ The security assessment and recommendations report
■ The plan of action and milestones report
■ An updated system security plan, risk management plan, or similar document

Certification agent input to this final accreditation package provides an unbiased and independent view of the extent to which the security controls in the information system are implemented correctly, operating as intended, and producing the desired outcome with respect to meeting the system security requirements.

Accreditation Decision Letter: Organizations shall determine if the risk to organization operations, organization assets, or individuals is acceptable and prepare a final security accreditation decision letter.

Authorizing officials shall determine if the final risk in operating the system is acceptable. Security considerations should be balanced against mission and operational needs. The authorizing official shall render an accreditation decision after reviewing all relevant information and consulting with key officials. The authorizing official may make one of three decisions.

■ If the risk is acceptable, an authorization to operate shall be issued, and the system shall be accredited without any restrictions or limitations on operations.
■ If the risk is unacceptable, but there is an important mission-related need to place the system into operation, an interim authorization to operate shall be issued. Specific terms and conditions, including corrective actions to be taken and a timeframe for the completion of those actions shall be issued. The system is not accredited during the period of interim authorization.
■ If the risk is unacceptable, then the system is not authorized for operation and therefore is not accredited.

The authorizing official prepares a final security accreditation decision letter. The letter includes the accreditation decision, the rationale for the decision, the terms and conditions for information system operation, and required corrective actions, if appropriate. The accreditation decision letter indicates to the information system owner whether the system is:

■ Authorized to operate
■ Authorized to operate on an interim basis under strict terms and conditions
■ Not authorized to operate

Supporting rationale provides the information system owner with the justification for the authorizing official's decision. The terms and conditions for the authorization shall provide a description of any limitations or restrictions placed on the operation of the information system that must be adhered to by the information system owner. The security accreditation decision letter is included in the final accreditation package. The contents of the accreditation package shall be protected appropriately in accordance with organization policy.

Documentation of System Changes: Organizations shall use configuration and change management practices to document proposed or actual changes to the information system (including hardware, software, firmware, and surrounding environment).

It is important to record any relevant information about the specific proposed or actual changes to the hardware, firmware, or software such as version or release numbers, descriptions of new or modified features or capabilities, and security implementation guidance. It is also important to record any changes to the information system environment such as modifications to the physical plant. The information system owner and CISO should use this information in assessing the potential security impact of the proposed or actual changes to the information system. Significant changes to the information system should not be undertaken prior to assessing the security impact of such changes.

Security Control Monitoring: Organizations shall conduct continuous monitoring to determine the extent to which selected controls are implemented correctly, operating as intended, and producing the desired outcome with respect to meeting the security requirements for the system.

Continuous monitoring of security controls can be accomplished in a variety of ways including:

- Security reviews
- Self-assessments
- Security testing and evaluation
- Audits

The methods and procedures employed to assess the security controls during the monitoring process are at the discretion of the information system owner. However, the monitoring process shall be documented and available for review by the authorizing official or CISO upon request. If the results of a security assessment indicate that selected controls are less than effective in their application and are affecting the security of the information system, corrective actions should be initiated and the plan of action and milestones updated.

Status Reporting and Documentation: Organizations shall update system security plans, risk management plans, action plans, and milestones based upon documented changes to the information system (including hardware, software, firmware, and surrounding environment) and the results of the security control monitoring process.

The system security plan, risk management plan, or similar document should contain the most up-to-date information about the information system. Changes to the information system should be reflected in the plan. The frequency of plan updates is at the discretion of the information system owner. The updates should occur at appropriate intervals to capture significant changes to the information system, but not so frequently as to generate unnecessary paperwork.

The plan of action and milestones should:

- Report progress made on the current outstanding items listed in the plan.
- Address vulnerabilities in the information system discovered during the security impact analysis or security control monitoring.

■ Describe how the information system owner intends to address those vulnerabilities (i.e., reduce, eliminate, transfer or accept the identified vulnerabilities).

The frequency of the plan of action and milestones updates is at the discretion of the information system owner. The updates should occur at appropriate intervals to capture significant changes to the information system, but not so frequently as to generate unnecessary paperwork.

9.3.5 Support from Change Management

Any organization's customers and employees expect to hold the organization to the highest standards for the confidentiality, integrity, and availability of data. As stewards of customer and employee information, organizations are accountable for exercising change management processes for IT systems and applications. Change management represents both a risk mitigation strategy, as well as a protection strategy for any organization. Without strict change management practices in place, the assessment of risk becomes an exercise in futility at best. Any risks that were mitigated in one version of a software program may have not been mitigated in a newer version of the software without configuration management controls. Likewise, old vulnerabilities may creep back into software if change management is not practiced by an organization.

Although it is acknowledged there may be additional costs associated with a stringent change management process to satisfy these expectations, there is also the justification for such activities to meet the accountability and assurance expectations of the organization's customers, employees, and business programs. This is, in effect, a form of risk management to protect the data of the organization.

Responsibility for following the change management processes is shared and extends to all personnel involved with the development, implementation, operations, use, or maintenance of information systems. Each person must satisfy the requirements of change management as they relate to the portion of each information system under his control.

9.4 Continuous Evaluation and Improvement

Risk assessment and risk mitigation represent only two of the processes associated with risk management. The final process associated with risk management is continuous evaluation and improvement. Part of this continuous evaluation and improvement process are the action plans contained in the risk management plan that describe continual risk assessment practices, as well as schedules for adopting new controls in order to mitigate risks. Another part of this is support for continual improvement in the form of policies and procedures calling for improvement. An example of such a policy is contained in Section 9.7 of this chapter.

Yet another part of this process lies in documenting the state of security controls that provide protection for a specific system. This is accomplished by the development of a System Security Plan (SSP). An SSP provides management with a current snapshot of the security controls associated with any given system. The system may then be evaluated based upon the controls currently implemented and documented to determine whether the system will be granted authorization to process information (i.e., accreditation). It also serves as a reference document for testing, evaluation, and audits by oversight bodies. The results of a recent risk assessment are required for the development of any SSP.

An SSP template has been included in Section 9.9 of this chapter as an example of the types of information that may be found in an SSP. The steps involved in creating an SSP are outlined in Figure 9.3. A more detailed description of the steps involved in developing an SSP follows.

9.4.1 System Security Plan Scope

All SSP development efforts will have a specific scope in mind. It is important to understand this scope at the outset of the project, as it will affect some of the steps required in developing an SSP.

During this phase, it is important to help the development team to understand why documenting the state of system security is important. Some of the reasons include the following:

- Business managers are typically unaware of all of the controls and safeguards in place in a system and how they relate to risk. An SSP will document all of the controls and safeguards in use and how effective they are at reducing and eliminating risks.
- Oversight organizations and auditors will want to review all of the controls and safeguards currently in place. A well-written SSP can save these organizations and auditors time by helping to focus their efforts, thus reducing the impact they need to make during an audit or review.
- Business managers are often unaware of the issues and the costs required to properly protect information system assets. SSPs clearly outline the controls and safeguards that are necessary to protect those assets.
- Typically only senior management personnel understand which aspects of the organization's mission are the most critical.

The goal for any SSP should be a clear understanding of the resources and controls currently in place providing protection to the organization's information system assets. This goal is best achieved through the documentation of those safeguards and controls so that decisions may be made wisely, and with the organization's mission in mind.

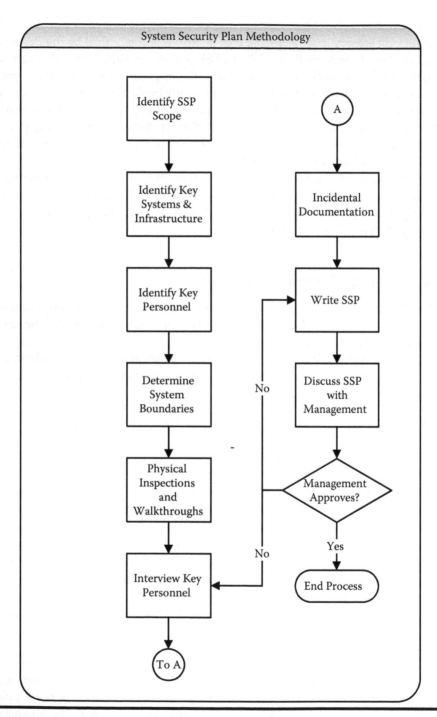

FIGURE 9.3 System security plan methodology

9.4.2 Identifying Key Infrastructure

Regardless of the scope of the SSP development, at this point it is necessary to identify all systems and the key elements of their IT infrastructure. Typically, this is done during the risk assessment process. However, some of the standard elements of this process include identification of the following:

- System name
- Record system type (i.e., VSAM, DB2, RDBMS, SQL server, etc.)
- System owner/contact info
- Business owner/contact info
- System maintainer/contact info
- System purpose and description
- System users (i.e., description of who uses the system)
- System environment
- System interconnections or information sharing
- Personnel security controls
- Physical and environmental security controls
- Production input/output controls
- Data integrity/validation controls
- Identification and authentication controls
- System security level (based on information sensitivity and system criticality)

It is necessary to obtain this information for each system and subsystem and major piece of key infrastructure or system involved. System and network diagrams should all be gathered during this phase of the SSP development.

9.4.3 Identification of Key Personnel

Every organization has key personnel who need to be a part of the SSP development process. It is essential to identify who those personnel are at the start of the project. The key is to determine if there is already a risk management program in place. If so, then it is simply a process of identifying the key personnel who are a part of that program and including them in interviews. If not, then it will be necessary to identify them through other means. At a minimum the following personnel should be considered for interviews:

- System owners
- Business owners
- System maintainers
- Information security personnel
- Physical security personnel

- Human resources personnel
- End users of key systems
- Supervisors of end users
- System administrators
- Development staff
- Database administrators

Some of these individuals will be identified in the risk management plan. Others must be identified by other means including asking questions to development team members, by observation during on-site walkthroughs, through a review of organizational charts, and by answers to interview questions with other individuals.

9.4.4 Determining System Boundaries

The next step is to define what constitutes a system. This means determining the system boundaries and interfaces with other systems. This requires an analysis of both technical system boundaries and organizational responsibilities. Constructing physical and logical boundaries around a set of processes, communications, storage, and related resources identifies a system. The set of elements within these boundaries constitutes a single system requiring a security plan. Each component of the system must:

- Be under the same direct management control (i.e., one system owner even though an application may cross several business lines)
- Have the same general business function(s) or business objective(s)
- Have essentially the same operating characteristics and security needs

All components of a system do not need to be physically connected.

- A group of stand-alone personal computers (PCs) in an office
- A group of PCs placed in employees' homes under defined telecommuting program rules
- A group of portable PCs provided to employees who require mobile computing capability for their jobs
- A system with multiple identical configurations that are installed in locations with the same environmental and physical safeguards

An organization may have systems that differ only in the responsible organization or the physical environment in which they are located. In such instances, it is appropriate to use plans that are identical except for those areas of difference.

9.4.5   Physical Inspections and Walkthroughs

Physical inspections and walkthroughs are an important part of the SSP process. At a minimum, a walkthrough of the following areas should be conducted:

- Building and area perimeters
- Data centers/computer rooms/server rooms
- Power supply centers
- Centralized printing/publishing centers
- Wiring closets
- Areas where sensitive data is received and processed
- Environmental controls
- Mail rooms
- Facsimile stations/areas
- Staircases, elevators, and emergency exits

9.4.6   Interview Key Personnel

The amount of interviews necessary to develop the SSP will depend upon how thoroughly the organization filled out the system identification template, and how thorough the organization's most recent risk assessment was. If there are any sections of the system identification template that are incomplete or raise questions, then the individuals identified in step three should be interviewed about the systems they own, support, or use. Where possible, interviews should be scheduled in advance.

Questions asked during the interview process should be limited to obtaining clarification of the following items:

- Information about the key infrastructure and system boundaries
- Information about the risk analysis
- Information necessary to complete any of the sections within the SSP template

Any clarification that is necessary after the walkthroughs and review of the system identification template and risk assessment should be handled in this step.

9.4.7   Incidental Documentation

There are several pieces of incidental documentation required for an SSP. These pieces of documentation include:

- Equipment (i.e., hardware) lists
- Software lists
- Glossary of terms
- Acronyms

The equipment list should include all of the hardware used within the boundaries of the system in question. A simple inventory should suffice. The software list should include all of the operating system software, as well as any specialized application software in use within the system boundaries. The glossary of terms and acronym list should spell out any terms used by the organization that are unique to the organization or the organization's line of business.

9.4.8   Prepare Documentation

The SSP is prepared based upon the template found in Section 9.9 of this chapter. The sections include:

- Section 1: System Identification
- Section 2: Management Controls
- Section 3: Operational Controls
- Section 4: Technical Controls
- Section 5: Appendices and Attachments

As each of the sections is completed, it should undergo a quality assurance check by an employee who did not write it, and then it should be forwarded as a draft to management for review. The purpose of this review is not to wordsmith the document, but rather to ensure that all of the technical details of each section are correct. An SSP is a large document, and it is easier to ensure that it is technically correct, by allowing the management to review each section separately.

9.4.9   Discuss SSP with Management

It is important to share any observations made during the development of the SSP with management as they are discovered and not wait until the written report is completed. Discuss observations with management immediately whenever breaches of security are in process, or when fraudulent activities are discovered. It is important to remember that the purpose of the SSP development is to document the current state of security and all of the controls and safeguards currently in place.

Draft copies of the SSP should be shared with management. Once management has had ample opportunity to review the draft, then a meeting with key information security, business managers, and system maintainers should be scheduled to review the SSP in detail. It should be clear to the client that the review will include all sections of the SSP.

9.4.10 Finalize Documentation

Once a face-to-face meeting has been held with management to discuss the SSP, then the document may be finalized. Make sure all of management's concerns during the discussion have been addressed in the document.

9.5 Risk Management Policy

Risk management is an important activity that can help identify the day-to-day operational uncertainties associated with any organization or project. Organizations that do not have a specific policy or standard which requires periodic risk management activities should consider developing such a policy or standard. A template for such a risk management policy has been included in Section 9.7 of this chapter.

9.6 Conclusions

We all want to feel secure when we walk into our homes or places of business. We don't want to find ourselves suddenly swept up in a crime or detective story, at least not as the subject of such a story! The same can be said for the information systems and the data that they contain; we want to make sure that they aren't the subject of a crime story. Yet all too often, we find that the information systems we rely upon have become the subject of a crime story. During the month of January 2008 alone, PrivacyRights.org reported that more than 1,000,000 records had been breached.

According to the National Cyber Security Partnership's Task Force on improving security across the software development lifecycle, "Security is a serious problem and if present trends continue, could be much worse in the future." This task force, consisting of subgroups in education, software processes, patching, and incentives, has made numerous recommendations for both the short and the long term. Yet in the meantime, organizations continue to entrust their precious information assets in software developed with the same vulnerabilities over and over again.

However, through the simple practice of assessing information assurance risks within the SDLC, assets, as well as common threats, vulnerabilities, and risks can be identified. Once the risks are known, then steps can be taken to mitigate them through the strategies of acceptance, transference, avoidance, or limitation. And where it isn't feasible to transfer, avoid, or limit risks within the software development process, then at least the risks are known, and security controls at other levels of the infrastructure such as perimeters, networks, policies and procedures, defense in depth, intrusion detection and prevention, as well as others may be able to mitigate the risks that could not be eliminated within the software itself. Unknown risks can't be transferred, avoided, or limited: they can only be accepted. That's why it's imperative we attempt to detect and analyze risks within each phase of the SDLC, starting with the requirements phase.

Just as it is cheaper to fix design flaws during software development the earlier those design flaws are recognized, the cheaper it becomes to make software more secure the earlier we recognize the risks associated with the development effort. Risk management activities must begin in the requirements phase and continue through the remaining phases of any software development effort until the software is retired from service. Even then, there may be risks associated with retiring the software from service that must be taken into consideration. If these risks remain unknown, then they cannot be transferred, avoided, or limited in any way.

It is hoped that this book has provided a foundation for security risk assessment and security risk management during software development by looking at current trends and problems that have plagued application development for a decade or more. It was the intent of the author to provide those individuals associated with software development efforts a step-by-step guide into understanding how some of the common threats and vulnerabilities associated with software development can be identified and prevented, through the process of risk assessment and risk mitigation. It is also the hope of the author that now that you have been informed of how to identify and mitigate risks associated with software development, that the resulting software produced by your team is more secure.

9.7 Risk Management Plan Template

A template of a typical risk management plan and the information it contains follows. The information listed with brackets ([ ]) is intended to indicate the type of information found in each section of the template.

9.7.1 Purpose

Risk represents a source of danger or threat, a possibility of incurring loss or misfortune. Risk management is the process of identifying risk, assessing risk, and taking steps to mitigate risks to the extent possible. This plan provides an effective risk management program, containing both the definitions and the practical guidance necessary for assessing and mitigating risks identified. The ultimate goal is achieving best practices in managing IT-related mission risks.

9.7.2 Objective

Performing risk management will allow the organization to accomplish its missions by:

- Securing the IT systems that store, process, or transmit data that are critical to mission success
- Enabling management to make well-informed risk management decisions to justify the expenditures that are part of the organization's budget
- Assisting management in self-regulating the department's IT systems on the basis of the results of annual risk assessments

9.7.3 References

[This section of the risk management plan can spell out any relevant guidance used in conducting risk assessment or risk mitigation efforts such as concepts presented in National Institute of Standards and Technology (NIST) Special Publication (SP) 800-30, Risk Management Guide for Information Technology Systems, or other publications.]

9.7.4 Legal Basis

[This section of the risk management plan spells out any legislative or regulatory requirements for conducting risk assessments and risk mitigation efforts including: HIPAA, SOX, GLB, SB 1386, among others, which may form the basis for the organization's policy or strategy for risk management.]

9.7.5 Definitions

This section of the risk management plan may contain definitions for terms used throughout the plan such as assets, threats, vulnerabilities, risks, and threat actions. Examples of some of these definitions include:

- An *asset* is something of value to an organization or enterprise. It can be a person or person(s), information, a system, hardware, or even a building or facility.
- *Risk* is the possibility of suffering harm or loss. It is the potential for realizing unwanted negative consequences of an event. It refers to a situation in which a person could do something undesirable or a natural occurrence could cause an undesirable outcome, resulting in a negative impact or consequence.
- A *threat* refers to something that is a source of danger to an asset.
- A *vulnerability* refers to a weakness in security systems, administrative controls, physical layout, internal controls, and so forth that could be exploited by a threat to gain unauthorized access to information or disrupt critical processing.

9.7.6 Risk Management Overview

[This section describes the risk management methodology used by the organization, how it fits into each phase of the System Development Life Cycle (SDLC), and how the risk management process is tied to the process of system authorization.]

[In addition, this section contains the results of the risk analysis including: the identification of critical assets, the risks associated with those assets, and an analysis of those risks. Also, the mitigation strategies selected to deal with those risks, and the planned implementation of those strategies is included.]

9.7.7 Importance of Risk Management

[This section of the risk management plan encompasses the processes of risk assessment, risk mitigation, and continuing evaluation and assessment. It is an overview of the risk assessment process, which includes identification and evaluation of risks and risk impacts, and recommendation of risk-reducing measures. It is also an overview of risk mitigation, which refers to prioritizing, implementing, and maintaining the appropriate risk-reducing measures recommended from the risk assessment process. Finally, it is an overview of the continual evaluation process and keys for implementing a successful risk management program.]

9.7.8 Integration of Risk Management into the System Development Life Cycle (SDLC)

[This section describes how risk management activities are introduced into the SDLC from investigation of initial requirements through analysis, design, implementation, and maintenance. Minimizing negative impact and the need for a sound basis in decision making are the fundamental reasons risk management is implemented for an organization's IT systems. Effective risk management must be totally integrated into the SDLC. Risk management must be an iterative process that can be performed during each major phase of the SDLC.]

9.7.9 Key Roles

[Risk management is primarily a management responsibility. This section describes the key roles of the personnel who should support and participate in the risk management process. Some examples are given below.]

■ *Senior Management.* Senior management, under the standard of due care and ultimate responsibility for the department's mission accomplishment, must ensure that the necessary resources are effectively applied to develop the capabilities needed to accomplish the mission. They must also assess and incorporate results of the risk assessment activity into the decision-making process. An effective risk management program that assesses and mitigates IT-related mission risks requires the support and involvement of senior management.

■ *Chief Information Officer (CIO).* The CIO is responsible for the department's IT planning, budgeting, and performance including its information security components. Decisions made in these areas should be based on an effective risk management program.

■ *System and Information Owners.* System and information owners are responsible for ensuring that proper controls are in place to address integrity, confidentiality, and availability of the IT systems and data they own.

■ *Business and Functional Managers.* The organization's managers responsible for business operations and IT procurement process must take an active role in the risk management process. These managers are the individuals with the authority and responsibility for making the trade-off decisions essential to mission accomplishment. Their involvement in the risk management process enables the achievement of proper security for the IT systems, which, if managed properly, will provide mission effectiveness with a minimal expenditure of resources.

■ *Security Officer.* The organization's computer security officer is responsible for the organization's security programs, including risk management. Therefore, the organization's security officer will play a leading role in introducing an appropriate structured methodology to help identify, evaluate, and minimize risks to the IT systems that support the organization's mission. The security officer will also act as a major consultant in support of senior management to ensure that this activity takes place on an ongoing basis.

■ *IT Security Practitioners.* IT security practitioners (e.g., network, system, application, and database administrators; computer specialists; security analysts; security consultants) are responsible for proper implementation of security requirements in the organization's IT systems. The existing IT system environment is dynamic (e.g., changes continually occur, such as expansion in network connectivity, changes to the existing infrastructure and organizational policies, introduction of new technologies). As changes to the organization's IT systems occur, IT security practitioners must support or use the risk management process to identify and assess new potential risks and implement new security controls as needed to safeguard all of the department's IT systems.

■ *Security Awareness Trainers (Security/Subject Matter Professionals).* All organization personnel are the users of the IT systems. Use of the IT systems and data according to the organization's policies, guidelines, and rules of behavior is critical to mitigating risk and protecting the organization's IT resources. To minimize risk to the IT systems, it is essential that system and application users be provided with security awareness training. Therefore, the organization's IT security trainers or security/subject matter professionals must understand the risk management process so that they can develop appropriate training materials and incorporate risk assessment into training programs to educate the end users.

9.7.10 Risk Assessment

[Risk assessment is the first process in the risk management methodology. This section of the risk management plan will describe the risk assessment methodology selected along with a justification for why that methodology was selected. In addition, this section of the document will spell out the following:

- The scope of the assessment effort
- Key success factors required for a successful assessment
- Who will be involved in the assessment effort
- The processes used to identify assets
- The processes used to identify threats
- The processes used to identify vulnerabilities
- The processes used to identify threat–vulnerability pairs and to develop threat action statements
- The process used in performing control analyses
- The processes used to risk evaluation criteria:
  - Likelihood of occurrence scale
  - Magnitude of impact scale
  - Risk matrices

An example of the types of items that might be found in this section of a risk management plan appears below.]

9.7.11 Preparing to Assess Risks

The initial focus of the [Insert Method Name] method is preparing for the evaluation. The following are key success factors in preparation:

- *Getting senior management sponsorship.* Successful risk analysis requires the time of people in the organization. If senior management does not support the process, staff support for the risk analysis will dissipate quickly.
- *Selecting the analysis participants.* The analysis participants will be responsible for managing the process and analyzing information. The members of this team need to have sufficient skills and training to lead the risk analysis and to know when to augment their knowledge and skills by including additional people.

■ *Setting the appropriate scope.* The risk assessment should include important operational areas but the scope cannot get too big. The analysis participants must work with the organization's senior management to select which operational areas will be examined as a part of the risk assessment.

■ *Selecting participants.* Staff members will contribute their knowledge about the organization. They should be assigned based on their knowledge and skills, not solely based on who is available. In general, participants should be familiar with the types of information-related assets in the organization, able to commit to the time required, and familiar with the ways in which information assets are used.

9.7.12 Phase 1: Build Asset-Based Threat Profiles

Participants from the organization contribute their unique perspectives about what is important to the department (assets) and how well those assets are currently being protected. The following activities are undertaken to elicit knowledge from participants during this phase:

■ *Identify assets and relative priorities.* An asset is something of value to the organization. It can be information, systems, software, hardware, and people. The first step is to brainstorm a list of assets from the participants.

■ *Identify areas of concern.* The participants will then express concerns about how the most important assets are threatened. Scenarios, using prompts based on known sources and outcomes of threat, will be developed. This information will form the basis for constructing threat profiles.

■ *Identify security requirements for the most important assets.* At this point, participants discuss what qualities are important about the assets that they have identified. Next, security requirements, in the form of confidentiality, integrity, and availability will be identified for each important asset. Finally, each security requirement for each asset will be ranked, relative to each other.

■ *Capture knowledge of current security practices and organizational vulnerabilities.* During this activity, the organization's current security practices will be evaluated against a catalog of known good security practices. In addition, the participants will discuss the current security practices and how they relate to organizational vulnerabilities.

9.7.13 Phase 2: Identify Infrastructure Vulnerabilities

This is the "technological view" of the risk assessment. During this phase, the participants will examine key components of the IT infrastructure. Once these key components have been identified, vulnerability tools will be used to scan the components for technological weaknesses. The results of the scans will then be reviewed and the results summarized. The ultimate goal of this phase is to identify techno-logical weaknesses in the organization's infrastructure.

Once the scans are complete, the participants will review the reports generated, interpret the results, and create a preliminary summary of the technology vulner-abilities for each key component.

9.7.14 Phase 3: Develop Security Strategy and Plans

During phase three, the participants will identify and analyze risks to the organiza-tion's critical assets. This phase includes the following activities:

- *Identifying the impact of threats to critical assets.* During this step, a narra-tive description of the potential impact of threats to the organization's criti-cal assets is developed. There are four possible threat outcomes: disclosure, modification, loss/destruction, and interruption. However, the impact will be broader, describing the effect of the threat on the organization's mission and business objectives.
- *Creating risk evaluation criteria.* During this activity, the organization's toler-ance for risk is defined by creating evaluation criteria. The criteria developed will act as a measure against in which the department will evaluate the types of impact described during the previous step. This will help the organization explicitly prioritize risks.
- *Evaluating the impact of threats to assets.* In this step, the evaluation criteria are compared to the impact descriptions. The impact on the organization for each threat to a critical asset can then be estimated. The ultimate result is that the organization can then establish priorities to guide its risk mitigation activities.

Once the impacts of threats to the organization's critical assets have been ana-lyzed, a protection strategy, mitigation plans for the risks to the critical assets, and an action list of near-term actions may be developed. Finally, the participants will present the proposed protection strategy, mitigation plans, and action list to senior management. Senior management will then review and revise the strategy as necessary and then decide how the organization will build on the results of the evaluation.

9.7.15 Risk Mitigation

[This part of the risk management plan describes how risk mitigation activities will be carried out. Through risk mitigation, the organization will prioritize, evalu-ate, and implement appropriate risk-reducing controls recommended from the risk assessment process. An example of the types of information that may be found in this section of a risk management plan is found below.]

The elimination of all risk is usually impractical or close to impossible. Therefore, it is the responsibility of the organization's senior management and functional and business managers to use the least-cost approach and implement the most appropriate controls to decrease mission risk to an acceptable level, with minimal adverse impact on the organization's resources and mission.

9.7.16 Risk Mitigation Options

Risk mitigation is a systematic methodology used by the organization's senior management to reduce mission risk. The organization will achieve risk mitigation through any of the following risk mitigation options:

- *Risk Assumption*. Accepting potential risk and continue operating IT system(s) or implementing controls to lower the risk to an acceptable level.
- *Risk Avoidance*. Avoiding the risk by eliminating the risk cause or consequence (e.g., forgo certain functions of a system or shut down the system when risks are identified).
- *Risk Limitation*. Limiting the risk by implementing controls that minimize the adverse impact of a threat's exercising a vulnerability (e.g., use of supporting, preventive, or detective controls).
- *Risk Transference*. Transferring the risk by using other options to compensate for the loss, such as purchasing insurance.

The organization's goals and mission shall be considered in selecting any of these risk mitigation options. Because it may not be practical to address all identified risks, the organization shall give priority to the threat and vulnerability pairs that have the potential to cause significant mission impact or harm. Because the organization has a unique environment and objectives, the option used to mitigate the risk and the methods used to implement controls may vary. The organization will use the "best of breed" approach by selectively using appropriate technologies from among various security products, along with the appropriate risk mitigation option and nontechnical administrative measures.

9.7.17 Risk Mitigation Strategy

As a general guideline, the organization will provide implementation of control actions at appropriate points in the SDLC using the following guidelines:

- When a vulnerability (or flaw/weakness) exists. The organization will implement appropriate assurance techniques to reduce the likelihood of the vulnerability being exercised.
- When a vulnerability can be exercised. The organization will apply layered protections, architectural designs, and administrative controls as appropriate, to minimize the risk of, or prevent, the vulnerability being exercised.
- When the attacker's cost is less than the potential gain. An attacker represents someone or something intentionally attempting to violate the security of an asset. The organization will apply appropriate protections to decrease an attacker's motivation by increasing the attacker's cost. For example, by applying system controls to limit what a system user can access and accomplish, the organization could significantly reduce a potential attacker's gain.
- When a potential loss would be too great. The organization will apply appropriate design principles, architectural designs, and technical and nontechnical protections to limit the extent of the attack, thereby reducing the potential for loss.

9.7.18 Control Implementation Approach

When control actions must be taken, the organization will address the greatest risks and strive for sufficient risk mitigation at the lowest cost, with minimal impact on other mission capabilities. The organization will use the following risk mitigation methodology when implementing controls.

Step 1: Prioritize actions. Based on the risk levels presented in the risk assessment report, the implementation actions will be prioritized. In allocating resources, top priority will be given to risk items with unacceptably high risk rankings. These vulnerability–threat pairs will require immediate corrective action to protect the organization's interests and mission.

Step 2: Evaluate recommended control options. The organization will analyze the feasibility (e.g., compatibility, user acceptance) and effectiveness (e.g., degree of protection and level of risk mitigation) of the recommended control options. The organization will then adopt the most appropriate control option for minimizing risk.

Step 3: Conduct cost-benefit analysis. The organization will conduct a cost-benefit analysis to aid management in decision making and to identify cost-effective controls.

Step 4: Select controls. On the basis of the results of the cost-benefit analysis, management shall determine the most cost-effective control(s) for reducing risk to the organization's mission. The controls selected should combine technical, operational, and management control elements to ensure adequate security for the system and the organization.

Step 5: Assign responsibility. Appropriate persons who have the appropriate expertise and skillsets to implement the selected control will be identified, and responsibility will be assigned.

Step 6: Develop an action plan. At a minimum, the plan shall contain:

- Risks (vulnerability–threat pairs) and associated risk levels
- Recommended controls
- Prioritized action list
- Selected planned controls based upon the results of the cost-benefit analysis
- Required resources for implementing the selected controls
- Lists of responsible teams and staff
- Start date for implementation
- Target completion date for implementation
- Maintenance requirements

Step 7: Implement selected controls. Depending upon individual situations, the implemented controls may only reduce the risk, instead of eliminating it. These reduced risks shall be documented for auditing purposes.

9.7.19 Evaluation and Assessment

[This section of the risk management plan will describe the ongoing activities that the organization will undertake to ensure that risks are managed. It may spell out such activities as when risk assessment and risk mitigation activities will be undertaken on a timeline, or within phases of the SDLC. An example of the types of information found in this section of a risk management plan is found below.]

The organization will repeat the risk assessment process annually, because it represents best practices as mandated by legislative and regulatory requirements and also because it supports the organization's business objectives and mission. The organization will establish a specific schedule for assessing and mitigating mission risks. However, this schedule shall be flexible enough to allow changes where warranted, such as major changes to the system and processing environment due to changes resulting from legislation and new technologies.

A successful risk management program in the organization will rely on the following:

- Senior management's commitment
- Full support and participation of the IT team
- The competence of the risk assessment participants in applying the risk assessment methodology to a specific site and system, identifying mission risks, and providing cost-effective safeguards that meet the needs of the organization

■ Awareness (including but not limited to training and education) and cooperation of members of the user community, who must follow procedures and comply with the implemented controls to safeguard the organization's mission
■ An ongoing evaluation and assessment of organization's IT-related mission risks

During the risk assessment process, the organization identifies risks, analyzes risks and sets priorities, and plans for improvement by developing protection strategies and risk mitigation plans. However, the process does not stop there. Between evaluations, the organization plans for implementation by developing detailed action plans, implements those action plans, monitors the progress of those action plans and risk indicators, and controls variations in those action plans and addresses significant changes denoted by risk indicators.

9.8 Risk Management Policy Template

The following represents a typical risk management policy. Many of the elements of a good risk management policy are also elements of a good risk management plan. Therefore, you may see several elements of the risk management plan template echoed in the risk management policy template found below.

9.8.1 Purpose

This risk management policy will allow the organization to accomplish its mission by securing the IT systems that store, process, or transmit data that are critical to mission success, enabling management to make well-informed risk management decisions to justify the expenditures that are part of the organization's budget, and assisting management in self-regulating the department's IT systems on the basis of the results of annual risk assessments.

9.8.2 Overview

Risk represents a source of danger or threat, a possibility of incurring loss or misfortune. Risk management is the process of identifying risk, assessing risk, and taking steps to reduce risk to an acceptable level. This plan provides an effective risk management program, containing both the definitions and the practical guidance necessary for assessing and mitigating risks identified within the organization's Information Technology (IT) systems. The ultimate goal is to achieve best practices in managing IT-related mission risks.

9.8.3 Scope

Responsibility for satisfying risk management policy is shared and extends to all personnel and customers using the organization's computing infrastructure. Each person shall satisfy the requirements as they relate to the portion of each information system under his or her control.

9.8.4 Statutory Authority

[This section of the policy would spell out which provisions of legislative or regulatory authority such as: HIPAA, SOX, GLB, FISMA, and so on apply, if any.]

9.8.5 Compliance

All employees, contractors, interns, consultants, and organization customers are responsible for understanding and complying with this policy.

9.8.6 Updates

This policy will be reviewed annually and updated as needed.

9.8.7 Definitions

- *Asset:* Something of value to an organization or enterprise. It can be a person or person(s), information, a system, hardware, or even a building or facility.
- *Actor:* Someone or something that may violate the security requirements of an asset.
- *Access:* How an actor accesses an asset. Examples include network access, physical access, and so on.
- *Motive:* Whether an actor's intentions are deliberate or accidental.
- *Outcome:* The immediate outcome (disclosure, modification, destruction, loss, or interruption) of violating the security requirements of an asset.
- *Risk:* The possibility of suffering harm or loss. It is the potential for realizing unwanted negative consequences of an event. It refers to a situation in which a person could do something undesirable or a natural occurrence could cause an undesirable outcome, resulting in a negative impact or consequence.
- *Threat:* Refers to something that is a source of danger to an asset.
- *Vulnerability:* Refers to a weakness in security systems, administrative controls, physical layout, internal controls, and the like, that could be exploited by a threat to gain unauthorized access to information or disrupt critical processing.

■ *System Authorizing Official:* Refers to the senior manager responsible for approving an application system.

9.8.8 Policy Details: Risk Management

Risk management encompasses three processes: risk assessment, risk mitigation, and evaluation and assessment. The risk assessment section of this policy describes the risk assessment process, which includes identification and evaluation of risks and risk impacts, and recommendation of risk-reducing measures. The risk mitigation section of this policy describes risk mitigation, which refers to prioritizing, implementing, and maintaining the appropriate risk reducing measures recommended from the risk assessment process. The continual evaluation process section of this discusses the continual evaluation process and keys for implementing a successful risk management program. The system authorizing official is responsible for determining whether the remaining risk is at an acceptable level or whether additional security controls should be implemented to further reduce or eliminate the residual risk before authorizing the IT system for operation.

Risk management is the process that allows the organization's management to balance the operational and economic costs of protective measures and achieve gains in mission capability by protecting the IT systems and data that supports the organization's mission(s).

9.8.9 Integration of Risk Management into the System Development Life Cycle (SDLC)

The SDLC is the overall process of developing information systems through a multi-step process from investigation of initial requirements through analysis, design, implementation, and maintenance. Minimizing negative impact and the need for sound basis in decision making are the fundamental reasons this risk management process is being implemented for the organization's IT systems. Effective risk management must be totally integrated into the SDLC. An IT system's SDLC has five phases: initiation, development or acquisition, implementation, operation or maintenance, and disposal. Some of the organization's IT systems occupy several of these phases at the same time. However, the risk management methodology used will be the same regardless of the SDLC phase for which the assessment is being conducted. Risk management is an iterative process that can be performed during each major phase of the SDLC.

9.8.10 Key Roles

Risk management is primarily a management responsibility. This section describes the key roles of the personnel who should support and participate in the risk management process.

- *Senior Management.* Senior management, under the standard of due care and ultimate responsibility for the organization's mission accomplishment, must ensure that the necessary resources are effectively applied to develop the capabilities needed to accomplish the mission. They must also assess and incorporate results of the risk assessment activity into the decision-making process. An effective risk management program that assesses and mitigates IT-related mission risks requires the support and involvement of senior management.
- *Chief Information Officer (CIO).* The CIO is responsible for the organization's IT planning, budgeting, and performance including information security components. Decisions made in these areas should be based on an effective risk management program.
- *System and Information Owners.* The organization's system and information owners are responsible for ensuring that proper controls are in place to address integrity, confidentiality, and availability of the IT systems and data they own.
- *Business and Functional Managers.* The organization's managers responsible for business operations and the IT procurement process must take an active role in the risk management process. These managers are the individuals with the authority and responsibility for making the trade-off decisions essential to mission accomplishment. Their involvement in the risk management process enables the achievement of proper security for the IT systems, which, if managed properly, will provide mission effectiveness with a minimal expenditure of resources.
- *Chief Information Security Officer (CISO).* The organization's CISO is responsible for the organization's security programs, including risk management. Therefore, the organization's CISO will play a leading role in introducing an appropriate structured methodology to help identify, evaluate, and minimize risks to the IT systems that support the organization's mission. The CISO will also act as a major consultant in support of senior management to ensure that this activity takes place on an ongoing basis.
- *IT Security Practitioners.* IT security practitioners (e.g., network, system, application, and database administrators; computer specialists; security analysts; security consultants) are responsible for proper implementation of security requirements in the organization's IT systems. The existing IT system environment is dynamic (e.g., changes continually occur, such as expansion in network connectivity, changes to the existing infrastructure and organizational policies, and introduction of new technologies). As changes to the

organization's IT systems occur, IT security practitioners must support or use the risk management process to identify and assess new potential risks and implement new security controls as needed to safeguard all of the organization's IT systems.

■ *Security/Subject Matter Professionals.* All of the organization's personnel and customers are users of the IT systems. Use of the IT systems and data according to the organization's policies, procedures, guidelines, and standards is critical to mitigating risk and protecting the organization's IT resources. To minimize risk to the IT systems, it is essential that system and application users be provided with security awareness training. Therefore security/subject matter professionals must understand the risk management process so that they can develop appropriate training materials and incorporate risk assessment into training programs to educate the end users.

9.8.11 Risk Assessment

Risk assessment is the first process in the risk management methodology. The [ORGANIZATIONAL NAME] will use the risk assessment process to determine the extent of the potential threats and the risks associated with its assets.

Regardless of the methodology used in actually performing the risk assessment, a number of key factors are required for success. They include:

■ *Getting senior management sponsorship.* Successful evaluation requires the time of people in the department. If senior management does not support the process, staff support for the evaluation will dissipate quickly.

■ *Setting the appropriate scope.* The evaluation should include important operational areas but the scope cannot get too big. Areas of the organization that are critical to achieving its mission should be selected.

■ *Selecting participants.* Staff members from multiple organizational levels will contribute their knowledge about the organization. They shall be assigned based on their knowledge and skills, not solely based on who is available. In general, participants should be familiar with the types of information-related assets within the organization, able to commit to the time required, and familiar with the ways in which information assets are used.

Once the key factors for success have been obtained, then information about the organization's assets and how well those assets are protected may be obtained. Regardless of the methodology utilized, the following are critical steps in identifying potential threats:

■ *Identify assets and relative priorities.* An asset is something of value to the organization. It can be information, systems, software, hardware, and people.

Once the assets have been identified, a relative priority should be assigned to each of them.

■ *Identify security requirements for the most important assets.* Security requirements, in the form of confidentiality, integrity, and availability are identified for each important asset.

■ *Capture knowledge of current security practices and organizational vulnerabilities.* The organization's current security practices are compared against a catalog of industry standard security practices.

Vulnerability tools will be used to scan the asset components for technological weaknesses. The results of the scans are reviewed and the results summarized. The ultimate goal is to identify technological weaknesses in the organization's computing infrastructure.

Risks to the critical assets can now be identified by:

■ *Identifying the impact of threats to critical assets.* A narrative description of the potential impact of threats to critical assets is developed. There are four possible threat outcomes: disclosure, modification, loss/destruction, and interruption. However, the impact will be broader, describing the effect of the threat on the organization's mission and business objectives.

■ *Creating risk evaluation criteria.* The organization's tolerance for risk shall be defined by creating evaluation criteria. The criteria developed will act as a measure against which the organization will evaluate the types of impact described. For each area of impact developed, evaluation criteria are defined as high, medium, and low impact.

■ *Evaluating the impact of threats to critical assets.* In this step, the evaluation criteria are compared to the impact descriptions. The impact on the organization for each threat to a critical asset can then be estimated. The ultimate result is that the organization can then establish priorities to guide its risk mitigation activities.

Once the impacts of threats to critical assets have been analyzed, a protection strategy, mitigation plans for the risks to the critical assets, and an action list of near-term actions may be developed. Finally, the proposed protection strategy, mitigation plans, and action list will be presented to senior management. Senior management will then review and revise the strategy as necessary and then decide how the organization will build on the results of the evaluation.

9.8.12 Risk Mitigation

Through risk mitigation the organization will prioritize, evaluate, and implement appropriate risk-reducing controls recommended from the risk assessment process.

The elimination of all risk is usually impractical or close to impossible. Therefore, it is the responsibility of senior management and functional and business managers to use the least-cost approach and implement the most appropriate controls to decrease mission risk to an acceptable level, with minimal adverse impact on organizational resources and mission.

9.8.13 Risk Mitigation Options

Risk mitigation is a systematic methodology used by senior management to reduce mission risk. The organization will achieve risk mitigation through any of the following risk mitigation options:

- *Risk Assumption.* Accepting potential risk and continue operating IT system(s) or implementing controls to lower the risk to an acceptable level.
- *Risk Avoidance.* Avoiding the risk by eliminating the risk cause or consequence (e.g., forgo certain functions of a system or shut down the system when risks are identified).
- *Risk Limitation.* Limiting the risk by implementing controls that minimize the adverse impact of a threat's exercising a vulnerability (e.g., use of supporting, preventive, or detective controls).
- *Risk Planning.* Managing risk by developing a risk mitigation plan that prioritizes, implements, and maintains controls.
- *Research and Acknowledgment.* Lowering the risk of loss by acknowledging the vulnerability or flaw and researching controls to correct the vulnerability.
- *Risk Transference.* Transferring the risk by using other options to compensate for the loss, such as purchasing insurance.

The organization's goals and mission shall be considered in selecting any of these risk mitigation options. Because it may not be practical to address all identified risks, the organization shall give priority to the threat and vulnerability pairs that have the potential to cause significant mission impact or harm. Because the organization has a unique environment and objectives, the option used to mitigate the risk and the methods used to implement controls may vary. The organization will use the "best of breed" approach by selectively using appropriate technologies from among the various vendor security products, along with the appropriate risk mitigation option and nontechnical administrative measures.

9.8.14 Risk Mitigation Strategy

As a general guideline, the organization will provide implementation of control actions at appropriate points in the SDLC using the following guidelines:

- *When a vulnerability (or flaw/weakness) exists.* The organization will implement appropriate assurance techniques to reduce the likelihood of the vulnerability being exercised.
- *When a vulnerability can be exercised.* The organization will apply layered protections, architectural designs, and administrative controls as appropriate, to minimize the risk of, or prevent, the vulnerability being exercised.
- *When the attacker's cost is less than the potential gain.* An attacker represents someone or something intentionally attempting to violate the security of an asset. The organization will apply appropriate protections to decrease an attacker's motivation by increasing the attacker's cost. For example, by applying system controls to limit what a system user can access and accomplish, the organization could significantly reduce a potential attacker's gain.
- *When a potential loss would be too great.* The organization will apply appropriate design principles, architectural designs, and technical and nontechnical protections to limit the extent of the attack, thereby reducing the potential for loss.

9.8.15 Control Implementation Approach

When control actions must be taken, the organization will address the greatest risks and strive for sufficient risk mitigation at the lowest cost, with minimal impact on other mission capabilities. The organization will use the following risk mitigation methodology when implementing controls.

Step 1: Prioritize actions. Based on the risk levels presented in the risk assessment report, the implementation actions will be prioritized. In allocating resources, top priority will be given to risk items with unacceptably high risk rankings. These vulnerability–threat pairs will require immediate corrective action to protect organizational interests and mission.

Step 2: Evaluate recommended control options. The organization will analyze the feasibility (e.g., compatibility, user acceptance) and effectiveness (e.g., degree of protection and level of risk mitigation) of the recommended control options. The organization will then adopt the most appropriate control option for minimizing risk.

Step 3: Conduct cost-benefit analysis. The organization will conduct a cost-benefit analysis to aid management in decision-making and to identify cost-effective controls.

Step 4: Select controls. On the basis of the results of the cost-benefit analysis, management shall determine the most cost-effective control(s) for reducing risk to the organization's mission. The controls selected should combine technical, operational, and management control elements to ensure adequate security for the system and the organization.

Step 5: Assign responsibility. Persons who have the appropriate expertise and skillsets to implement the selected control will be identified, and responsibility will be assigned.

Step 6: Develop an action plan. At a minimum, the plan shall contain:

- Risks (vulnerability–threat pairs) and associated risk levels
- Recommended controls
- Prioritized action list
- Selected planned controls based upon the results of the cost-benefit analysis
- Required resources for implementing the selected controls
- Lists of responsible teams and staff
- Start date for implementation
- Target completion date for implementation
- Maintenance requirements

Step 7: Implement selected controls. Depending upon individual situations, the implemented controls may only reduce the risk, instead of eliminating it. These reduced risks shall be documented for auditing purposes.

9.8.16 Evaluation and Assessment

The organization will repeat the risk assessment process every other year, because it represents best practices and also because it supports organizational business objectives and mission. The organization will establish a specific schedule for assessing and mitigating mission risks. However, this schedule shall be flexible enough to allow changes where warranted, such as major changes to the IT system and processing environment due to changes resulting from legislation and new technologies.

A successful risk management program in the organization will rely on the following:

- Senior management's commitment
- Full support and participation of the members assigned to the risk assessment team
- The competence of the risk assessment team in applying the risk assessment methodology to a specific site and system, identifying mission risks, and providing cost-effective safeguards that meet organizational needs
- Awareness (including but not limited to training and education) and cooperation of members of the user community, who must follow procedures and comply with the implemented controls to safeguard the organization's mission
- An ongoing evaluation and assessment of the organization's IT-related mission risks

During the risk assessment process, the organization identifies risks, analyzes risks and sets priorities, and plans for improvement by developing protection strategies and risk mitigation plans. However, the process does not stop there. Between evaluations the organization plans for implementation by developing detailed action plans, implements those action plans, monitors the progress of those action plans and risk indicators, and controls variations in those action plans and addresses significant changes denoted by risk indicators.

9.9   System Security Plan Template

Executive Summary

[A summary of each of the first four (4) sections of the SSP. Do not restate methodology; only provide a summary of facts about the system being documented.]

DATE: (of plan or modification)
METHODOLOGY DATE/VERSION: (used to write the SSP)

9.9.1 Section 1: System Identification

System Name/Title
Official System Name
System Acronym
System of Records (SOR)

9.9.1.1 Responsible Organization

[In this section, list the organizational component responsible for the system. If another organization performs the function, identify the business partner or other organization, and describe the relationship. Be specific about the organization and do not abbreviate. Include all physical locations and addresses.]

- Name of Organization
- Address
- City, State, Zip
- Contract Number, Contractor contact information (if applicable)

9.9.1.2 Information Contact(s)

- Name (System Owner/Manager)
- Title

- Name of Organization
- Address
- Mail-stop
- City, State, Zip
- E-mail address
- Phone number

- Name (Business Owner/Manager)
- Title
- Name of Organization
- Address
- Mail-stop
- City, State, Zip
- E-mail address
- Phone number

- Name (System Maintainer/Manager)
- Title
- Name of Organization
- Address
- Mail-stop
- City, State, Zip
- E-mail address
- Phone number

- Name (SSP Author)
- Title
- Name of Organization
- Address
- Mail-stop
- City, State, Zip
- E-mail address
- Phone number

9.9.1.3 *Assignment of Security Responsibility*

[This section may include up to four (4) different security contacts: two (2) different security contacts and two (2) different emergency contacts. Each emergency contact should know how to contact the primary contact or his or her supervisor but does not have to be a technical person.]

- Name
- Title
- Name of Organization
- Address
- Mail-stop
- City, State, Zip
- E-mail address
- Phone number
- Emergency Contact Information (name, phone and e-mail only)

9.9.1.4 System Operational Status

[Document the operational status of the system: new, operational, or undergoing a major modification.]

9.9.1.5 General Description/Purpose

[This section of the SSP must contain a brief (one to three paragraphs) description of the function and purpose of the system and the organizational business processes supported, including functions and processing of data. Include major inputs/outputs, users, and major business functions performed. Include all applications supported, including functions and information processed.]

9.9.1.6 System Environment and Special Considerations

[Provide a (one to three paragraphs) general technical description of the system. Discuss any environmental factors that raise special security concerns (e.g., Internet connectivity, dial-up access) and document the physical location of the system. Provide a network diagram or schematics to help identify, define, and clarify the system boundaries for the system. Provide a description of the system and subapplications and other software intradependencies.]

NOTE: This section must provide stand-alone information regarding the operational environment within the scope of the SSP. Do not provide references to other documents without providing all the pertinent information within this section.

9.9.1.7 System Interconnection/Information Sharing

[Describe any system interconnections or information sharing (inputs/outputs) outside the scope of this plan. Show how the various components and subnetworks are connected or interconnected to any other system. Include information on the authorization for connections to other systems or the sharing of information. Document any written management authorizations with other companies in this section.]

9.9.1.8 Applicable Laws or Regulations Affecting the System

[List any specific laws and regulations that are applicable to the information processed by the system which establish specific requirements for Confidentiality, Integrity, Availability (CIA) auditability and accountability of information in the system.]

9.9.1.9 General Description of Information Security Level

[Determine the appropriate information security level for the information stored and processed by the system.]

9.9.2 Section 2: Management Controls

[Management controls focus on the management of the computer security system and the management of risk for the system. In the subsections below, describe the overall management controls that are currently implemented (i.e., in place) for the system. Each security control measure must be described in enough detail to determine if they are adequate.]

9.9.2.1 Risk Assessment (RA) and Risk Management

The risk assessment must describe the methods used to assess the nature and level of risk to the system. State and describe the risk assessment methodology used. If the risk assessment is contained in a separate document, attach that document to the SSP, and provide a summary of that document here with a reference to the attachment.

[Complete Table 9.1 for all of the system-specific vulnerabilities (excluding low risk levels). The vulnerabilities included in the table should map directly to the RA report. That is, Vulnerability 1 (V1) in the RA report should be identified as V1 in the table, V2 in the RA report should be identified as V2, and so on.]

9.9.2.2 Review of Security Controls

[If other types of security evaluations were conducted on the system during the past 12 months (e.g., audits), information about who performed the review, when the review was performed, the purpose of the review, a summary of general findings, actions taken as a result of the review, and a reference to the location of the full report and corrective action plans, include a summary of the most recent self-assessment in this section.]

9.9.2.3 Rules of Behavior (ROB)

[Provide a definition of each type of user of the system (e.g., user, developer, system administrator, database administrator, etc.) and a summary of the rules of behavior or "code of conduct" specific to the system for each type of user, including how often the system users are required to reacknowledge the rules and how is this process documented. These ROB (e.g., password construction/maintenance, changing system data, searching databases, divulging information, working at home, dial-in access, connection to the Internet, assignment and limitation of system privileges) must include the consequences of noncompliance and must clearly state the exact behavior expected of each person. If the ROB are contained in a separate document, provide a summary of that document here with a reference for the responsible component.]

9.9.2.4 Security in the Software Development Life Cycle (SDLC)

[Identify how security was implemented into each life cycle phase(s).]

9.9.3 Section 3: Operational Controls

[In the subsections below, describe the day-to-day procedures and mechanisms to protect operational systems. If this information is contained in a separate document, summarize the controls here and provide the document name/title, document control number (if applicable), document date, office responsible for maintaining the document (not a person's name), and location of the document (where it is available for review). Specify the document reference before providing the document summary.]

9.9.3.1 Personnel Security Controls

[Describe the personnel security controls for the system. It is important to note that the information in this section applies to all personnel who use the system, including contractor personnel and other external users. Personnel controls include individual accountability, least privilege, and separation of duties. All IT-related positions must be evaluated and sensitivity level assigned to the position description. Document if, when, and how personnel screening will be conducted.]

9.9.3.2 Physical and Environmental Protection Controls

[Describe the physical security and environmental protection controls for the system or application (e.g., access controls, fire safety factors, failure of supporting utilities, water sensors, structural collapse, plumbing, raised floor access, emergency exits). List the attributes of the physical protection afforded the area(s) where processing of the system or application takes place.]

9.9.3.3 Production, Input/Output Controls

[Describe the controls over the handling, processing, storage, and disposal of input and output data, media, and any special production rules.]

9.9.3.4 Incident Response Capability

[Begin this section by describing any automated Intrusion Detection Systems (IDS) in place. Then, describe the following: the formal incident response capability and the capability to provide users with help when an incident occurs; the formal incident response capability available; and the procedures for recognizing, handling, and reporting incidents. Also document who responds to alerts/advisories and what preventative measures are in place (e.g., automated audit logs, penetration testing).]

9.9.3.5 Contingency Planning and Disaster Recovery Planning

[Describe the contingency plan(s) and disaster plan(s). Discuss arrangements and safeguards to ensure the alternate processing site will provide an adequate level of security, if applicable. Describe any documented backup procedures. Describe coverage of backup procedures and physical location of stored backups. Describe the generations of backups kept.]

9.9.3.6 Hardware, Operating System, and System Software Maintenance Controls

[In the subsections below, describe the security controls used to monitor the installation and updates to hardware, operating system software, and other system software to ensure that the hardware and software functions as expected and that a historical record is maintained of system changes.]

9.9.3.7 Configuration Management (CM)

[Describe the CM procedures for the system including: testing or approving system components prior to production, impact analyses to determine the effect of proposed changes on existing security controls and change identification, approval, and documentation.]

9.9.3.8 Environmental System Software Management

[Describe the controls used to coordinate and control updates to the environmental system software and monitor the installation and updates of the software to ensure that it functions as expected and that a historical record is maintained of changes and policies for handling copyrighted software or shareware.]

9.9.3.9 Application Software Management

[Describe the CM version controls used to coordinate and control updates to application software and monitor the installation and updates of the application to ensure that the software functions as expected and that a historical record is maintained of software changes.]

9.9.3.10 Data Integrity/Validation Controls

[Describe integrity controls for the systems to prevent and detect destruction or unauthorized data modification, including controls used to protect the information, operating system, application, and other system software (including security software) from accidental or malicious destruction or alteration.]

9.9.3.11 Documentation

[List the existing documentation that describes the system: its components, operations, and use. Include the title, date, and the office responsible for maintaining the documentation (e.g., formal SDLC documents).]

9.9.3.12 Security Awareness and Training (SAT)

[Describe the system-specific security training for all users who are involved with the management, use, or operation of the system. List the types and frequency of system-specific training established and how the training will be conducted.]

9.9.4 Section 4: Technical Controls

[In the subsections below, describe how the following technical controls have been implemented for the system. Discuss the logical controls in place to authorize or restrict the activities of users and information technology personnel within the system. If this information is contained in a separate document, summarize the controls here and provide the document name/title, document control number (if applicable), document date, office responsible for maintaining the document (not a person's name), and location of the document (where it is available for review). Specify the document reference before providing the document summary.]

9.9.4.1 Identification and Authentication Controls

[Describe user identification and authentication controls for the system, including mechanisms that provide the ability to verify users. If the system uses application-specific passwords, describe in detail the characteristics of the passwords (e.g., minimum and maximum length, character set limits/requirements, password aging)].

9.9.4.2 Authorization and Access Controls

[Describe user authorization and access controls for the system. Be sure to include any specific system hardware or software features (e.g., Access Control Lists [ACL]) used to control access to the system resources by defining which users can access which resources. A description must be included indicating how users (in various roles) request and are approved for access to the system. Describe any system-specific warning or notice banners. Provide a screen image of any system-specific warning banners or notices of system criticality or data sensitivity.]

9.9.4.3 Remote Users and Dial-Up Controls

[Describe remote users and dial-up access controls for the system. Describe the type of remote access (e.g., dial-up, VPN, Internet) permitted and the functions that may be authorized for remote use (e.g., e-mail only, data retrieval only, full access).]

9.9.4.4 Wide Area Networks (WAN) Controls

[Describe WAN security controls for the system. If the system is connected to the Internet or other wide area network(s), discuss what additional hardware or technical controls have been installed and implemented to provide protection against unauthorized system penetration and other known Internet threats and vulnerabilities (e.g., VPN, network firewalls).]

9.9.4.5 Public Access Controls

[Describe the public access controls in place, including the access controls used to secure the system and information, if the system provides access to the public. Privacy statements and warnings must be described here. In addition, provide a screen image of any warning banners for systems that allow public access.]

9.9.4.6 Test Scripts/Results

[Describe the test scripts and results that were used to test the effectiveness of the security controls. Unavailable test scripts for legacy systems should be noted.]

9.9.4.7 Audit Trails

[Describe the auditing mechanism controls to allow management to conduct an independent review of recent activities. Include what is recorded, who reviews the audit trail, how often it is reviewed, and what procedures are employed for corrective actions as a result of a finding. Describe when audit trails are employed (e.g., on a given cycle, continuously, when an incident occurs, etc.). Describe the audit trail archive procedures, including how long they are kept, where they are stored, and on what media type they are stored.]

9.9.5 Section 5: Appendices and Attachments

[The following appendices represent documentation that may be developed and maintained as separate documents but must be included with the SSP for evaluation by the CIO or designee before accreditation. Maintaining these documents as appendices facilitates configuration management of all the related materials. These appendices can be updated without a recertification or reaccreditation if there is no change in the security profile.]

- Appendix A: Equipment List
- Appendix B: Software List
- Appendix C: Glossary of Terms
- Appendix D: Acronyms

[Do not attach or include large documents with the SSP including appendices. Instead, summarize the document in the appropriate SSP section, and provide the document name/title, document control number (if applicable), document date, office responsible for maintaining the document (not a person's name), and location of the document (where it is available for review).]

9.9.6 Secure Product Development Policy Template

9.9.6.1 Purpose

These policy statements outline both senior management's commitments to and expectations of [ORGANIZATION NAME] projects. These commitments also reflect [ORGANIZATION NAME] management and business objectives to implement and established a mature and structured work environment in compliance with the [ORGANIZATION NAME]'s process improvement requirements.

9.9.6.2 Scope

The policies apply to all product development and maintenance projects for which [ORGANIZATION NAME] is the prime contractor or has control over project management, processes, and procedures to be followed for the project.

9.9.6.3 Senior Management Commitments

Senior management will support [ORGANIZATION NAME] product development and maintenance projects by:

- Ensuring adequately trained and qualified project managers are assigned to each project
- Ensuring adequate funding and resources are available for the success of the projects
- Providing timely decision making and support as necessary to remove barriers to the success of the projects

9.9.6.4 Directives and Expectations

In return, senior management expects responsible individuals for each project and the organization to comply with the following in each process area:

9.9.6.5 Requirements Development

- Actively elicit, identify, and collect stakeholder needs, expectations, constraints, and interfaces and translate them into customer requirements.
- Refine, elaborate, and allocate customer requirements to establish and maintain product and product component requirements to include interfaces.
- Establish operational concepts and associated scenarios in order to establish and maintain a definition of required functionality.

- Analyze requirements to ensure that they are necessary and sufficient and that they balance stakeholder needs and constraints.
- Validate requirements to ensure the resulting product will perform as intended in the user's environment using multiple techniques as appropriate.
- Institutionalize, define, and improve the requirements development process for all projects, through appropriate planning, control, staffing, training activities, the involvement of upper management and other relevant stakeholders, and the use of configuration management.

9.9.6.6 Requirements Management

- Manage the project's requirements by maintaining the relationship between the requirements and all of the project components, identifying inconsistencies between the requirements and all of the project components, and taking corrective action when needed.
- Institutionalize, define, and improve the requirements management process for all projects, through appropriate planning, control, staffing, training activities, the involvement of upper management and other relevant stakeholders, and the use of configuration management.

9.9.6.7 Project Planning

- Establish and maintain estimates of project planning parameters. Project planning parameters include all information needed by the project to perform the necessary planning, organizing, staffing, directing, coordinating, reporting, and budgeting. Estimates should include:
  - Scope of the project
  - Work product and task attributes (primarily size and complexity)
  - Defined project life cycle
  - Effort and cost
- Establish and maintain a project plan based on the project requirements and the established estimates as the basis for managing the project. The project plan should consider all phases of the project life cycle and ensure that all plans affecting the project are consistent with the overall project plan (e.g., configuration management plan, quality assurance plan, etc.). The project plan should identify:
  - Budget and schedule (assumptions, constraints, dependencies, etc.)
  - Risks
  - Data management
  - Resources
  - Needed knowledge and skills
  - Stakeholder involvement

- Review all plans that affect the project to understand project commitments, reconcile the project plan to reflect available and estimated resources, and obtain commitment from relevant stakeholders responsible for performing and supporting plan execution.
- Institutionalize, define, and improve the project planning process for all projects, through appropriate planning, control, staffing, training activities, the involvement of upper management and other relevant stakeholders, and the use of configuration management.

9.9.6.8 Project Monitoring and Control

- Evaluate the project's progress against the plan by monitoring project planning parameters, commitments, risks, data management, and stakeholder involvement. Conduct periodic progress and milestone reviews.
- Manage corrective actions to closure by analyzing issues and taking corrective actions.
- Institutionalize, define, and improve the requirements management process for all projects, through appropriate planning, control, staffing, training activities, the involvement of upper management and other relevant stakeholders, and the use of configuration management.

9.9.6.9 Supplier Agreement Management

- Determine the acquisition type, select suppliers based on established criteria and capability, and establish and maintain formal agreements with suppliers.
- Review candidate (Commercial Off-the-Shelf) COTS products to ensure they satisfy the requirements of the supplier agreement, perform activities with the supplier as specified in the supplier agreement, ensure that the supplier agreement is satisfied before accepting the product(s), and transition the acquired product(s) from the supplier to the project.
- Institutionalize, define, and improve the supplier agreement management process for all projects, through appropriate planning, control, staffing, training activities, the involvement of upper management and other relevant stakeholders, and the use of configuration management.

9.9.6.10 Measurement and Analysis

- Align measurement objectives and activities with identified information needs and objectives. Specify how measurement data will be obtained, stored, analyzed, and reported.

- Address identified information needs by collecting measures that are analyzed, interpreted, and reported to all relevant stakeholders.
- Provide management with appropriate measures and analysis data to help monitor process performance, fulfill contractual obligations, make informed management and technical decisions, and enable corrective actions to be taken.
- Institutionalize, define, and improve the measurement and analysis process for all projects, through appropriate planning, control, staffing, training activities, the involvement of upper management and other relevant stakeholders, and the use of measurement and analysis tools.

9.9.6.11 Process and Product Quality Assurance

- Objectively evaluate the processes and work products of all projects, to ensure and record adherence to applicable process descriptions, standards, and procedures.
- Provide objective insight into noncompliance issues, and ensure those issues are objectively communicated, recorded, tracked, and resolved.
- Institutionalize, define, and improve the process and product quality assurance process for all projects, through appropriate planning, control, staffing, training activities, the involvement of upper management and other relevant stakeholders, and the use of configuration management.

9.9.6.12 Configuration Management

- Identify any items, components or work-related products in the project that will be placed under configuration management and develop a configuration management system for controlling them.
- Ensure that changes to configuration items are controlled and tracked.
- Establish and maintain configuration management integrity using records describing configuration items and performing configuration audits.
- Institutionalize, define, and improve the configuration management process for all projects, through appropriate planning, control, staffing, training activities, the involvement of upper management and other relevant stakeholders, and the use of configuration management tools.

9.9.6.13 Technical Solution

- Select product component solutions by developing detailed alternative solutions and selection criteria, evolving operational concepts and scenarios specific to each product component, and selecting the product component solutions that best satisfy the criteria established.

- Develop a design for the product or product component; establish and maintain a technical data package; design product component interfaces in terms of established and maintained criteria; and evaluate whether the product components should be developed, purchased, or reused based on established criteria.
- Implement the designs of the product components, and develop and maintain end-use documentation.
- Institutionalize, define, and improve the technical solution process for all projects, through appropriate planning, control, staffing, training activities, the involvement of upper management and other relevant stakeholders, and the use of configuration management.

9.9.6.14 Product Integration

- Prepare for product integration by determining the product component integration sequence, establishing and maintaining the environment needed to support the integration of product components, and establishing and maintaining procedures and criteria for integration of the product components.
- Ensure interface compatibility by reviewing interface descriptions for coverage and completeness, and managing internal and external interface definitions, designs, and changes.
- Assemble product components and deliver the product by confirming readiness of product components for integration, assembling product components according to the product integration sequence and available procedures, evaluating assembled product components for interface compatibility, packaging the assembled product, and delivering it to the appropriate customer.
- Institutionalize, define, and improve the product integration process for all projects, through appropriate planning, control, staffing, training activities, the involvement of upper management and other relevant stakeholders, and the use of configuration management.

9.9.6.15 Verification

- Select the work products to be verified and the verification methods to be used for each, establish and maintain the environment needed to support verification, and establish and maintain verification procedures and criteria for the selected work products.
- Prepare for and conduct peer reviews for selected work products, identify issues, and analyze peer review data.
- Perform verification on the selected work products, analyze the results of all verification activities, and identify corrective action.
- Institutionalize, define, and improve the verification process for all projects, through appropriate planning, control, staffing, training activities, the

involvement of upper management and other relevant stakeholders, and the use of configuration management.

9.9.6.16 Validation

- Select the products and product components to be validated and the validation methods that will be used for each, establish and maintain the environment needed to support validation, and establish and maintain procedures and criteria for validation.
- Perform validation on the selected products and product components, analyze the results of validation activities, and identify issues.
- Institutionalize, define, and improve the validation process for all projects, through appropriate planning, control, staffing, training activities, the involvement of upper management and other relevant stakeholders, and the use of configuration management.

9.9.6.17 Organizational Process Focus

- Establish and maintain the description of the process needs and objectives of the organization, appraise the processes of the organization periodically and as needed to maintain an understanding of their strengths and weaknesses, and identify improvements to the organization's processes and process assets.
- Establish, maintain, and implement process action plans to address improvements to the organization's processes and process assets.
- Deploy organizational process assets across the organization; and incorporate process-related work products, measures, and improvement information derived from planning and performing the process into the organizational process assets.
- Institutionalize, define, and improve the organization process focus process for all projects, through appropriate planning, control, staffing, training activities, the involvement of upper management and other relevant stakeholders, and the use of configuration management.

9.9.6.18 Organizational Process Definition

- Establish and maintain the organization's set of standard processes, which include: descriptions of the life-cycle models approved for use in the organization, tailoring criteria and guidelines for the organization's set of standard processes, the organization's measurement repository, and the organization's process asset library.

■ Institutionalize, define, and improve the organizational process definition process for all projects, through appropriate planning, control, staffing, training activities, the involvement of upper management and other relevant stakeholders, and the use of configuration management.

9.9.6.19 Organizational Training

■ Establish and maintain the strategic training needs of the organization, determine which training needs will be the responsibility of the organization and which will be left to the individual project, establish and maintain an organizational training tactical plan, and establish and maintain training capability to address training needs.
■ Provide training necessary for individuals to perform their roles effectively by delivering the training following the organizational training tactical plan, establishing and maintaining records of the organizational training, and assessing the effectiveness of the organization's training program.
■ Institutionalize, define, and improve the organizational training process for all projects, through appropriate planning, control, staffing, training activities, the involvement of upper management and other relevant stakeholders, and the use of configuration management.

9.9.6.20 Integrated Project Management

■ Tailor the organization's set of standard processes as necessary to establish and maintain the project's defined process.
■ Use the organizational process assets and measurement repository to estimate and plan the project's activities.
■ Integrate the project plan and the other plans that affect the project to describe the project's defined process; and manage the project using the project plan, the other plans that affect the project, and the project's defined process.
■ Contribute work products, measures, and documented experiences to the organizational process assets.
■ Manage the involvement of the relevant stakeholders in the project; participate with relevant stakeholders to identify, negotiate, and track critical dependencies, and resolve issues with relevant stakeholders.
■ Institutionalize, define, and improve the integrated project management process for all projects, through appropriate planning, control, staffing, training activities, the involvement of upper management and other relevant stakeholders, and the use of configuration management.

9.9.6.21 Risk Management

- Determine risk sources and categories; define the parameters used to analyze and categorize risks, and the parameters used to control the risk management effort; and establish and maintain the risk management strategy.
- Identify and document risks; and evaluate, categorize, and prioritize each identified risk using the defined risk categories and parameters.
- Develop a risk mitigation plan for the most important risks, as defined by the risk management strategy, monitor the status of each risk periodically, and implement the risk mitigation plan as appropriate.
- Institutionalize, define, and improve the risk management process for all projects, through appropriate planning, control, staffing, training activities, the involvement of upper management and other relevant stakeholders, and the use of configuration management.

9.9.8.22 Decision Analysis and Resolution

- Establish and maintain guidelines to determine which issues are subject to a formal evaluation process, the criteria for evaluating alternatives, and the relative ranking of these criteria.
- Identify alternative solutions to address issues, select the evaluation methods, evaluate alternative solutions using the established criteria and methods, and select solutions form the alternatives based on the evaluation criteria.
- Institutionalize, define, and improve the decision analysis and resolution process for all projects, through appropriate planning, control, staffing, training activities, the involvement of upper management and other relevant stakeholders, and the use of configuration management.

Index

A

Abuse cases, 220
Access Control Lists (ACL), 288
Access control policy, 129
Accreditation
  definition of, 247
  security, 242
ACL, *see* Access Control Lists
ALE, *see* Annualized Loss Expectancy
American Express, security guidelines, 6
Annualized Loss Expectancy (ALE), 23, 24
Annualized Rate of Occurrence (ARO), 22
Anti-virus software, 12, 127
Application
  firewall, 205
  software management, 287
  testing, 222
Application development, identification of
    assets in, 49–52
  assets found during previous risk
    assessments, 51
  assets found on information security Web
    sites, 51
  business and user management
    involvement, 49–50
  current headlines, 52
  legislative, regulatory, or compliance
    initiatives, 51
  organizational documentation, 50
  system architecture, 51–52
Application security, current trends in, 1–18
  application vulnerability, 3
  asset protection, 12
  blocked threats, 14
  buffer overflows, 10
  compromised records, 2
  definition, 3–4

failure to comply with standards, 7
firewall, 7
industry standards, 6–10
legislative and regulatory requirements,
  4–5
recent data security breaches, 1–2
risk management process, 15
risks associated with current trends, 10–14
standards organizations, 6
test case, 14–18
threat-vulnerability pair, 13
vendor-provided security patches, 8
ARO, *see* Annualized Rate of Occurrence
Arthur Andersen LLP, 42
ASSET, *see* Automated Security Self-
    Evaluation Tool
Asset(s)
  -based threat profiles, 267
  brainstormed list of, 55
  checklist, 55
  definition of, 11
  information, value of, 19
  inventory of, 124
  libraries, 57
  passwords as, 50
  PII as, 53, 224
  protection, 12
  test case, 224
  typical, 43
Assets, identification of, 41–57
  asset checklist, 55–56
  asset determination for test case, 52–55
  asset types typically found in software
    development, 43–49
    accounts, transactions, and
      calculations, 49
    business rules, 46

encryption software and encryption
keys, 48
external databases, 44–45
information assets, 44
people, 48–49
proprietary formulas, 47
services and functions, 46
software, 46–47
definition, 42–43
funds transfer, 49
how to identify assets in application
development, 49–52
assets found during previous risk
assessments, 51
assets found on information security
Web sites, 51
business and user management
involvement, 49–50
current headlines, 52
legislative, regulatory, or compliance
initiatives, 51
organizational documentation, 50
system architecture, 51–52
summary, 56–57
virtual bank, 45
Web portal, 53
Attack(s)
backdoor, 68
Denial-of-Service, 69
Distributed-Denial-of-Service, 69
histories, 73
spam, 19, 30, 156
XSS, 9, 111, 141
consequences of, 116
protection from, 117
types of, 116
Audit trails, 289
Authorization official, definition of, 247
Automated Security Self-Evaluation Tool
(ASSET), 35
AV, *see* Value of the Asset
Availability, definition of, 247

B

Backdoor, 105
attack, 68
discovery, 228–229
methods of detecting, 210
programming, 103, 210, 228
removal, 227

BCP, *see* Business Continuity Planning
BIA, *see* Business Impact Analysis
"Big Five" international accounting firms, 42
Buffer overflows, 10, 69, 113, 138, 211, 229
Business Continuity Planning (BCP), 154
Business continuity planning framework, 134
Business Impact Analysis (BIA), 154
Business impact threat model, 33
Business rules
application of incorrect, 161, 225
assets and, 46
Calculation object, 98
calculation of retirement benefits, 16, 47
data contamination and, 105
IRS, 16, 54, 98, 224
proprietary, 17, 37, 53
Business threats, 61–62

C

Cable cuts, 71, 106
Calculation object, 98
California Security Breach Information Act, 5
Cardholder Information Security Program
(CISP), 6
Carnegie-Mellon University, Computer
Engineering Institute, 31
CEI, *see* Computer Engineering Institute
Centers for Medicare and Medicaid Services
(CMS), 74
CERT CC, *see* Computer Emergency
Readiness Team Coordination
Center
Certification
agent, 246, 247
definition of, 247
security, 242
Change control procedure, 133
Change management processes, 254
Chief information officer (CIO), 244, 275
Chief information security officer (CISO),
245, 275
CIA, *see* Confidentiality, Integrity,
Availability
CIA triangle, 155
CIO, *see* Chief information officer
CISO, *see* Chief information security officer
CISP, *see* Cardholder Information Security
Program
Clinger–Cohen Act of 1996, 4
Clock synchronization, 131

CM, *see* Configuration management
CMS, *see* Centers for Medicare and Medicaid
    Services
Code reviews, 119, 221
Combined likelihood scale, 151
Combined scale, example of, 27
Commercial Off-the-Shelf (COTS) products,
    292
Common Vulnerability Scoring System
    (CVSS), 34, 35
Computer Emergency Readiness Team
    Coordination Center (CERT CC),
    110
Computer Engineering Institute (CEI), 31
Computer Fraud & Abuse Act of 1986, 4
Computer Resource Security Center (CSRC),
    74
Computer Security Act of 1987, 4
Computer Security Institute (CSI), 36
Confidentiality
    agreements, 124
    definition of, 247
    impact of threat action on, 155
    Integrity, Availability (CIA), 284
    national security and, 155
Configuration management (CM), 287, 293
Contingency planning, 286
Control, definition of, 12
COTS products, *see* Commercial Off-the-
    Shelf products
Countermeasures, definition of, 247
Cross-Site Request Forgery (CSRF), 111, 141
Cross-site scripting (XSS) attacks, 9, 111, 116,
    141
    consequences of, 116
    protection from, 117
    types of, 116
CSI, *see* Computer Security Institute
CSRC, *see* Computer Resource Security
    Center
CSRF, *see* Cross-Site Request Forgery
Customer database, 13, 14, 21, 23
Customer Web Portal Database, 86
CVSS, *see* Common Vulnerability Scoring
    System

D

Data
    contamination, 67, 103, 105, 210
    entry errors, 63, 104

    integrity, 287
    privacy, confidentiality and, 155
    tampering of, 31
Database(s)
    customer, 13, 14, 21, 45
    damage to, 207
    DB2, 89, 99
    destroyed, 23
    exposure factor and, 21
    external, 44–45
    fault logs in, 128
    least privilege and, 115
    mainframe DB2, 99, 103, 139, 162, 226
    National Vulnerability Database, 140
    pension plan member, 17, 77
    test, 227
    user review saved to, 114
    value of, 22
    Web portal, 87, 88, 95
DDoS attacks, *see* Distributed-Denial-of-
    Service attacks
Denial-of-Service (DoS) attacks, 32, 69, 76
Department of Defense (DoD), 74
Disaster Recovery (DR), 154
Disaster recovery planning, 286
Discover, security guidelines, 6
Distributed-Denial-of-Service (DDoS)
    attacks, 69
DNS, *see* Domain Name Service
DoD, *see* Department of Defense
Domain Name Service (DNS), 70
DoS attacks, *see* Denial-of-Service attacks
DR, *see* Disaster Recovery
DREAD, 32, 35
Dynamic code scanning, 121

E

Eavesdropping, 67, 103
EF, *see* Exposure factor
Electromagnetic interference, 71
Electronic commerce
    authentication credentials, 146
    security, 128
Elevation of privilege, 76
E-mail, 211
    address, customer representative, 83
    security, 129
    spam attack, 156
    virus, 156
Encryption software, 48

Environmental system software management, 287
Environmental threats, 70–72
  cable cuts, 71
  electromagnetic interference, 71
  environmental conditions, 71–72
  hazardous materials, 72
  power fluctuations, 72
  secondary disasters, 72
Equipment security, ISO standards, 125
Error log files, 210, 229
Espionage, 63, 105
Evidence collection, 134
Exposure factor (EF), 21

F

Fault logging, 127, 128
FBI, *see* Federal Bureau of Investigation
Federal Bureau of Investigation (FBI), 36
Federal Information Security Management
  Act of 2002 (FISMA), 5
File Transfer Protocol (FTP), 130
FISMA, *see* Federal Information Security
  Management Act of 2002
FOIA, *see* Freedom of Information Act of
  1974
Fortune 500 company, 16
Fraud, 64, 105
Freedom of Information Act (FOIA) of 1974, 5
FTP, *see* File Transfer Protocol

G

GAO, *see* General Accounting Office
General Accounting Office (GAO), 11, 236
GISRA, *see* Government Information
  Security Reform Act of 2000
GLB, *see* Gramm–Leach–Bliley
Google, 1
Government Information Security Reform Act
  (GISRA) of 2000, 5
Gramm–Leach–Bliley (GLB), 5, 51, 53, 236

H

Hardware
  mainframe, depreciated cost of, 203
  test case, 95
  theft, 2
Health Insurance Portability and
  Accountability Act (HIPAA), 4, 44,
  51, 236, 241

HIPAA, *see* Health Insurance Portability and
  Accountability Act
HTML code, 31
HTML Injection, 113
Human threats, 63–66, 104, 161
  curiosity, 63
  data entry errors and omissions, 63
  espionage, 63–64
  fraud, 64
  improper disposal of sensitive information,
    64
  inadvertent acts or carelessness, 64
  misrepresentation of identity, 65
  other human threats, 66
  policy violations, 65
  shoulder surfing, 65
  theft or vandalism, 65–66

I

IDS, *see* Intrusion Detection Systems
IDS/IPS, *see* Intrusion Detection and
  Intrusion Prevention Software
Incidence response capability, 286
Incident management procedures, 126
Information
  access restrictions, 131
  assets, value of, 19
  backups, 127
  custodian, 245
  disclosure, 32, 76
  handling procedures, 128
  integrity, threat affecting, 68
  security
    education and training, 125
    independent review of, 123
    Internet sites, 74
    management, code of practice for, 122
    responsibilities, allocation of, 123
  sensitive, improper disposal of, 64
Information Technology Management Reform
  Act, 4
Injection flaws, 113
Input validation, 114
Installation errors, 105
Integrated project management, 296
Integrity, definition of, 247
Intellectual property rights, 134
Internal Revenue Service (IRS), 77
  business rules, 16, 54, 98, 224
  limitation file, 102, 225

International Organization for Standardization (ISO), 6, 122, 125
Internet
    access to organizational applications over, 3
    alert services available on, 8
    -based applications, attacks on, 37
    connectivity, 283
    Customer Web Portal, 96
    permits, 205
    published exploit instructions on, 33
    -related applications, risk management, 243
    retirement plan calculations done on, 167
    rules of behavior, 285
    search engine, 1
    sites, information security, 74
    sources of threat identification, 106
    threats, 288
Intrusion Detection and Intrusion Prevention Software (IDS/IPS), 9–10
Intrusion Detection Systems (IDS), 286
IRS, *see* Internal Revenue Service
ISO, *see* International Organization for Standardization
ISO 27002, 122, 123, 135
IT security practitioners, 275

K

Kennedy–Kassenbaum Act, 4
Keystroke monitoring, 67

L

Legislation
    California Security Breach Information Act, 5
    Clinger–Cohen Act of 1996, 4
    Computer Fraud & Abuse Act of 1986, 4
    Computer Security Act of 1987, 4
    Federal Information Security Management Act of 2002 (FISMA), 5
    Freedom of Information Act (FOIA) of 1974, 5
    Government Information Security Reform Act (GISRA) of 2000, 5
    Gramm–Leach–Bliley Financial Services Modernization Act, 5, 51
    Health Insurance Portability and Accountability Act (HIPAA), 4, 51
    Kennedy–Kassenbaum Act, 4

    Paperwork Reduction Act of 1978, 4
    Privacy Act of 1974, 4
    Public Company Accounting Reform and Investor Protection Act of 2002, 5
    Sarbanes–Oxley, 51
    Social Security Act, 4
Life-cycle models, 295, 296
Likelihood of occurrence, 26
Logic bombs, 68, 105, 168

M

Magnitude of impact, 27
Mainframe
    error, data contamination and, 210
    hardware, depreciated cost of, 203
    VSAM records on, 96
Managed services, 204
Management controls, definition of, 247
MasterCard, Site Data Protection program, 6
Media disposal, 128
Message authentication, 132
Microsoft
    Baseline Security Analyzer, 122
    DREAD, 32, 35
    Patch Tuesday, 3
    Security Development Lifecycle process, 75
    STRIDE, 31
Misrepresentation of identity, 65, 69, 105
Mobile computing, 131
Model(s), *see also* Threat modeling
    business impact threat, 33
    DREAD, 33
    life-cycle, 295, 296
    STRIDE, 76, 77, 137
    TRIKE, 33

N

National Cyber Security Partnership's Task Force, 261
National Institute of Science and Technology, 35
National Institute of Standards and Technology (NIST), 6, 74, 111, 160
National security
    confidentiality and, 155
    risk avoidance and, 205
National Vulnerability Database, 140
Natural threats, 61, 72
Network

connection protocol, 130
controls, 128
sniffers, 67, 103
vulnerability scanning, 121
NIST, *see* National Institute of Standards and Technology
Node authentication, 130

O

OCTAVE, 31, 35, 177
Office of Management and Budget (OMB), 5, 74
OMB, *see* Office of Management and Budget
Open Web Application Security Project (OWASP), 6, 74, 140, 220
Operational change control, 126
Operational controls, definition of, 247
Operator logs, 127
Organization
　asset, software as, 46
　cost of insurance, risk mitigation as, 239
　life-cycle models, 295
　managed services, 204
　protection strategies, 207, 208
　standard processes, 295
Outsourcing, 124
　change control procedures, 133
　processing and storage facilities, 244
　security requirements, 124
　software development, 133
OWASP, *see* Open Web Application Security Project

P

Paperwork Reduction Act of 1978, 4
Password(s)
　aging, 288
　encrypted, 54
　establishment, 167
　incorrect, 167
　invalid, 115
　management, 129, 131
　policy, 50
　removal of, 8
　reset, 229
　root, 69
　rules of behavior, 285
　spoofing and, 31, 76
　stolen, 65, 102
　system, 7

use guidelines, 130
Patch management, 12
Payment Card Industry Data Security Standard (PCI DSS), 6, 9, 205, 236
PCI DSS, *see* Payment Card Industry Data Security Standard
PCI Security Standards Council, 6
PCs, *see* Personal computers
PDD 63, *see* Presidential Decision Directive/NSC-63
Personal computers (PCs), 258
Personal Health Information (PHI), 51
Personally Identifiable Information (PII)
　damage to, 55
　modification of, 92
　protection of, 44, 51
　retrieval by mainframe service, 139, 227
PHI, *see* Personal Health Information
PII, *see* Personally Identifiable Information
PIN numbers, stolen, 65, 105
PKIs, *see* Public Key Infrastructures
PRC, *see* Privacy Rights Clearinghouse
Presidential Decision Directive/NSC-63 (PDD 63), 5
Privacy Act of 1974, 4
Privacy Rights Clearinghouse (PRC), 2, 52, 73
Privilege management, 129
Product
　integration, 294
　quality assurance, 293
Proprietary formulas, 47
Protection strategy
　definition of, 207, 208
　objective of, 184
Public access controls, 289
Public Company Accounting Reform and Investor Protection Act of 2002, 5
Public Key Infrastructures (PKIs), 48
Publicly available systems, 129

Q

QA, *see* Quality assurance
Qualitative risk analysis, 19
　cost-benefit analysis, 29
　definition, 20
　risk level in, 28
Quality assurance (QA), 112, 137, 218, 293
Quantitative risk analysis, 19
　benefits to using, 25
　definition, 20

drawback to, 25
greatest strength of, 24
values required in, 30

R

RA, *see* Risk assessment
Repudiation, 76
Retail sales Web site application, 114
Risk(s)
  avoidance, definition of, 205
  definition of, 11, 248
  limitation, definition of, 206
  project management, 240
  transference, 203–205, 278
Risk assessment (RA), 10, 176–199, 284,
      see also Security risk assessment
    methodologies
  critical assets, 177–178
  current protection strategies, 184–186
  identified assets, 177
  impact descriptions, 182–184
  methodology, inputs and outputs
    associated with, 20
  OCTAVE risk assessment methodology,
    177
  overview, 176
  reporting template, 172–175
    implementation analysis, 174—175
    risk determination, 173
    safeguards determination, 174
    system documentation, 172
    system environment, 173
    system interconnection and
      information sharing, 173
    system purpose and description, 172
    system sensitivity and criticality, 173
  risk analysis, 186
  risk level examples, 188–199
  risk mitigation plans, 186
  security requirements, 178–180
  sources and potential impacts of threats,
    180–182
  tools, automated, 34–35
  vulnerability assessment, 178
Risk management, 10, *see also* Security risk
    assessment and risk management
    process, maintaining of
  definition of, 202
  plan template, 262–272

building of asset-based threat profiles,
    267
  control implementation approach,
    270–271
  definitions, 263
  development of security strategy and
    plans, 268
  evaluation and assessment, 271–272
  identification of infrastructure
    vulnerabilities, 267–268
  importance of risk management, 264
  integration of risk management into
    SDLC, 264
  key roles, 264–266
  legal basis, 263
  objective, 262–263
  preparing to assess risks, 266–267
  purpose, 262
  references, 263
  risk assessment, 266
  risk management overview, 264
  risk mitigation, 268–269
  risk mitigation options, 269
  risk mitigation strategy, 269–270
policy template, 272–281
  compliance, 273
  control implementation approach,
    279–280
  definitions, 273–274
  evaluation and assessment, 280–281
  integration of risk management into
    SDLC, 274
  key roles, 275–276
  overview, 272
  policy details, 274
  purpose, 272
  risk assessment, 276–277
  risk mitigation, 277–278
  risk mitigation options, 278
  risk mitigation strategy, 278–279
  scope, 273
  statutory authority, 273
  updates, 273
process of, 234
Risk mitigation, 13
  checklists, 212
  definition of, 234
  inputs and outputs associated with, 202
  plan, focus of, 208
  reporting template, 213–215
    control implementation approach, 215

risk mitigation documentation, 213
risk mitigation options, 213–214
risk mitigation strategy, 214
status, 237
strategy, 202, 220
ROB, *see* Rules of behavior
Rules of behavior (ROB), 285

S

Safeguards, definition of, 248
SANS Institute, *see* SysAdmin, Audit,
        Security, Network Institute
Sarbanes–Oxley, 51
SAT, *see* Security awareness and training
SDLC, *see* Software Development Life Cycle
SDLC, risk assessment and risk mitigation
        activities in, 217–232
    abuse cases, 220
    application testing, 222
    authentication service, 226
    backdoor, 227
    buffer overflows, 227, 229
    code reviews, 221
    design, 220–221
    development, 221–222
    dynamic code scanning tools, 222
    error log files, 229
    invalid plan ID, 229
    production and maintenance, 223
    quality assurance, 218
    requirements gathering and analysis,
        218–220
    risk assessment and risk mitigation
        activity checklist, 230–232
    risk discovery, 228
    risk management activities within test
        case, 223–230
        test case assets, 224–225
        test case risks and mitigation efforts,
            228–230
        test case threats, 225–227
        test case vulnerabilities, 227–228
    risk mitigation activity checklist, 230–232
    takeover of authorized sessions, 226
    test, 222–223
    threat-action statements, 222
SDL process, *see* Security Development
        Lifecycle process
SDP, *see* Site Data Protection
Secondary disasters, 72, 106

Security
    accreditation, 242
    awareness and training (SAT), 287
    certification, 242, 246
    controls, definition of, 248
    incidents, definition of, 248
    plan, definition of, 248
    responsibility, assignment of, 282
Security Development Lifecycle (SDL)
        process, 75
Security risk, analysis of, 145–199
    alternative magnitude of impact, 158
    combined likelihood scale, 151
    common risk scales and tables, 169–176
        alternate risk assessment reporting
            template, 175
        likelihood of occurrence scales, 169
        magnitude of impact scales, 170
        risk assessment reporting template,
            172–175
        risk matrixes, 170–172
    control analysis, 152–154
    determining risk levels, 158–160
    determining security risks for test case,
        160–168
        control analysis, 164–166
        human threats, 161
        likelihood of occurrence, 164
        magnitude of impact, 166–168
        risk levels, 168
        technical threats, 161–162
        threat-action statements, 162–164
        vulnerabilities, 162
    evaluation criteria examples, 183
    impact or severity of threat actions,
        154–158
        availability, 156–158
        confidentiality, 155
        integrity, 155
    insignificant impact, 167
    likelihood scales, 148
    logic bomb, 168
    magnitude of impact scale, 157, 171
    natural disasters, 154
    numerical risk matrix, 159
    operational practices, 185
    organizational records, 153
    risk assessment summary, 176–199
        critical assets, 177–178
        current protection strategies, 184–186
        identified assets, 177

impact descriptions, 182–184
OCTAVE risk assessment
   methodology, 177
overview, 176
risk analysis, 186
risk level examples, 188–199
risk mitigation plans, 186
security requirements, 178–180
sources and potential impacts of
   threats, 180–182
vulnerability assessment, 178
risk level examples, 188–199
risk likelihood or probability, 147–152
risk matrix, 159, 172
safeguards determination table, 175
significant impact, 167
sources of scales and tables, 160
strategic practices, 185
test case likelihood scale, 165
test case magnitude of impact scale, 166
test case risk matrix, 168
threat-action statements, 148, 149, 162
threat–vulnerability pairs, 146–147
Security risk, assessment methodologies,
   19–40
automated risk assessment tools, 34–35
checklist for methodology decision, 39–40
combined scale, example, 27
definitions, 20
DREAD, 32, 35
intrusion detection software, 24
likelihood of occurrence, 26
likelihood scales, 26, 28
loss of company reputation, 25
magnitude of impact, 27
methodology selection for test case, 37–39
   arguments against using qualitative
      risk analysis method, 39
   arguments against using quantitative
      risk analysis method, 38–39
   arguments for using qualitative risk
      analysis method, 39
   arguments for using quantitative risk
      analysis method, 38
methodology selection tips, 35–37
published methodologies, 31–34
   Australian/New Zealand standard
      4360:2004, 34
   CVSS, 34
   DREAD, 32–33
   OCTAVE, 31

STRIDE, 31–32
   TRIKE, 33–34
qualitative risk analysis, 19
qualitative risk assessment methodologies,
   25–30
   likelihood of occurrence, 26–27
   magnitude of impact, 27–28
   risk level, 28–30
quantitative risk analysis, 19
quantitative risk assessment
   methodologies, 21–25
   annualized loss expectancy, 23
   annualized rate of occurrence, 22–23
   cost-benefit analysis, 23–25
   exposure factor, 21
   single loss expectancy, 21–22
Security risk, assessment and risk
      management process, maintaining
      of, 233–297
acceptable risk, 252
accreditation decision letter, 252
accreditation package, 251
authorizing official, 244
certification agent, 246
chief information officer, 244
chief information security officer, 245
continuous evaluation and improvement,
      254–261
   determination of system boundaries,
      258
   discussion of SSP with management,
      260
   finalizing of documentation, 261
   identification of key infrastructure, 257
   identification of key personnel,
      257–258
   incidental documentation, 259–260
   interview of key personnel, 259
   physical inspections and walkthroughs,
      259
   preparation of documentation, 260
   system security plan scope, 255
definitions, 234
documentation of system change, 252
information custodian, 245
information system description, 249
information system owner, 245
initial risk determination, 250
IT procurement process, 240
IT-related mission risks, 280
IT security practitioners, 275

plan of action, 251
project uncertainty, 234
risk management plans, 235–238
risk management plan template, 262–272
  building of asset-based threat profiles,
    267
  control implementation approach,
    270–271
  definitions, 263
  development of security strategy and
    plans, 268
  evaluation and assessment, 271–272
  identification of infrastructure
    vulnerabilities, 267–268
  importance of risk management, 264
  integration of risk management into
    SDLC, 264
  key roles, 264–266
  legal basis, 263
  objective, 262–263
  preparing to assess risks, 266–267
  purpose, 262
  references, 263
  risk assessment, 266
  risk management overview, 264
  risk mitigation, 268–269
  risk mitigation options, 269
  risk mitigation strategy, 269–270
risk management policy, 261
risk management policy template, 272–281
  compliance, 273
  control implementation approach,
    279–280
  definitions, 273–274
  evaluation and assessment, 280–281
  integration of risk management into
    SDLC, 274
  key roles, 275–276
  overview, 272
  policy details, 274
  purpose, 272
  risk assessment, 276–277
  risk mitigation, 277–278
  risk mitigation options, 278
  risk mitigation strategy, 278–279
  scope, 273
  statutory authority, 273
  updates, 273
secure product development policy
  template, 290–297
  configuration management, 293

decision analysis and resolution, 297
directives and expectations, 290
integrated project management, 296
measurement and analysis, 292–293
organizational process focus, 295
organizational process definition,
  295–296
organizational training, 296
process and product quality assurance,
  293
product integration, 294
project monitoring and control, 292
project planning, 291–292
purpose, 290
requirements development, 290–291
requirements management, 291
risk management, 297
scope, 290
senior management commitments, 290
supplier agreement management, 292
technical solution, 293–294
validation, 295
verification, 294–295
security accreditation decision letter, 252
security assessment and recommendations,
  251
security certification, 242, 246
security control monitoring, 253
status reporting and documentation, 253
supporting risk management practices,
  238–254
certification and accreditation support,
  242–246
definitions, 247–248
guidelines, 248–254
legislative, regulatory, or compliance
  support, 241–242
support from change management, 254
support from policies and procedures,
  240–241
top-down support, 238–240
system security documentation analysis,
  250
System Security Plan, 255, 256, 260
system security plan template, 281–289
appendices and attachments, 289
executive summary, 281
management controls, 284–285
operational controls, 285–287
system identification, 281–284
technical controls, 288–289

threat identification, 249
unacceptable risk, 252
user representatives, 246
Security risk, management of, 201–215
    application firewall, 205
    authentication service, 211
    buffer overflows, 211
    definitions, 202
    detection of backdoors, 210
    error log files, 210
    mitigating risks in test case, 209–211
    programming of backdoor, 209
    protection strategies, 207–209
    risk mitigation checklists, 212–213
    risk mitigation reporting template,
        213–215
        control implementation approach, 215
        risk mitigation documentation, 213
        risk mitigation options, 213–214
        risk mitigation strategy, 214
    risk mitigation strategies, 202–207
        risk assumption, 203
        risk avoidance, 205–206
        risk limitation, 206–207
        risk transference, 203–205
    vulnerability–threat pairs, 215
Security standards, publication of, 5
Security threats, identification of, 59–107
    authenticated user, 83, 100
    authentication service, 81, 92
    backdoor attack, 68
    buffer overflows, 69
    Calculation object, 98
    data contamination, 103, 105
    data flow, 84
    DB2 database, 89
    definition, 60–61
    dummy dataset, 79
    gateway device, 96
    how to identify security threats, 73–76
        attack histories, 73
        current headlines, 73
        Internet sites, 74
        threat modeling, 75–76
    impersonation, 102
    information security threats to software
        development, 61–72
        business threats, 61–62
        environmental threats, 70–72
        human threats, 63–66
        natural threats, 72

        system threats, 62
        technical threats, 66–70
    logic bombs, 68
    malicious code, 105
    Participant object, 97
    PDF file, 86, 87
    Plan object, 97
    test case hardware components, 95
    test case threats, 77–103
        calculation of retirement benefits,
          79–83
        customer review of calculations, 86–88
        modification of PII used to calculate
          retirement plan benefits, 92–96
        posting retirement plan benefits to
          member accounts, 89–92
        saving calculated results and notifying
          customer, 83–86
        test case architecture, 97–101
        test case business objectives, 78
        test case components, 96
        test case use cases, 79–96
        test case user roles, 78–79
    threat identification checklists, 104–107
        sources of threat identification, 106
        threat modeling, 106–107
        typical threats, 104–106
    user credentials, 100
    VSAM records on mainframe, 96
SEI, *see* Software Engineering Institute
Shoulder surfing, 65
Single Loss Expectancy (SLE), 21
Site Data Protection (SDP), 6
SLE, *see* Single Loss Expectancy
Social Security Act, 4
Software development
    asset checklist, 55
    asset libraries, 57
    attack histories, 73
    balancing act of, 217
    best practice standards, 122
    buffer overflows and, 113
    business threats, 61
    change control procedures, 133
    common coding vulnerabilities in, 9
    common vulnerabilities associated with,
        135
    data from external sources, 44
    design flaws, 262
    eliminating security controls from, 217
    encryption software, 48

environmental threats, 71
fire and, 117
information security risk assessment for,
35
information security threats to, 61–72
business threats, 61–62
environmental threats, 70–72
human threats, 63–66
natural threats, 72
system threats, 62
technical threats, 66–70
installation errors, 68
malicious code and, 135
managed services, 204
methods of detecting vulnerabilities
during, 118–135
best practice standards, 122–135
code reviews, 119
dynamic code scanning, 121
network vulnerability scanning,
121–122
review of current controls, 119
static code scanning, 120–121
testing, 120
Web application scanning, 121
methods of identifying threats, 73
outsourced, 133
physical security and, 66
proprietary formulas, 47
quantitative analysis and, 36, 37
risk assessment, 10, 223
risk mitigation efforts, 220
security requirements, 137
system architecture, 51
system threats recognized during, 62
team problem, 112
threat identification checklists, 104
trade-offs, 11
typical assets, 43
typical threats affecting, 62
vulnerabilities associated with, 222
vulnerability scanners, 122
Software Development Life Cycle (SDLC),
3, 217, 236, 264, *see also* SDLC,
risk assessment and risk mitigation
activities in
code reviews, 135
documents, 287
information assurance risks within, 261
information security risk assessment
practices applied to, 11

integration of risk management into, 264,
274
methods of detecting vulnerabilities, 118
National Cyber Security Partnership's
Task Force, 261
risk management activities within, 219
risk management methodology, 236, 237
risk mitigation strategy, 214, 269
threat modeling process, 75
Software Engineering Institute (SEI), 6, 160
Spam, 68, 105
attacks, 19, 30, 156
control, 129
Spoofing, example of, 31, 76
SpyWare, 68, 105
SQL, *see* Structured query language
SSP, *see* System Security Plan
Static code scanning, 120
STRIDE, 31, 76, 77, 137
Structured query language (SQL)
injection, 9, 13, 113
flaws, 229
vulnerabilities, 206, 207
query, 228
statements, development of, 115
SysAdmin, Audit, Security, Network (SANS)
Institute, 51
System
acceptance, 127
architecture, identification of assets using,
51
audit controls, 134
audit tools, protection of, 134
boundaries, determination of, 258
documentation, 172
environment, 173
failures, corruption by, 67
interconnection and information sharing,
173
owner, definition of, 248
purpose and description, 172
sensitivity and criticality, 173
test data, protection of, 132
threats, categories, 62
use, monitoring of, 131
utilities, 131
System Security Plan (SSP), 255, 256
System security plan template, 281–289
appendices and attachments, 289
executive summary, 281
management controls, 284–285

risk assessment and risk management, 28
rules of behavior, 285
security controls, 285
security in SDLC, 285
operational controls, 285–287
    application software management, 287
    configuration management, 287
    contingency planning and disaster recovery planning, 286
    data integrity/validation controls, 287
    documentation, 287
    environmental system software management, 287
    hardware, operating system, and system software maintenance controls, 286
    incident response capability, 286
    personnel security controls, 285–286
    physical and environmental protection controls, 286
    production, input/output controls, 286
    security awareness and training, 287
system identification, 281–284
    applicable laws or regulations affecting system, 284
    assignment of security responsibility, 282–283
    general description of information security level, 284
    general description/purpose, 283
    information contact(s), 281–282
    responsible organization, 281
    system environment and special considerations, 283
    system interconnection/information sharing, 284
    system operational status, 283
technical controls, 288–289
    audit trails, 289
    authorization and access controls, 288
    identification and authentication controls, 288
    public access controls, 289
    remote users and dial-up controls, 288
    test scripts/results, 289
    wide area networks controls, 288

T

Tampering, 70

Technical compliance checking, 134
Technical controls, definition of, 248
Technical threats, 66–70, 161–162
    compromising emanations, 66–67
    corruption by system failures, 67
    data contamination, 67
    eavesdropping, 67
    failures and intrusions not properly logged, 68
    installation errors, 68
    intrusion, 68
    malicious code, 68–69
    misrepresentation of identity, 69
    misuse of known weaknesses, 69
    saturation of resources, 69–70
    takeover of authorized sessions, 70
    tampering, 70
Telecommuting, 132
Templates, *see* Security risk assessment and risk management process, maintaining of
Terminal log-on procedures, 131
Threat(s)
    action, 146, 155
    -action statements, 148, 149, 162–164, 222
    blocked, 14
    business, 61–62
    definition of, 11, 60, 248
    environmental, 70–72
        cable cuts, 71
        electromagnetic interference, 71
        environmental conditions, 71–72
        hazardous materials, 72
        power fluctuations, 72
        secondary disasters, 72
    human, 63–66, 104, 161
        curiosity, 63
        data entry errors and omissions, 63
        espionage, 63–64
        fraud, 64
        improper disposal of sensitive information, 64
        inadvertent acts or carelessness, 64
        misrepresentation of identity, 65
        other human threats, 66
        policy violations, 65
        shoulder surfing, 65
        theft or vandalism, 65–66
    identification checklists, 104–107
        sources of threat identification, 106
        threat modeling, 106–107

typical threats, 104–106
modeling, 75
   application to test case, 77
   attack vectors, 137
   definition of, 75
   example of, 76
   steps, 106–107
   threat–vulnerability pairs, 146, 147, 163
natural, 61, 72
outcomes of, 180
profiles, asset-based, 267
risks associated with, 228
system, categories, 62
technical, 66–70, 161–162
   compromising emanations, 66–67
   corruption by system failures, 67
   data contamination, 67
   eavesdropping, 67
   failures and intrusions not properly
      logged, 68
   installation errors, 68
   intrusion, 68
   malicious code, 68–69
   misrepresentation of identity, 69
   misuse of known weaknesses, 69
   saturation of resources, 69–70
   takeover of authorized sessions, 70
   tampering, 70
test case, 101, 225
TJ Maxx, 43
TRIKE, 33, 35
Trojan horses, 67, 68, 105

U

US CERT, *see* U.S. Computer Emergency
      Readiness Team
U.S. Computer Emergency Readiness Team
      (US CERT), 140
User
   access rights, 129
   equipment, unattended, 130
   ID, 139, 211
   registration, 129

V

Value of the Asset (AV), 21
Vandalism, 65, 105
Vendor-provided security patches, 8
Virtual bank, 45
Viruses, 68, 105

VISA, Cardholder Information Security
      Program, 6
Vulnerabilities
   definition of, 12, 109, 248
   identification phase, 110
   infrastructure, 267
   scanning tools, 121
Vulnerabilities, identification of, 109–143
   black-list approach, 114, 135
   buffer overflows, 113, 138
   checklists, 140–143
      methods for finding vulnerabilities, 142
      OWASP top 10 (2007), 141
      SANS top 20 (2007), 141
      secure coding practices to avoid
         vulnerabilities, 143
      sources of education, 140
   code reviews, 119
   common vulnerabilities, 113–118
      administrative vulnerabilities, 118
      buffer overflows, 113
      cross-site scripting, 116–117
      information leakage and improper error
         handling, 115–116
      injection flaws, 113–115
      nontechnical vulnerabilities, 117–118
      physical vulnerabilities, 117
   definition, 109–110
   exception-handling messages, 115
   identifying vulnerabilities, 111–112
   importance of identifying vulnerabilities,
      110–111
   input validation, 114
   methods of detecting vulnerabilities
      during software development,
      118–135
      best practice standards, 122–135
      code reviews, 119
      dynamic code scanning, 121
      network vulnerability scanning,
         121–122
      review of current controls, 119
      static code scanning, 120–121
      testing, 120
      Web application scanning, 121
   quality assurance, 137
   retail sales Web site application, 114
   secure coding techniques to avoid
      vulnerabilities, 135–137
      coding standards, 137
      defense in depth, 136

definition of security requirements, 137
keeping it simple, 136
principle of least privilege, 136
quality assurance, 137
threat modeling, 137
validation of input, 135
validation of output to be displayed on
    browsers, 135–136
user ID, 139
vulnerabilities associated with test case,
    138–139
white-list approach, 114, 135

W

WAN, *see* Wide area network
Web application scanning tools, 121, 222
Web portal, 53, 86
Wide area network (WAN), 288
Worms, 68, 105

X

XSS attacks, *see* Cross-site scripting attacks